MASS

A SNIPER, A FATHER, AND A PRIEST

Jo Scott-Coe

Pelekinesis

MASS: A Sniper, a Father, and a Priest by Jo Scott-Coe

ISBN: 978-1-938349-73-7

eISBN: 978-1-938349-76-8

Library of Congress Control Number: 2017952963

An adapted version of "Father's Rules" was previously published under the title, "This American Monster," in *Tahoma Literary Review* No. 10 (Summer 2017).

Layout and book design by Mark Givens and Jo Scott-Coe

Front cover illustration by Nick Smith Williams, @nicksmithwilliamsart

Author photo by Wes Kriesel

First Pelekinesis Printing 2018

For information:

Pelekinesis, 112 Harvard Ave #65, Claremont, CA 91711 USA

www.pelekinesis.com

MASS

A Sniper, a Father, and a Priest

Jo Scott-Coe

Intention

For the dead and for the wounded,
For those who remember too well
And those who have tried to forget.

Table of Contents

MASS: NOUN

1. a coherent, typically large body of matter with no definite shape.

   "A mass of extra cells"

   "A mass of spectators"

   "A mass of complex evidence"

2. the majority of; pl. the ordinary people

   "THE mass of students"

   "THE masses"

3. the Christian Eucharist

   "We attended mass more than once a week."

MASS: ADJECTIVE

1. relating to, done by, or affecting large groups of people

   "Only parts of the story had mass appeal."

Part I

Little Father

They had a word for his kind—a whisky priest, but every failure dropped out of sight and mind: somewhere they accumulated in secret—the rubble of his failures. One day they would choke up, he supposed, altogether the source of grace. Until then he carried on, with spells of fear, weariness, with a shamefaced lightness of heart.

Graham Greene, *The Power and the Glory* (1940)

Fr. Joseph G. Leduc presiding at wedding ceremony of Kathy Leissner to Charles Whitman: St. Michael's Catholic Church in Needville, Texas, Friday 17 August 1962. *Credit: Courtesy of Nelson Leissner*

HE had been taught to consecrate the perfect victim, to re-enact the divine son's execution according to the order of priests who preceded him. Like ancient Melchizedek, he wore special robes. But like Pontius Pilate, he spoke in Latin. Like Pontius Pilate, he rinsed and dried his hands. Then he folded a rectangular cloth, put his palms together, and bowed to the altar boy. After blessing the ingredients each time, he enacted the murder that was bloodless through a daily offering of unleavened bread and wine diluted by water. The original murder had been a sacrifice that made possible the redemption of guilty mankind. The priest learned to perpetuate the sacrifice in the name of a God who could raise believers from the dead. He did this as long as he could, until the troubles overcame him.

The first ten years of his priesthood he faced the altar at the sanctuary wall during mass, which meant that he kept his back to the people except at moments of greeting or blessing, or during his homily. During the consecration, he raised the white host towards Christ's knees on the crucifix above the tabernacle. Christ's legs looked different in sanctuaries of different churches. Sometimes the calves and feet overlapped, and sometimes there was a slight crooked space in-between. Sometimes Christ's body was forged from metal, which smelted smooth the marks of torture. Other times the body was carved from wood or marble, or molded from chalk, painted with scrapes and bruises to differentiate points of bone under skin, crude iron nails and muscle, thorns and hairs and earlobes. Always, there was a cloth tied above a hip or knotted in the center, to cover the holy parts that were private.

Hundreds of times, the priest had enacted the moment with the host between his thumbs and forefingers, and he had spoken the words after he elevated the wafer that had been transubstantiated into a holy body, a Real Presence, slightly sticky under his fingertips: *hostiam puram, hostiam sanctam, hostiam immaculatam*—the pure victim, the holy victim, the all-perfect victim. There was the jangle of sacred chimes. The priest could sometimes sense the gentle tug of an altar boy's hand behind him, on the step below, lifting the hem of his chasuble slightly (as if to peek beneath it, but not to) so that he could more easily raise his arms. He would look up where his hands came together in the point of a gently inverted V, where the host that was a circle of bread that was the victim became the center of death and eternal life.

He would rest the blessed victim's body—that is, the host—on a golden paten, like a small plate, and then genuflect and press his lips against the linens at the edge of the altar. Next he would consecrate the water mixed with ruddy wine that would become the victim's blood. The chalice could not be overfilled and could not be spilled. He would raise the chalice with both hands. Again, the hem of his chasuble would be lifted. Again the chimes. His hands could not be unsteady. He was commemorating the solemn supper before the sacred agony among the moonlight olive trees and the sacred kiss that was a betrayal somehow, which led to the scourging and crucifixion. The priest would break the host into pieces and place a section on his own tongue, then drink from the chalice and wipe the edge with a cloth. Before Holy

Communion, he would hold the host over the chalice and lift it up and repeat the words about beholding the lamb who could take the people's sins away: *Ecce Agnus Dei*—Behold the Lamb of God. Then, one by one, he would place the host that was the victim in the mouths of worshippers kneeling in a row on the long cushion at the altar rail.

On special days, after the last gospel and the final blessing, he would conduct a benediction. This meant he took a large consecrated host in a special glass case and placed it into the opening of a monstrance, which was shaped like a giant sunburst at the top of a candlestick. He would wear a special mantle called a cope around his shoulders, and he would wrap his hands inside the fabric—not to prevent fingerprints, but to make his own flesh disappear. At the top of the monstrance, the host would be a pure white circle surrounded by a golden sun. He would bless it with incense. There would be singing as he lifted the monstrance above his head and exposed the sacred body for veneration.

This was his daily bread, his daily victim. He learned first by serving mass for other priests. He was taught to practice and to imitate. At some point, he had begun to drink alcohol that was not sacramental. At some point, there would be other victims he could not consecrate, and for whom he would not be prepared.

The trauma of the priest, unlike the trauma of the man who committed the crimes and the trauma of those who suffered them, was never quite clear, and its consequences did not become visible until afterwards.

The priest always wanted to be a priest, according to relatives. The priest knew the Baltimore Catechism, and the altar boy and Boy Scout handbooks. The rules of the church were complex and formed a canon of laws and also traditions that could be learned by text and by example, and there seemed to be ways to manage discrepancies. In the two seminaries he attended, his teachers taught that if he followed the Rule, he would become a good priest. When ordination came, under the chapel apse inlaid with a golden mosaic of the vine and branches and leaves and the lamb, the Houston bishop laid hands upon his head, and presented him with the stole and chasuble, and anointed his palms with oil, then took his hands and asked for the sacred promises. The priest vowed to be obedient and to be chaste.

In the house of his Waterbury childhood, they had spoken French. For several years his family lived two blocks behind the grey stone spires of the French parish of St. Anne's, and he could walk to the parish school. His parents were petit and slender, and he became petit and slender. He was not a handsome child. (Though, much later, a seminary classmate would say that he looked good in a black cassock, his slender waist bound with the cincture.) His father's skills were precise, even delicate— he repaired and adjusted gears and filaments inside clocks and watches. His mother wore a back brace under her clothes and kept her home immaculate. She would wipe the counters and the walls and the stovetop and the windows. The priest would be her only child.

In his mother's family, in Canada, there were many men and women who had chosen religious life. Not much is known about the father's family or religious affiliations (no extended relatives were identified in his obituary). We do not know if the priest drank altar wine with a relative or pastor after mass or with other servers, or whether a cousin or uncle offered him beer or whiskey, or whether the drinking would come later—at his boarding prep school, at college, or in the first seminary (before he left), or in the ten months between seminaries, or at the second seminary that took him in. But three sources confirm that he was drinking heavily years before the shooting.

A neighbor with the same last name drove a truck for a brewery, and he allegedly came home drunk at the end of every week and beat his dog. Decades later, a classmate from St. Anne's described being summoned by the neighbor's wife on Fridays to take the animal out of the house to protect it from being beaten, and that on one occasion the classmate saw the man pinning his wife against a wall. The classmate said no one talked about it. The neighbor who drove the truck had two sons slightly younger than the priest, and they attended the same school. One of those surviving sons could name the street the priest lived on as a boy, and said that the priest's first name sounded like a girl's. He said they did not get along very well and also were not related.

We do not know whether the priest's parents protected him as a child from any relatives or neighbors or clerics, but it is doubtful that his parents would have considered such figures suspicious. Larger considerations (the Great Depression, the Second World War) did not foster vocabulary for more personal concerns. We do not know if there were distant or immediate family members who drank too much, beat or sexually abused children. We know that the priest was a member of the very first Boy Scout Troop founded in the parish. We know that, following 8th grade, his parents sent him for four years to an all-boys French prep boarding school in Worcester. The school was run by Augustinian fathers, whose robes were bound by belts with tongues that nearly touched the floor. As a student, he belonged to a small club of young men who wanted to become priests, as well as the drama club that put on plays, including *The Mikado.* He is listed and photographed as a photographer on the staff of the school yearbook, *Memini.* One surviving prep school classmate who was part of the priest group said that neither his name nor his portrait rang a bell.

After prep school (and before seminary), the priest studied languages at the University of Ottawa. Around that time, a doctor advised that his mother should move to a different climate because of her physical condition, so the priest's parents moved to, and built a small house in, southeastern Florida—down the street and around the corner from the home where the little boy who was not yet a killer lived with his family, and who witnessed (and also suffered from) beatings from his father.

Approximately one year later, the priest transferred to a second seminary halfway across the country, in Texas, where he was finally ordained. His first month as a priest, he returned to serve temporarily, briefly at his parents' church, where the killer (now only a teenager) served as altar boy at one of the priest's first masses.

We do not know exactly why the drinking started, and to what extent he enjoyed or thought he controlled or felt entitled to it. But we know that after ordination, he would be required to drink the wine that became Christ's blood every day. It was part of the sacred ritual, the holy sacrifice. It was also one of the rules, and so it would be difficult to believe it could hurt him.

With each assignment the Houston diocese gave him, he moved farther from the city center into the surrounding countryside of rice fields, cattle grazing, reservoirs, petrochemical bay areas and ports of call. Yet at each parish he could still feel like the center, even if he was only an assistant, even if he were only present for a short while. His mother tongue had taught him that he was not "priest" but "curé"—the one who cured, who healed, who made the trouble go away. It didn't matter if he was not the most attractive young man, and if women other than his mother disliked or mostly ignored him. He wouldn't have to worry about injuring his body after long hours in a factory, or how to please and also to care for a wife who became sick. If a woman or man did become attached to him, he would not be obliged, since the Church was his bride already, and any decent person should certainly know better. He would not have to explain himself, not really.

He could go alone or among a small company of fisherman on a chartered deep-sea vessel and would not need to walk on swooning waves. He loaded his tackle box and baited his hooks and tended his lures, balancing the slack and taut geometry of each line. Patient and watchful, he trolled for kingfish and for mackerel, attending the slightest twitch or vibration before he grabbed the rod and turned the reel.

So he learned that his place at the table, both sacred and secular, would be arranged ahead of time and secured for eternity. He could have children without having children, without worrying about how to protect them from bad companions or how to keep them from falling astray. As a scout chaplain, he could teach boys how to tie knots and build fires and build a shelter, and he could coax them about cold showers and soap and combing their hair, as well as nervous habits such as nailbiting. He could put them at ease with occasionally strange jokes, and by speeding through the mass ritual during camp-outs.

As a scout chaplain, he made a positive impression. Just six months after being ordained, he received the scouting Vigil Honor, which meant he had to complete an ordeal ritual by going into the woods and tending a small fire through the night. Like others who received this honor, the priest was given an Indian name (whose precise Native American language origin was not identified), and his assigned name was translated as Little Father.

The priest would have remembered his own father's special magnifying glasses and tiny screwdrivers, and how the back of a watch could be removed and then replaced, and how the panel of a grandfather clock could be detached and a man could stick his head inside to see what was wrong. He would have remembered the clock tower in the Brass City of his childhood, how the tower rose above the train station, the factories, church spires, and tenements.

He knew how to keep his fingers clean, and his small body fit into compact places. His skill with languages and with codes of conduct would enable him to blend in and to pass through. Like the criminal, the priest knew how to hold a gun, and how to load and shoot a firearm properly. For a time, he had his own collection of rifles and pistols and ammunition, though few people seem to know about this. Except for the sacred murder every day, with the holy victim made of bread, the priest never killed anybody.

The priest did not expect the bride to be murdered by the groom on the bed, as in some gruesome fairy tale. He did not mean to make her a victim, nor to bless any part of her body for this purpose—not the hair under her veil, not her neck, not the décolletage where the groom thrust his knife five times. (Or was it three times? Or two?)

With the bride he was lenient, as he did not force a conversion the way another priest might have. He also could not see the bride very well, if at all, as he had been raised (like the groom) in a world of plaster statuary, pinup posters, and dogmas written on parchment by men. The bride was the first in her family to marry a non-Protestant. The priest indulged the groom, who was his friend, in making the marriage happen easily, to please (or simply appease) the groom's mother. His friend had been only nine or ten when they first met, and the priest was eleven years older. The priest said he had much contact with the killer during his first year of college. Such contact would require the friend to drive from the campus dorm in Austin to the diocese in Houston, a long way, and vice versa. We do know that the priest drank to excess in front of him during this time, even (on one occasion) in a rectory. We know they talked on the phone, that the priest was one of the killer's first phone calls his second day upon arriving at college.

Around this time, the priest had purchased a secluded property one hour south of Houston, on a dead end behind an old cemetery, where the dark, brackish waters of the Chocolate Bayou bent into an elbow. There were no lights along the road. The killer and his friends visited there, attended cookouts and parties there, and sometimes borrowed the keys.

The priest later told investigators that he saw the "playboy" in his friend and perceived some lapses in his faith and morality. Perhaps the priest knew about the dirty pictures his friend will later be accused of trying to sell off, or about the gambling, or the fits of temper, or carrying a gun in a holster when he went to class. Perhaps the killer had popped amphetamines in front of him, or had shared his stash of pills from an amber bottle. Perhaps the priest counseled him about sex and women and pornography, or else made light of these topics or avoided them altogether.

In any case, he would have known St. Paul's teaching that it was better to marry than to burn (unless one chose the priesthood), so the priest agreed to give the groom what he wanted. The engagement lasted one month. Though required by church law, instructions in Catholicism may or may not have been provided to the bride, who continued to attend Methodist services at different times during her marriage. We can only assume that the couple's answers on the required questionnaire were satisfactory enough, or that the priest did not admonish or advise them too heavily, if at all.

Inside the small, countryside church that could have been carved from blocks of sugar, the priest listened to their vows and accepted them at the railing where communicants knelt every day to take the host that was the sacred body on their tongues. But this ceremony was not a mass. There was no holy communion, though there would be cake and punch afterwards.

The bride and groom stood and pronounced their promises and exchanged rings and kissed each other, and the priest might have felt the heat of the August afternoon rising. At the top of the main altar behind him stood St. Michael the Archangel, pale and lean, poising a golden spear over a sooty-looking demon. A photograph taken from the organ loft shows the priest's eyes downcast towards the prayer book, the ribbon bookmark flat across his forefinger. There was another photo taken after the couple had been pronounced man and wife. In the latter image, the priest smiled at the two white faces touching each other, the groom's hand on the bride's cheek. In close-up, the priest's tongue appears to show between his teeth.

The priest might have recalled these moments even after the precise date and time blurred in memory, after he had consecrated many more hosts and witnessed other weddings, and after the bride's body and the mother's body were discovered. There were pictures he did not see but could likely imagine: one arm stretched limp across the mattress, dark stains across the bride's bare skin; a mass of dishwater curls behind the mother's worn face on a bloody pillow.

⬧

The priest never revealed whether the groom ever confided, or confessed, about assaulting his wife. The priest never revealed whether the groom shared fears that we know he shared with other people: that he was sterile, that he would never be financially independent, that he thought his wife would be better off without him, and that he was sometimes overcome by violent impulses. The priest did reveal that the killer once said that he had been beaten by his own father and nearly drowned in a swimming pool, and also that the killer's mother was seeking a divorce because she had told him that her husband "was continually beating her." The priest presents this information to the FBI as nothing he had witnessed or could personally verify.

The priest said that two months before the killings, he visited the couple's small Austin house (which had no air conditioning), where his friend showed off a garage filled with guns. The priest also said that one month before the killings, the priest took his friend, along with wife and mother, to dinner at the Officer's Club on the San Antonio Air Force base where the priest had temporary duty before being sent away. Around this same time, he defaulted on a large promissory note and abandoned the secluded property he had purchased down in the bayou.

Military records show that exactly seven days before the bride, the mother, and all the strangers were victimized, the priest arrived at his Air Force base assignment in Alaska, where the sun did not set until midnight. During those days, he began to minister to families on the base. He also ministered to wounded men arriving from Vietnam on special aircraft en route to the lower forty-eight. He could have already offered mass on seven occasions by the time it happened.

We do not know when the priest first heard the story. Walter Cronkite on CBS News reported about the man who had gone to the top of the clock tower on the college campus and shot down at people. Air Force News would have reported the story, too, but with the usual delay—two days, maybe three. Perhaps the priest received a phone call. The night before the shootings, the man had strangled and bludgeoned his mother, then stabbed her in bed. Then he had stabbed his wife in her bed. When he got to the tower, he went on making victims until two policemen came to the top and shot him around a corner. His body fell next to a drain on the brick observation deck, where there was no shade from the merciless sun. The priest knew this was the same body that had prepared the water and wine in cruets before he celebrated his first mass, the same body that had bowed to him at the altar, and spoken responses on behalf of the congregation, and touched the hem of his chasuble, and chimed the bells when the victim was consecrated.

Two weeks later, following leads from Texas law enforcement, an FBI agent or agents interviewed the priest in Alaska. He sat with the priest in a room and took his statement, or asked him questions, or waited as the priest wrote a narrative in his own hand with a pen on lined paper provided to him. The document was typed and transmitted to the FBI director via teletype labeled "urgent." By that date, his friend's picture had already appeared on the cover of *TIME*, looking pudgy in a white cardigan, with a fluffy toy dog at his elbow and a newspaper spread across his lap. *LIFE* magazine printed the photo of bride and groom kissing each other at the wedding while the priest's small face (including no identification) smiled in the background. In his white surplice and with his small stature, he could have passed for an altar boy.

He would or would not want to remember that moment. Perhaps he thought only of the August humidity like a heavy wall, the heat of the steering wheel under his hands as he pulled his blue convertible into the church parking lot, a flash of perspiration above his lips.

The priest's name did not yet appear in any articles. The *LIFE* magazine cover was filled with a close-up of a window shattered by two of his friend's bullets, with the tower casting its own dark reflection across the cracks. The glassy edge of each round hole gleamed in the late-day sunlight. The empty center was rimmed by a lacy starburst, where a hand could almost press a host to fit inside.

☦

These were not victims the priest had prepared for, and they would be difficult to understand. No one had taught him about senseless crimes that were not holy mysteries, that could not be consecrated on an altar with traditional words of blessing. Perhaps someone had tried, but he had missed the lesson.

News showed footage of a woman collapsed for protection behind a searing hot flagpole, and men with rifles crouched on the street behind parked cars, and students with cameras and binoculars gathered around a fountain. There was a young man who had returned from Vietnam who said he cleared two bodies from the line of fire. There were images of a white ambulance with its back door hanging open, and someone's bloody leg. There were images of the clock-tower on high, like a tabernacle atop an altar.

On the Alaskan base, the priest's duties continued, and life for servicemen continued, and the victims did not stop coming, even after the shooter and his victims' funerals. The priest put on his uniform and his glasses and his side cap, which resembled the hat he had worn as a Boy Scout. Most of the wounded who were not officers had been conscripted into combat by order of the government, and they had made themselves an offering to fight against an official enemy. Now planes carried them on stretchers and gurneys they were strapped to, under scratchy blankets. There were victims whose skin was seared raw, with bandages that oozed and had to be changed to prevent infection. Some had needles taped to their arms, with tubes and bags for fluids or for morphine. Some had tubes with bags in other places for urine or for feces. There were men with makeshift splints and plaster casts, and men whose shattered limbs had already been cut away and padded with dressings. Some men had wounds that bled inside their bodies, and they passed in and out of consciousness. Some were now blind.

In the middle of the night, when the planes arrived, all clergy were expected to leave their quarters to meet the men on the planes. Their charge was to offer clarity and to bring comfort, in any way asked for. Most wouldn't talk. Some just wanted a cigarette, please. The priest could be unreadable, also irreverent, and he had learned how to blend in and to play and to pretend. He also knew the church's teaching on human suffering and victimhood as a union with Christ's suffering and victimhood that would become a triumph over death. Christ was bread. Christ was the sign of peace. Christ could be liquid courage.

Still: one victim was not like another victim. Imagine some

men grabbing his hand and catching it tightly or awkwardly, in a way that felt wet or trembling or ice cold. Imagine other men who would not look at him, or who seemed to sleep even with their eyes open. Some stared ahead into something he could not see, as if they would never not be able to see it.

☦

The catechism taught that the Eucharist was a sacrament: an outward sign instituted by Christ to give grace. But there were other signs that were not sacraments in and of themselves. Holy water. Beeswax candles. Incense, at special times. Stained glass and statues of saints.

In the churches of the priest's childhood and ministry, the monogram IHS was also everywhere. The Greek letters stood for Christ's name, and together were called a Christogram, and sometimes there were three nails underneath. The sign was so omnipresent it could be ignored and then suddenly become haunting. The letters could be imprinted on the host, and blazoned onto his chalice, and woven into his vestments (at the center of his chest and the back of his ribs), and on the hems of altar cloths, and melded into altar railings, and on the side altars with images of the lamb and sometimes the shepherd or the virgin. They could appear on the monstrance when he held up the sacred victim for benediction. The letters made a seal like a target, to direct concentration and worship.

Some had also associated the symbol with the Emperor Constantine, who according to legend saw a blazing cross and heard a voice that said, In this Sign (*In Hoc Signo*) You Will Conquer. The vision took place before a bridge battle, and Constantine had been inspired to urge his warriors forward to conquer Rome in the name of Christ. His victory meant defeating a brother-in-law, whose drowned body was dragged from the Tiber and then decapitated, and whose head was paraded through the streets. The church and Constantine's empire became ascendant, described by forceful adjectives such as One and True.

Whose victory now, what signs and what victims? The priest could have asked if he allowed himself to wonder. He had his own Air Force uniform, and his dog tags, and (still) his Roman collar. He had the field kit he had inherited from another priest, a World War II veteran, who had been killed in a civilian plane crash. There would be a small crucifix on the wall in his barracks apartment. There was the officer's club, where happy hour participation was socially expected on Friday nights, and where he would or would not have been comfortable among the pilots, navigators, commanders, Protestant clergy, and other airmen. The priest's body knew the liturgical calendar as the way of dividing days and seasons from anticipation and penance to celebration and feast. Every day in the liturgical calendar was represented by a color, and the days of August were considered ordinary, and therefore green.

If the priest opened his breviary book, the pages would provide Biblical text and meditations for each hour of the day—it would tell him when to pray, whether he did or not. The breviary could not give any sign that he was already ten years past the midpoint of his life.

There were also liquids that warmed the priest's body and helped him sleep in the late, late twilight, and that would soothe him if he pictured his friend alone at the top of the college clock tower that was not the same clock tower of the priest's own lost childhood, the tower that was not the top of a holy altar under the crucified Christ, the giant clock that tolled the hour and drew the eyes upward but did not offer any redemption.

And the bottles would become empty, and time did not stop. And he slept alone, or he found someone's bed to sleep in.

In accepting a military commission, the priest had wanted a change or wanted to change or had been sent to be changed. But the close and the faraway worlds were mingling, or had never been separate in the first place. This was not a sacred mystery. It was not a mystery at all, which would not have made it easier to bear.

As a young priest, he first heard confessions across the small screen in the dark closet that sometimes looked like a miniature church made of wood with velvet curtains. But he could drape the purple sash around his shoulders and hear confessions anywhere, and he could bless and absolve the penitent sinner if he deemed the confession sincere. That was his obligation and his power, also his burden. He could not break the seal.

In the early years, before his military service, most of the penitents were women and children. There were venial sins and mortal sins, and perfect and imperfect contrition. Some of the sins were mumbled and some of them were blubbered and many seemed repetitive, yet if he listened, he could tell when the voices believed they were the only ones, or the first ones, or the worst.

He could not confess to himself. He could not absolve himself. We do not know in whom he confided.

On the base, in the weeks after his friend committed the crimes, there would be more men who needed him and who refused to need him and who did not know what they needed. The words Hero and Warrior were not always helpful. The word Sacrifice was not always accepted. It would not help to tell them that they were beloved sons in whom America was well pleased. Confession was not therapy, and therapy could not always guarantee reconciliation. Some men hated their own bodies, or dreaded the touch of their women. Some men had attractions to other men, which had to remain secret. Some had experienced sexual pleasure in deploying bombs into the jungle, or they felt blame and remorse because the gun had jammed and they had not been able to fire, or because they had felt fear and not been able to fire, and other men had been killed. Perhaps one had lifted a screaming child from a dirt road but in the chaos and the smoke had not been able to carry her all the way to an aircraft or to a shelter, and had left the child behind.

The men would whisper from their pillows, or across the corner of his desk, and sometimes he would absolve them, if they asked him to. He could press his thumb in a small container of holy grease and draw a cross on the forehead of a man who had lost too much blood. He could remove the consecrated victim from a portable case and offer a man Holy Communion and the man would say, Amen. Or: the man would put a cigarette in his mouth and ask the priest for his lighter. Or: the man would refuse to speak or would ask questions for which the priest had no response. Or: the man would breathe heavily with his mouth slightly open and would not wake up.

The Alaskan sun refused to set, and it was difficult to sleep. The giant moon would hang its tortured face, *Ecce Homo,* above the horizon. The engines of planes would roar and scream.

The priest would drink with others and also by himself, and he would sometimes try not to. On the television there would be images of military and also civilian victims in the Vietnam jungle, people who would never make it to a Jeep, or to a helicopter, or to a makeshift hospital, or to the base. There were coffins in rows, draped by flags. Perhaps he did not watch, or he would turn the channel.

The priest would sense when it was going to be morning again already, whether his body had rested or not. More pilots took their positions on the runway. More men returned torn by mortar explosions and plane crashes, or were severed by wounds that could not be seen. Some had melted patches of skin and would try to smile. Some cried out or said words he didn't understand and turned their faces to the wall.

The bride and the mother did not rise from the dead. The other victims of his friend did not rise from the dead. His friend who was a murderer did not rise from the dead. The bodies kept coming. Not all wounds could be easily identified.

Across the country, there were Jesuit priests protesting by damaging warheads and pouring their own blood onto government documents. There was a Trappist monk writing books of poetry and meditation in the name of peace. The popular archbishop who had been a TV star in a long fuchsia cape publicly asked the president to announce an immediate withdrawal of troops from Vietnam. In Washington, DC and on college campuses, masses demonstrated against the war and against drafting young men to fight it. Dark smoke wafted as someone ignited an American flag in Central Park.

Around this time, a British movie titled *If...* was released about an English all-boys prep school that was not a Catholic seminary, but where the students were completely segregated from girls to train for their rightful place in the world, and they wore uniforms of black vests and suitcoats with ties. The National Catholic

Office for Motion Pictures did not deem the film O for morally offensive, but classified it as A-IV, meaning appropriate for a limited audience, with problematic content many adults would find troubling. We do not know whether the priest ever saw this film in a theater, but he would have already been familiar—literally or intuitively—with certain elements of the story.

In the film, the boys studied Latin and world history, and attended chapel and sat together at the long wooden tables in the mess halls, and they performed calisthenic exercises on the pommel horse and military drills on the field. The younger boys studied together during sessions of communal study hall, under supervision of a proctor. The senior student leaders whipped disobedient boys with a cane, and after the boys were whipped, they shook hands with their punisher and said Thank You. One of the young men played the "Sanctus" from a mass sung by Congolese voices over and over on a licorice-looking record in his dorm room. He and his friends sliced their hands with a knife and smashed their palms together and swore a blood oath. At the end of the film, after a sadistic thrashing by official student whips, the young men went to the rooftop of the school and shot at people in the courtyard with machine guns taken from a campus weapons locker.

Unlike the priest's friend, the central character in the film aimed at specific enemies representing the institutional elite, and he did not act alone. Unlike the wounded men on the Air Force Base, the central character participated in an attack that was not ordered and blessed by the establishment.

So much could have been different: If the priest hadn't drunk so much or moved around so much. If he had brushed his teeth. If he had left seminary to become a car salesman or a deep-sea fisherman or a bartender. If he had paid his debts, as he promised to. If he had seen active combat. If he hadn't married them.

The same year, the pope composed an encyclical letter titled *Humanae Vitae: Of Human Life*, which addressed not war or other forms of brutality but the immorality of artificial birth control. The same year, Martin Luther King, Jr. was assassinated. That same year, Robert Kennedy was assassinated. Richard Nixon was elected President of the United States.

A few weeks before Christmas, the priest made out his own last will and testament. He borrowed another sum of money he would not be able to repay. He was not yet forty years old.

Before he died, the external ritual of the ordinary mass had changed, though the ceremony to perpetuate the sacrifice remained essentially the same. Unlike Pontius Pilate, the priest would now speak English. He would also conduct the ceremony face-to-face with the people. In the new rite, he would still wear robes. He would still wash and dry his hands during the offering. But the last few consecrations the priest would have performed, his back would be turned to the tabernacle and the sanctuary wall, and he would hold his eyes towards the people in the pews.

When he elevated the host that was the perfect victim, he would now see the petals of strangers' faces, the tops of their heads. When he elevated the chalice, it would be the same. When he elevated the host over the chalice and presented these sacred species to the people, it would be the same idea in the new language: *This is the Lamb of God, who takes away the sins of the world. Happy are those who are called to his supper.* If the priest's hands trembled, the worshippers might have seen it. Perhaps there were chimes, but the altar boy no longer touched or lifted his chasuble. The worshippers would respond together in their own voices now: *Lord I am not worthy to receive you, but only say the word, and I shall be healed.*

In his mouth, after communion and the final blessing, after he returned to the sacristy and placed his vestments on hangers in a closet, the priest would still taste the wine that was also the sacred blood, and he would not be able to stop. The sweet acids would burn his gums. It was not supposed to matter how much of each holy element he took in—even the smallest dose of Christ was supposed to be the whole Christ: body, blood, soul and divinity, as the catechism said. But there were too many victims he had seen and not seen. The priest could not help himself, and no cure would suffice.

Part II

Two Men in Britches

'*The cleverest killers of to-morrow will kill without any risk. Thirty thousand feet above the earth, any dirty little engineer... will merely have to press a button to wipe out a town...And you people, who refused Christian burial to poor mummers in the seventeenth century, how do you mean to bury a guy like that?*'

Georges Bernanos, *Diary of a Country Priest* (1937)

Gilles Real Leduc, first-year theology student 1950-51. One year before leaving St. Mary's Seminary & University, Roland Park (age 21/22). *Credit: St. Mary's Seminary & University Archives, Associated Archives at St. Mary's Seminary & University.*

Charles J. Whitman, 23 Nov. 1963. Saturday before USMC special court martial at Camp Lejeune, North Carolina (age 22). *Credit: Photo courtesy of Nelson Leissner*

IN a doorway I can only imagine stands a priest who really existed. The white square at his collar makes a clean print, like a blank postage stamp, but at first his face is obscured. I picture a black jacket or cassock below the hypothetically slim neck, clean lines on a young body. In this doorway the priest does not hide, yet he is only partly visible, as if the space is not meant to contain him.

Consider him twenty-six years old in 1955, his first year ordained, perhaps shaving as his French-Canadian immigrant father taught or didn't teach him, pressing a straight-edge blade along his cheeks and jaw. Perhaps there are early, small indulgences (a daub of Gillette in the hair), minor vices (small flask in the jacket, a silver lighter, the picture of a girl), and contingencies (breath mints in a small tin, a wadded handkerchief, a pocketknife). Somewhere there must be a rosary with ebony or olivewood beads—a gift from his mother or a religious relative—loose in his slacks pocket, stored in a petite leather pouch, perhaps looped on a bedpost or scrambled up with papers on a desk. His breviary book, first in Latin, then English: Does he use it for daily reading and prayer, as recommended to all priests in the Roman Rite? Has he simply left it in a drawer somewhere, wrapped in the original plastic?

The summer of 1965, after ten years at parishes in the diocese of Galveston-Houston, Texas, the priest becomes an Air Force chaplain. Whether this transition is a personal request or a professional suggestion, his bishop approves. Some time during his chaplaincy training, the priest receives a marksmanship medal, suggesting ease with firearms, a steady hand, and the gift of farsightedness (not to be confused with foresight). He never will see active combat in the Vietnam War, but he will see casualties en route from the killing fields during his first official base assignment, starting late July 1966, at Elmendorf Air Force Base in Alaska.

Exactly one week after the priest arrives in Alaska, other drastic but domestic casualties—here one must say, plainly, murders—occur in the state he left behind. In the center of UT Austin, from the observation deck of the clock tower, Charles Whitman fires a rifle to wound and kill random strangers for ninety-six minutes. And before that, he murders his wife and his mother.

The priest has known the killer for almost sixteen years, starting about the time the killer was nine years old, several years before the priest even became a priest. Ultimately, horribly, the altar boy who had served at one of the priest's very first masses was shot dead in the act of mass murder. For half a century, the priest disappears into the narrative of bloodshed.

I. THE SINS OF SPECIAL MEN

According to Roman Catholic teaching, the moment a man is ordained to the priesthood, he undergoes an "ontological change." This alleged transformation sets the priest permanently, existentially apart from ordinary people; he becomes a completely different human being, a second Christ.

This teaching, which even some Catholics label as a heresy,

has multiple consequences. First, a priest gains grave and exclusive powers: the ability to change bread and wine into the body and blood of Christ, and the privilege to grant or refuse absolution of sin. As a social and cultural result, the priest becomes protected and isolated in a celibate brotherhood whose all-male hierarchy has often relied upon secrecy to guard its own. During most of church history, it has been difficult to speak openly of an individual priest as anything but beyond reproach, whatever his actual struggles, flaws, or outright crimes.

The resulting tension is an uneasy one. The French writer Georges Bernanos, in his novel *Diary of a Country Priest* (1937), captured the predicament from a clerical perspective: "We pay a heavy, very heavy price for the super-human dignity of our calling. The ridiculous is always so near to the sublime. And the world, usually so indulgent to foibles, hates ours instinctively."

Despite hundreds of years of art, literature, research, and films exploring the vast spectrum of characters inside the clergy, church tradition has ironically denied a priest his humanness in the name of his super-humanity. This position makes honest inquiry and exchange about the priesthood rather difficult, to say the least, not only for laity but for priests themselves.

The logic mirrors how, in the wake of mass violence, many American voices insist that we deny the humanness of the murderer in the name of his super-inhumanity—how unlike us and how exceptional he really is, whether for metaphysical or scientific reasons. His violent acts ordain him to be a different kind of person entirely. Preoccupation with naming a final diagnosis for the violence becomes, in effect, a silencing of narrative details. There is no story to explore because: His soul was possessed. His body had been invaded. He experienced psychosis.

Some believe we mustn't even speak the murderer's name. Instead we must say: Evil. Satan. A mass in his brain. One group preserves the sacred façade of priesthood; the other preserves the notion of violent men as demonic monsters or biological aberrations. These patterns of thought do not exclude each other. In the US, we find a way to embrace the monster selectively, revering those ordained to kill "with good reason," especially on our behalf and at our expense, within the most exclusive ranks of the military.

No wonder I found it difficult to resist a story where a man who was not always a priest crossed paths with a boy who was not always a killer but had been trained to become one.

At the beginning of this journey, I didn't know that I would be writing such a book. I thought that my questions about the sniper's priest would lead to simple facts along another pathway. My interests were straightforward: Who was Reverend Joseph G. Leduc, and what happened to him? What was he like before the killings of 1966, and what was he like afterwards?

For one thing, he was already dead. For another, finding answers was not as simple as I imagined or wanted, and I realized slowly that this was part of the story. I traveled hundreds of miles to talk with strangers, to visit parishes, seminaries, libraries, schools and houses, to dig through archives. I sent emails and follow-ups and made cold calls, I scoured databases and microfiche, ordered documents by snail mail and waited for padded envelopes. After four years of discoveries, digressions, leads, dead ends, and awkward conversations, I realized that asking questions about a priest sixty years after his ordination—as a layperson, marginal Catholic, and a woman—still cuts deeply into the tradition of priestly existential transformation. It also challenges the privileges and reveals the burdens ingrained by the clerical system. Imagine being an average priest struggling with sexual anxiety or desire, an addiction, financial worries, or depression. To whom does a man turn to talk about normal human difficulties when he is supposed to exist as an "ontologically changed" being? And what dysfunctions may be cultivated in a system so deeply dedicated to preserving its external image?

It appears that some variation of these thoughts also crossed the mind of the future Texas sniper. Aside from expressing the usual doubts about papal authority and the church's stand on artificial contraception, Whitman reportedly raised questions about priests' special status in one of many conversations he shared in the early 1960s with an older friend and real estate agent named A.J. Vincik. Whitman's skepticism in itself was not new or illuminating, but his focus caught my attention the first time I read about it, and it is something that a non-Catholic might breeze right past.

To be specific, Whitman challenged the lack of reciprocity when it came to confession and absolution. According to Vincik, as quoted by the *Texas Observer* in 1966, "[Whitman] could not conceive of one man being able to grant another man something that he himself could not grant in return, forgiveness—that a man in a pair of britches was no different from another man in another pair of britches." It is a striking comment from a young Catholic who had closer-than-average association with a seminary student who transformed into a priest.

Perhaps this real-life association helped Whitman to understand all too clearly that, whatever his catechism had taught him as a child, priests were not so different after all. While they were consecrating bread and doling out penances in confessionals, they themselves needed to be granted forgiveness—and by laypeople, no less.

The average Catholic would not have needed a litany of grievances in order to sense superficial priestly imperfections or deep character flaws, even if these could not be addressed in public. The two methods encouraged for parishioners in a mid-century book of Catholic etiquette were: "If you cannot help any other way, do so by failing to criticize," and "Pray for your pastor at all times."

Throughout his life, Whitman witnessed how the status quo was reinforced by prerogatives of power—among secular as well as religious groups of men. Even when inconsistent, appalling, or outright destructive, such prerogatives were enticing. It makes sense that, although Whitman paid lip service to questions about hypocrisy, his public and private brutality replicated a terrible privilege claimed by all callous and self-serving systems: he shed the blood of others in the name of making things right.

His friend Father Leduc, on the other hand—despite his privileges and also, perhaps, as a partial result of them—privately, secretly imploded.

✟

In 1950, Charles Whitman ("Charlie") was a nine year-old altar boy at Sacred Heart Parish in Lake Worth, Florida. In this respect he resembled most average Catholic schoolboys of his generation, serving mass in Latin, in the Tridentine Rite. At each service, his direct responses to the priest would stand in as a proxy for the collective voice of the entire congregation—and, in effect, all the faithful of the Catholic Church.

From the time he was born in 1941 until the late 1940s, Charlie moved with his parents at least six times between Georgia and

Florida. Documents discovered after the shooting suggest that these moves had as much to do with domestic turmoil as with his father's efforts to establish an independent business. Eventually the family settled on South "L" Street in Lake Worth, and by 1950 Charlie had two younger brothers: Patrick, 5, and Johnnie Mike, 1. Charlie's paternal grandmother occupied the house next door (his father, who had spent most of his childhood in a Savannah orphanage, purchased it for her). Charlie attended the Sacred Heart Elementary School run by Sisters of St. Joseph, and his Catholic mother was active in the parish as an officer in the Mothers' Teachers Club. His father did not practice any faith, though he was not averse to his children's mass attendance or the expense of Catholic education. He ran a plumbing and septic tank cleaning business, and his wife maintained the financial records. He was also active in the local Chamber of Commerce and the Democratic Party.

By all accounts developed after the murders sixteen years later, Charlie's home life was violent as well as highly structured. Guns were embedded in daily life, a bit more than average during a generation when most boys learned to hunt and fish. Guns were mounted on walls throughout the home. An infamous photograph shows toddler Charlie wearing a cloth diaper and standing with the help of two full-size rifles propped in the sand on the beach. Neighbors and relatives described the father beating his wife as well as the children, particularly Charlie. High school classmates described seeing marks or welts on his back—one witness said "frequently." The family doctor recounted treating the mother for abuse-related "bruising." A neighbor recalled beatings of the family dog.

In photographs—on a living room couch, at the foot of a

Christmas tree—members of the family looked clean, healthy, comfortable, and handsome. The father reportedly bragged about his success and his children. He indulged them and also made strict demands, exerting what one witness later called "physical pressure" to get compliance. There were extravagant presents at Christmas, hunting trips, bikes, allowances, and piano lessons. Charlie was given enough money to attend the Boy Scout Jamboree in California in the summer of 1953 as a reward "in advance," anticipating that he would achieve Eagle Scout status by the end of the year. The father prescribed what activities and friendships were acceptable, and the family did not appear to socialize much with other families as a whole group.

After the murders in 1966, Charlie's father affirmed publicly that he should have "spanked" his children more, in order to make them more obedient. The lawyer for Charlie's mother, who that spring separated from her husband after twenty-five years, stated that he heard the man "boast" about beating her. The father also told reporters that he knocked around his wife because she was so "stubborn."

Before hitting puberty, and more than a decade before he killed anyone, Charlie Whitman had witnessed vividly disturbing messages about what it meant to be married and to raise children. At the time, the traditional catechism taught that marriage was an inferior state to the religious life, and that women should be submissive to men. Like thousands of other Catholic children, Charlie saw drastic evidence of marital trouble in daily life, which weirdly confirmed the church's messages.

By 1950-51, Charlie was old enough to crave and appreciate alternative models of maturity and manhood if any were available. That same year, the future Father Leduc from Alaska entered the scene in Lake Worth, and he was not even a priest yet. He was not exactly living there, either. He was a small and odd looking 21 year-old seminarian enrolled at St. Mary's Seminary Roland Park, located in Baltimore. On breaks, Leduc visited his parents, who had just moved to Florida from Connecticut. They had built a small house down the street and around the corner from the Whitman family.

Records show that the Tuesday after Veteran's Day, in November 1951, Leduc left seminary. For about ten months, he did not attend seminary at all. During this gap, according to his FBI statement, he became "instrumental in organizing" Scout Troop 119 at Sacred Heart Parish and "became more closely associated with Whitman" and members of his family. He seemed to be enjoying himself, too. A newspaper reported that in June Leduc went deep-sea fishing with a party of scout leaders on the ship, *Britches*, and caught a kingfish.

Leduc helped with Charlie's beginning progression to Eagle Scout rank and told the FBI that "with much coaxing" the young boy stopped biting his fingernails. He also stated that he learned of Charlie's "interest in weapons" and "marksman[ship] at an early age" while on hunting trips with the boy and his father. Charlie turned 11 in June 1952, one month after the release of *The Sniper*, a psychological thriller and film noir about a disturbed man killing femmes fatales and leaving a trail of clues so that investigators could catch him.

That fall, Leduc transferred to a much smaller seminary more than one thousand miles west, on the gulf coast of La Porte, Texas. The seminary facility was old and dilapidated, a reconstituted hotel resort battered by hurricanes and standing two hundred paces from the water. Leduc journeyed home for family visits on holidays and in the summers. In May 1955, Leduc was one of only six men ordained at a brand new seminary campus built in a lush area west of downtown Houston.

After ordination, he returned to Sacred Heart Parish in Lake Worth to spend approximately one summer month with his parents, a prelude to his first official parish assignment back in Texas. During this time, the summer before his freshman year at St. Ann's High School, Charlie Whitman served as Leduc's altar boy.

✠

If I were an average layperson asking for a priest the year Leduc was ordained, there would have been very little mystery involved. I would likely have been one of the working middle class Catholics in the US, a group whose legitimacy had finally arrived and whose membership was hitting its high water mark prior to the turmoil of Vietnam, Vatican II, *Humanae Vitae* (the 1968 papal encyclical against artificial birth control), and the full bloom of the Sexual Revolution. I would have likely been looking for a priest to hear my confession, baptize my baby, bury a relative, post my wedding banns, or administer the final rites in a hospital. I might have been seeking an intelligent guest for my dinner table. Like one of my aunts, and eventually my mother, I might have sought a priest to take instructions in the faith—either because I planned to marry a Catholic, or because I wanted to become one.

This was more than a decade before the priest celebrated mass facing the congregation, before vernacular English and guitar masses or shaking hands and hugging during the "sign of peace." Women still covered their hair with hats or lace mantillas. Parishioners knelt along a rail at the front of the church to take communion. Altars and statuary were elaborate, often crafted or imported by immigrants who sought to evoke the European cathedrals they had left behind. There was no *Jesus Christ Superstar* yet.

But in the mid-fifties, even before John F. Kennedy became a household name, Catholics looked attractive and talented. At the time, I wouldn't have had to search far in popular culture for images of priests as surrogate father-uncle-brother figures. (This doesn't even count depictions of nuns.) Secular Hollywood had already provided many portrayals to choose from, representing a continuum of acceptable and heroic masculinity: lean, world-wise crooner Bing Crosby in *Going My Way* (1944) and *The Bells of St. Mary's* (1945); conscientious and handsome former soldier Montgomery Clift in Hitchcock's *I Confess* (1953); and barrel-chested tough-guys Spencer Tracy in *Boys Town* (1938), Charles Bickford in *The Song of Bernadette* (1943), and Karl Malden in *On the Waterfront* (1954). In this last group, one must also place Bishop Fulton J. Sheen, who played himself on the Emmy-winning weekly program *Life is Worth Living*, which aired on network television from 1952 to 1957—competing for ratings with comedian Milton Berle. This was a time in America when being a priest was "cool."

But I began my search in 2012, when looking for a man ordained in the fifties also meant looking back into a period that no longer simply represented a positive assimilation of Catholics into the American mainstream, but revealed wounds of sexual abuse and church secrecy that have only come to light in the past two decades. It has been more than fifty years since Vatican II set out to change the nature of interaction and accountability between laity and clerics. Yet in my own process, I learned quickly that emails to diocesan archivists or librarians or religious orders might need to include some peremptory assurance that I was not tracing a private violation or grudge, that I was not crafting a lawsuit or working for a lawyer.

Even bothering to offer such assurances, however, whether directly or in code, felt both dishonest and contaminating. (As Jung says, "Beware unsolicited denials.") Trying to locate records and timelines for a missing priest already seemed like an affront to a context when looking for good Father O'Malley was (supposedly) as uncomplicated as finding a car mechanic or locating a man to do my taxes: no apologies or parenthetical disclaimers necessary. It seemed that in attempting to declare a lack of dark motives, as if to absolve my subject in advance of what I didn't yet know, I had already planted a bad seed. There was no easy way around that.

I can see how other researchers, coming across references to Father Leduc, would perhaps overcompensate and dismiss him, or else safely fold him into the story of the killer. This also felt wrong—or, at least, unnecessarily deferential. Indeed, after a friendly email exchange regarding other materials in the Whitman case, I asked one writer whether he had ever seen a photograph of Father Leduc. His answer was no reply at all, which seemed to suggest that my interest in the priest was irrelevant, if not prurient. More directly, a librarian at Leduc's second seminary responded to one of my first, unguarded email inquiries by sending me an FBI link I had already accessed, then insisting that Leduc had attended a different seminary altogether and become a different kind of priest somewhere else.

Nothing to see here; move right along, Ma'am. From a Catholic point of view, the ontological boundary of priesthood reared its head very early. But I sensed, too, a block in the secular imagination, where Catholic priests remain a weirdly avoided, almost taboo class—except as stock characters in horror films featuring exorcism, or at the end of too-obvious punch lines about touching little boys. Wherever the diversions came from, they indicated nostalgia for a saint or dread of a shadow: a face in the dark, projected onto a screen.

I had no desire to protect a phantom. But in the preliminary stages, I conjured up a romantic picture of my own. I wanted to find an earnest but immature priest who had reached out to a troubled kid that he wouldn't ultimately know how to help. I suppose, on some level, I desired a story I had already heard, of the reverend who aspired deeply but stumbled due to ego or ignorance and could not recover when it went so wrong. Straight-up tragedy is, after all, a much easier tale to write. I had to look closer as the emerging portrait became less predictable and more uncomfortable. I couldn't turn away.

Curiosity implicated me, of course. Denial would have been easier, but false. I had to embrace a narrative awkwardness and resist binary conclusions. If Leduc wasn't a cliché—a flawed saint or a brutal criminal—who was he, and who would care? The journey to understand took me underneath/between/around/over/behind rather than straight through. Leduc's life came into focus apart from Whitman's crimes, taking shape within the context of other people, social organizations, and cultural moments. But their paths had crossed and intertwined, and I faced that, too.

Why bother? one may ask. The murders are long over, and we know who committed those. And it's only murders or, say, molestations that are worth discussing, right? At least, that's what sensationalism tells us.

The ability, or the strategy, not to see beyond this surface may develop from a need to hide and survive. But it's compelling to me how this mass strategy contributes to a cycle of enforced denial. Every time there is another shooting on a campus, in a theater, or in a mall; every time we hear of an atrocity committed in a country not our own but in our name; every time another man takes his family hostage before he kills his children, his wife, and himself, many American voices repeat the same words: How could this senseless act happen? It's not really an inquiry anymore. It's a rote and useless American prayer.

In *The Power and the Glory* (1940), Graham Greene's whiskey priest confronted his own illusions as he eluded authorities and endured his sins across the Mexican desert. I found no evidence that Leduc—who was socialized by church traditions that both ensured his status and reinforced selective silences—ever learned to go that deep. I learned that as a man, Leduc played the margins of his special status in a way that allowed him to remain both untouched and untouchable, in multiple senses of the word.

Forget theology. By my very interest, by daring to ask, I was breaking open a narrative seal.

II. LOOKING FOR FATHER LEDUC

If you go looking for an American priest who lived from 1929 to 1981, here are the resources you may consult:

1. Secular and religious newspapers, for profiles, articles about assignments, public events, and (of course) obituaries. Not all newspapers are accessible online; many local newspapers have to be viewed onsite, via microfiche. Prepare to purchase

database subscriptions. Prepare to travel.

2. Census records and city directories, via genealogy websites.

3. The Official Catholic Directory (OCD), published at the beginning of each calendar year since 1817. This resource contains annual updates of clergy contact information for all dioceses in the U.S. Because this is published once a year, it cannot capture more than one assignment record within a 12-month period. Occasional quirks include: names missing from indexes, or names listed where not indexed. Font is small. Wear your glasses.

4. Seminary archives. Basic enrollment and ordination date records only if available. Perhaps photographs, catalogs, or institutional publications. If the seminary has an alumni association, your name and contact information can be shared via email with surviving classmates who may or may not be open to interviews.

5. Local chancery archives for any diocese where the priest worked. Laypeople have access to ordinary records of assignments only. Any material containing complaints or matters of "conscience," unless already disclosed under subpoena in a civil or criminal lawsuit, would be kept in secret files ("secret" is actually an official term). Important: the federal Freedom of Information Act (FOIA) does not apply to church records.

6. Interviews with surviving family members, friends, elementary or high school classmates, former neighbors, clerical and non-clerical colleagues, former parishioners, or surviving members of his seminary class.

7. Any dissertation documents or other writings that preserve the voice, intellect, vocabulary, or expressed values and thoughts of the priest.

8. Military assignment records, if any, available through the National Personnel Records Center.

9. County court records, both civil and criminal. Some materials are purged, sealed, or deemed "confidential," especially following settlements. Even innocuous case records were sealed more arbitrarily in past decades than now. You may need to consult legal experts. Some names and cases will not yield records from the usual search tools.

10. County clerk records, for real property deeds, trusts, and liens.

The first time I discovered Father Leduc's name was accidentally, in a preliminary Internet search about Charles Whitman. A lengthy, now unredacted FBI document pops up easily as a PDF online dated two weeks after the murders, on August 15, the Catholic Feast of the Assumption of Mary.

Upon first encountering the narrative, I thought: Sure, Leduc must have been some kindly old parish priest for the Whitman family, he baptized all the children, he was close to the parents—or at least to the mother. Or: He taught at the school the killer and his brothers attended. Or: He was one of the killer's longtime classmates from parochial school or a kid from the neighborhood or from college, a childhood friend who decided to enter the seminary. The most common accounts of the case that bother to mention Leduc at all merely brush past him as "a friend of the family" or "Whitman's scoutmaster." At casual glance, Leduc seems a device to underscore both Whitman's all-American and Catholic boyhood, perhaps making him an even creepier villain to a WASP-y true-crime audience. But, as I discovered, Leduc does not fall into the usual categories, and as a character, he strikes an odd figure in his own story as well as in Charles Whitman's. He stood out immediately to me as more than a neutral character or bit player.

Cultural understandings as a Catholic fed my native curiosity. Whitman had grown up surrounded by men and women who had chosen religious life and whose everyday clothing—cassocks for priests, habits for nuns—signaled their exclusive status and privileged role. In the spectrum of Catholic identity, Whitman would qualify as deeply immersed in the formal and informal traditions of the faith. He was baptized, made his first communion and first confession, was confirmed and then eventually married in the church. He attended parochial schools through the twelfth grade, which meant absorbing not simply formal catechism but the rituals and rhythms of the Catholic calendar—daily masses, "high" and "low" masses, saints' feast days and holy days of obligation, the changing colors of liturgical vestments and altar linens for the appropriate season. He was also raised in a pre-Vatican II world, when the many-hundred-years-old requirement to fast before receiving communion was reduced to three hours rather than starting the midnight before. Eating meat was still forbidden on all Fridays, not just during Lent. There were rosary processions, Stations of the Cross, an abundance of holy water and rosary beads, incense and statuary, patron saints, and Knights of Columbus breakfasts in the parish Madonna Hall. Whitman's Eagle Scout picture was taken not outside a cabin at a campground but in front of the altar rail at Sacred Heart Church. He served mass well into young adulthood, so he had long enjoyed a boy's exclusive access to clerics' special territories of rectory offices and church sacristies.

This in no way meant, however, that a sustained personal

connection over time with any priest was inevitable or even necessary. Priests were simply part of the ordinary wallpaper in Whitman's upbringing. I can count and name the priests I remember with affection on one hand, but I do not know if they would remember me. There are many more others, some faceless and some with names, who left hazy or negative impressions, whose sermons were forgettable or narrowly obsessed on boilerplate topics including "immodest fashions" or rock music or abortion. None of this mattered, because if I wanted to attend mass or make a confession, any Father would serve. Catholics can enjoy anonymity and still participate in the exact unifying rituals—which we call "sacraments"—anywhere in the world because a priest's individual identity is always transcended by the sacred duties he performs. Catholics, unlike Protestants, need—no, *depend upon*—the priesthood to practice their faith. We can lay claim to any priest as a spiritual father to meet a specific spiritual need. Knowing or liking him, or his knowing and liking *us*, is beside the point, a lucky bonus. For the mid-century American Catholic, any positive attention from a priest was a sacred and unquestioned privilege.

Except for those men who belong to secluded monastic orders, diocesan priests pass through parishioners' lives as public figures in local communities that know, remember, or forget them. For this reason in part, choosing to keep a relationship with any individual church Father, as a friend rather than a functionary, can feel like a distinct personal treasure, especially after childhood rituals mandated by parents have long passed. But even treasured connections have practical limits. It is rare anymore that pastors spend decades at a single parish. In Whitman's childhood, many priests were imported from Ireland to serve the vast frontier diocese (at the time the *only* diocese) in Florida, the Diocese of

St. Augustine. In my lifetime, both clergy and congregations have tended to accept more frequent assignments and re-assignments of priests with resignation, in service to a higher communion of believers. Such movement has now been documented as evidence of institutional evasion when a priest has serious personal problems or even commits crimes. At the most benign level, Catholics learn to understand: people move on.

Despite this reality of impermanence, I know that in rare times of crisis, my mother wrote letters to priests she still trusted—months or even years after we (or they) had gone elsewhere. I remember that, when they were still alive, these priests wrote or called back to offer comfort or counsel. But I do not remember seeing the priests again. No priest was making a three-hour drive, one way, to re-establish contact. Neither was my mother. Priests were busy men with limited resources of time and money. Laypeople had mouths to feed and bosses to please.

By contrast, I could tell early on that Father Leduc's contact across time and geography with Charles Whitman was different, even unusual, which didn't mean there was anything inherently suspicious about it. But I could not help asking: how did the bond form in the first place, and why did Whitman keep returning to it? Leduc didn't come from Ireland, and he didn't come from Florida. He also did not stay in Florida for long. For the first years of their acquaintance, Leduc was not even a priest yet. He was then a seminarian on hiatus.

Whitman and Leduc met during a generation when seminary students were largely sequestered from "the world." Requirements were strict. Catalogs from St. Mary's Seminary Baltimore/Roland Park (SMSU)—the oldest Roman Catholic Seminary in the U.S., founded in 1791—list the materials necessary for admission in the early 1950s: bishop's permission to enroll; recommendation from seminarian's pastor and rector of school of philosophy; certificates of baptism, confirmation, and parents' marriage; official transcripts of academic credits in classics and philosophy; and "testimonial letters from the chancery office of each diocese, other than his own, in which he has resided for six months or more since his fourteenth birthday."

To get a grasp of seminary life at the time, I located and spoke for hours with priests who attended the same two seminaries as Leduc: SMSU and St. Mary's La Porte/Houston (SMH). Students in the 1950s and early 1960s had their activities expressly limited by rules about mail, food in dorms, access to cars, clothing, even money. One former priest and now avowed atheist, Edward Tarte (SMH 1963), described to me how Houston seminary instructors forbade him even to accept a subscription to *Time* magazine from his parents.

There would be "free days" during the week and vacation during the regular cycle (summer and Christmas), but as another retired (now deceased) Houston priest recounted, restrictions on mobility were so severe during the standard course of study that seminarians would resort to breaking their eyeglasses in order to get permission to leave campus. To emphasize the isolation combined with lack of psychological and sexual education, he said something else: "If more people understood how the training was, then they'd understand the scandal. To give you an idea: they told guys to sleep on their backs with hands outside the sheets."

This dynamic wasn't conducive to education of the whole person. Fr. Jack McGinnis, also a classmate of Tarte's at SMH and now a resident priest at Xavier College Prep School in Palm

Desert, described how certain strict prohibitions could be disregarded privately while off campus: "I'd go off on Saturday, go to the doctor and get drunk all afternoon, then come back and go in without ever seeing anybody. I'd go to bed and nobody ever knew it." He stressed how the disconnection between faculty and candidates for the priesthood could have profound consequences: "They asked me: 'Were your parents married?' Not 'How do you think it affected you that your father burned to death in a fire? How did it affect you that your mother was gone?' They never asked those questions. So: I kept the Rule. Externally. I got good grades... And I was so sick it was just amazing."

Much research has been done examining the immature or ill formed motivations for entering seminary. Each man would or would not come to terms with this in his own way, often after decades. "I became a priest so I could be somebody," McGinnis said. "I became a priest to be loved. Eighty percent of the reason for my attraction to the priesthood was pathology. Thank God for the other twenty percent."

Several priests repeated to me in different ways how, while modeling lives of comprehensive and admirable spiritual discipline, their instructors simply did not know them at all. Sometimes this was a matter of scale (a ratio of 341 seminarians to 16 faculty members at Leduc's first seminary, SMSU in 1950-51) and sometimes a matter of culture (SMH was considerably smaller, with roughly 100 students when Leduc arrived in 1952).

Individual seminarians were discouraged from having too-close "particular friendships" with other men, in the spirit of avoiding worldly attachments and loyalties, not to mention homosexual behaviors if not homosexual attraction. Such feelings could be channeled into religious life and celibate discipline. One priest told me outright, "If you were gay and you were trying to live a respectful life, becoming a priest was the way to do it."

Not everyone I talked to shared that positive outlook. A former Jesuit seminarian now living in Houston described to me how he left seminary of his own volition exactly when he realized that he was gay. He explained the loneliness: "It was easy to feel like you were isolated in whatever your struggle was. And the more serious it was, the less likely you would be to tell anyone. It would get you kicked out right away."

I spoke with Jeffrey Meadows, the former partner of a Houston priest who eventually asked to be laicized because he didn't want to live a double life anymore. Ordained for Galveston-Houston in 1961 and deceased in the late 1980s, this priest had shared his perceptions with Meadows, who recounted them to me: "He would name the priests…that were 'gay, out, and playing' and those that were 'gay and closeted.'"

It clearly wasn't so easy for men who wanted to come to terms with sexuality or the outside world. Mixed messages in seminary training and culture could be difficult for candidates to resolve. Regardless of sexual orientation, everything depended upon an individual's motivations, maturity, and mentors. Furthermore, despite discouragements against "particular friendships," ordained priests formed an exclusive and insular social group, discouraged from mixing with anyone outside the clergy.

"The idea was: get together with other priests—that's where you're safe," Fr. McGinnis said. But the dynamics could be toxic. "There was a lot of criticism, a lot of mistrust, a lot of jealousy. That's when I discovered my disillusion with the whole thing, that this was not a very loving community…They used to make a joke: 'You better go to the party, because if you don't go, they'll talk about you.' I was extremely idealistic and not very practical, but it just wasn't there for me."

A former instructor at St. Mary's Houston described how he and his colleagues knew that one local priest visited the campus seeking sexual liaisons during the early 1970s. When the bishop was informed, he reportedly dismissed the news with indignation: "How dare you say something like that about one of my priests?" Whatever the professed and official restrictions, "ontologically-special" kinship couldn't help but inspire an unsettling blend of loyalty and denial.

McGinnis described the dysfunction this way: "It was a good old boy network-type family, redneck if you want to call it that. Not redneck in the sense of country. It was a fraternity…That was the clergy culture that was created. It eventually moved into cover-up, looking the other way, moving [guys] around, we-take-care-of-our-own type of thing. It was very deep."

The tension between seminary discipline and secrecy (not to mention homophobia and homosexual tension) could be frightening as well as isolating, as I heard men describe again and again. When a seminarian suddenly disappeared or was "clipped" to prevent his advancement to holy orders, his name would not be spoken again. No one would know what happened to him: his bedroom, or his bunk space in the open dorm, was suddenly empty; his assigned seat at chapel or in the classroom became a haunting, blank space. No warning. No explanation.

Records of reasons for seminary withdrawal, expulsion, or "clipping" are not retained in writing. But Leduc's departure from his first seminary is abrupt, and after a limited initial acquaintance in 1950, Leduc's most extended contact with Charlie in Lake Worth took place during Leduc's "limbo" period between seminaries, from November 1951 to August or September 1952.

Charlie was 10 years old, and Leduc was 22. Their bond began here. It ended forever the summer Leduc left for a military base in Alaska and the week Charlie committed mass murder.

Considered in its entirety, from 1950 to 1966, the Whitman-Leduc connection was distinct because it blurred traditional clerical-layperson boundaries of the time. They were neither social nor generational peers, yet across fifteen years, on some level, theirs could be considered a "particular friendship": homosocial (not expressly homosexual) and sustained, fraternal attachment. The disparity in ages underscores Whitman's impressionability, as well as his possible projection or overestimation of a truly reciprocal connection, especially in the beginning.

As the FBI investigation documented well, most of Whitman's friendships emerged from his immediate situations. People who knew him in grade school or high school in Florida remembered him but were not "keeping close touch" once he entered the Marines, or after he enrolled at UT Austin. Whitman socialized mostly with immediate classmates, bunkmates, employers, professors, and neighbors. Despite his exterior and superficial charm, when it came to people other than family, he tended not to extend a great deal of extra effort.

Leduc is one person not biologically related whose continued contact (at times sustained, at times intermittent) fell outside this pattern over a fifteen-year period. Significantly, one of Whitman's surviving friends described Charlie in an email as a "follower." He added that Whitman always talked about Father Leduc, and that Leduc appeared to be one incentive for Whitman's choice to employ his military scholarship at a college in Texas—one hundred sixty-two miles north of Leduc's assigned parish (not exactly a short drive).

As the trouble of Leduc's life unfolded, I wondered whether, in hindsight, Leduc was "marked" by church officials for his association with Whitman after the shootings—simply as an additional excuse to disown him quietly. After all, what bishop would want people making any links between one of his difficult priests and a mixed-up Catholic college student who became a mass killer?

This was a haunting question I would not be able to answer. Leduc's appeals for secrecy at the beginning and the end of his statement to the FBI seem to indicate his own concern, perhaps even paranoia, about scrutiny. His statement was not unredacted until the 1990s, which means that his connection to Whitman was not revealed publicly until more than a decade after Leduc's own death in 1981.

Leduc generally shared so little with anyone, however, that it begs the question: unless he disclosed it himself, how would any diocesan superiors have known? There are two "official" possibilities: first, that the FBI informed his bishop of the interview as a courtesy; second, that Leduc's commanding officer at Elmendorf AFB knew of the interview, passing on word to the Military Ordinariate and/or the Chief of Military Chaplains, who could have shared the information with his home diocese.

Unofficially, Leduc would have been remembered in Florida by SMSU classmates who served as priests in the Lake Worth-West Palm Beach area and who knew the Whitman family.

Furthermore, there were occasions in Houston where Charlie could have easily met Leduc's supervising pastor or clerical colleagues on a social visit. And while Charlie's name might have been forgotten in the moment, his handsome face tended to leave an unforgettable impression. Picture that gameshow smile suddenly blooming into newsprint and on television screens everywhere in awful context, suddenly screaming familiarity, and then: I remember.

✛

The following documents are the surviving public artifacts written in Charles Whitman's own hand and preserved in the Austin History Center:

An autobiographical essay dated March 1, 1956, the spring of his freshman year at St. Anne's Catholic School in West Palm Beach, Florida, and nearly one year after Leduc's ordination and permanent assignment to Houston. The impeccable penmanship and childlike punctuation errors (e.g. using quote marks in the title and for his name) suggest a subconscious awareness of narrative posing: "Autobiography" of "Charles Joseph Whitman."

Fall 1959: Two notebooks from Marine Corps training, one leather-bound pocket loose leaf and one top-bound cardboard spiral. Notes include sex hygiene and types of venereal disease, basic pay, uniform code of conduct, combat procedures, rifle descriptions and shooting technique, and rules for speaking to military officers or drill instructors.

Fall 1961: At-a-Glance Diary for daily appointments, purchased for his first year as a student at UT Austin. Lists daily expenses, phone calls, scheduled meetings, and small notes on the day ("Met Dean Sininger," "Called Gayle for first time," "Failed English theme," "Met Carol"). As is common for college students, and average people, the notes become spotty after a promising few months' effort—and after December, the daily diary goes blank.

June 1963: In February that year, only six months after getting married, Whitman's grades at UT Austin were reportedly not strong enough to sustain his scholarship, and he returned to active duty in the USMC at Camp Lejeune, in North Carolina. The first artifact from this period is his U.S. Marine Corps Score Book, where he tracked his training scores as a rifleman.

November 1963: Hard cover Memoranda book, with sewn binding: the first document where we see Whitman putting sentences together about his experience in traditional "diary" or journal style. He expresses his negative feelings about the Marine Corps ("a waste and a shame," "the corp [sic] definitely sucks!!"), his brother Pat running away from home and getting in a car accident ("that boy has physcologial [sic] problems"), his time in the military brig, and his fear of pregnancy after a visit with his wife. He refers to his father as "Daddy" in this document, especially in places where he expresses gratitude about money. Whitman also states unambiguously his change in religious behaviors ("I don't pray anymore").

February through March 1964: A large canvas-covered blank book with "Daily Record of C.J. Whitman" printed on the front. After the final entry, composed before a trip to visit his wife in Texas on leave, three quarters of the lined pages are left blank though he remained separated from his wife for another nine months. Also contains dated, handwritten comments he added two years later, the night of the killings.

March 1966: Forms filled out at UT Austin when Whitman sought psychiatric help following his mother's separation from his father. Rather than checking "mother" or "father" in response to a question about whom he consults regarding personal problems, he filled out "NEITHER" in the "specify" box. He also lists his "most recent employer" as NASA in Houston, a reference to his brief internship almost a year earlier, the summer of 1965.

July 31, 1966: Letter before the shootings, started several hours prior to killing his wife and mother. Typed and then handwritten. Started at 6:45 PM and finished at 3:00 AM the next day, after both women were dead.

August 1, 1966, 12:30 AM: Handwritten letter on yellow legal paper left on the body of his mother in bed.

August 1, 1966: Letters to his brother, Johnnie Mike, and to his brother, Pat.

Dig as I might through the public materials, I located only one, abbreviated reference to Father Leduc among these pages, written Whitman's first week at UT Austin. There were other mentions of the priest to discover, and many more private letters to read, but I did not see them at the beginning.

Initially, I had to question whether investigators had overestimated Leduc's importance in Whitman's life. I wondered how police or federal authorities had established the connection in the first place.

During a week of combing through and copying archive materials, I located one piece of the puzzle in a letter to Assistant FBI Director DeLoach, dated approximately two weeks after Whitman's tower rampage. The document refers to a follow-up investigation by O.N. Humphreys, then an officer with the Texas Department of Public Safety, who determined that a redacted source "has known Whitman since childhood and reported to know Whitman better than anyone else." Humphreys adds that Whitman "had confided in" the redacted source and "told him more than any other person." Citing both "presidential interest" in the case, as well as the interest of Texas's Governor Connelly, the letter requests an interview with the alleged, name-redacted confidant in Anchorage, Alaska. What follows this document is the first teletype summary from the interview with Leduc while stationed at Elmendorf Air Force Base, complete with white boxes that redact his name and identifying information.

What's unclear in the cover letter is any detail from Humphreys about his basis for discovering the connection between Leduc and Whitman. Who knew, who observed, or who was claiming that they were so close: had someone in Whitman's immediate or extended family made this suggestion? Had a neighbor back home? Had Leduc himself made contact?

Leduc's name comes up again, nearly one month after his interview, in a sworn, handwritten document provided to investigators in South Carolina by one of Whitman's Marine Corps and college friends, Francis J. Schuck, dated and signed September 13. Schuck's statement had to wait until he returned to land after several months of duty on the USS John C. Calhoun, a nuclear submarine. Schuck at one point refers to Whitman's more than average mass attendance rate (during the first year of college) and identifies one of Whitman's "close friends from other than a professional standpoint" as "Father Joseph Gileus [sic] Leduc." Aside from underscoring Leduc's importance to Whitman, Schuck's statement offered a nickname—Gileus, rather than Gilles—an error understandably perpetuated in first reports of the priest's identity.

Despite the significance ascribed to Father Leduc by these two documents, a thorough scouring of Charles Whitman's archived personal material turns up a single reference to the priest in September 1961—not only Whitman's first week at UT Austin, but the second day after he arrived. Among a list of expenses for

Thursday, September 7, is a single line in slanted, printed capital letters: ".25 TIP & CALL TO FATHER GIL."

This discovery in Whitman's handwriting was crucial. First, it clarified the name Leduc used with people who knew him—not "Joseph" or "Joe" or even "Leduc," but "Gil," an anglicized version of "Gilles," his French middle name. This explained why, when I first searched "Joseph G. Leduc" on the Internet, I located the FBI statement, while other materials were elusive. Nominal slippages and errors seem to play a role in blurring Leduc's record.

From a storytelling point of view, the disproportion was striking: other people emphasized Leduc as a crucial figure in Whitman's life; Leduc himself references names (and approximates ages) of Whitman's brothers and also identifies friends as well as two other priests (both now deceased) connected to Whitman, suggesting more knowledge and contact than the average busy clergyman. The FBI expended resources and time to locate Leduc—in Alaska—and interview him. There is also documented involvement marked by verifiable life milestones (Eagle Scout status, Leduc's first mass, Whitman's first year of college, Whitman's twenty-first birthday, and Whitman's wedding). Leduc outlined his history with Whitman, including "a great deal of contact" his first year at UT, and observations of school-related stress and "turmoil concerning religion" during two visits closer to the time of the shootings.

But in the materials written in Whitman's own hand, the priest seems barely visible. And in the surviving summary of Leduc's interview, the mixture of selective detail and emotional detachment makes for a disjointed read. The more I learned, the more I came to understand that Leduc had an extraordinary ability to camouflage himself when he wanted to.

Merely being scoutmaster and neighbor for approximately one year seems more means-to-an-end rather than pathway to sustained, intimate, peer-level friendship. The twelve-year age difference underscores the dilemma here: in his early twenties, Leduc was certainly not young enough to be a peer for Whitman, but neither was he old enough to be a peer to Whitman's parents. Did he babysit, mow the lawn, or skim leaves from the swimming pool for Charlie's mother? Did Leduc have any friends in the neighborhood his own age?

However their connection evolved, the traditional Catholic identity of Charlie's mother would have provided a spoken or unspoken encouragement, even imprimatur, for continuing the relationship. Any friendly connection with a young priest or priest-to-be would have been seen as a blessing by the young mother of three boys, stuck in a violent marriage. Questioning it at the time would have been un-thinkable. If Leduc had merely been a college drop-out still at home with his parents, this perception would have likely been much different.

The FBI investigation turned up one essay from Charlie's freshman year of high school, written approximately one year after he had served as an altar boy at Leduc's first masses in Lake Worth. In the essay, he describes his Catholic elementary school experiences with a great amount of specificity—even to the point of emphasizing a "lack of leaders" for scouts prior to the founding of the troop at Sacred Heart. His impeccable penmanship matches the impeccability of his almost predictable good boy résumé: he lists his First Holy Communion, becoming an altar boy in the fourth grade and winning a $5 prize for learning Latin the best, attending the 1953 Scout Jamboree in California (with thanks to his parents for paying his way), his Ad Altare Dei Award (the Catholic scouting award), and eventually his Eagle Scout achievement. Most importantly, he refers to key adults by name: the doctor who brought him into the world, Dr. Grady H. Brantley; his father; and even the auxiliary bishop who presided over his fifth grade confirmation, Thomas J. McDonough. He makes no mention of Leduc as a troop leader, brand new priest, or friend.

I discovered another memorable connection as well. In September 1952, at age 23, just after transferring to continue his seminary studies in Texas and one year before Charlie received his Eagle Scout award, Leduc returned briefly to Lake Worth to be presented with his own Eagle Scout honor in a ceremony at the civic auditorium.

Within the details of shared parish life experience, and in the context of the "perfect" Catholic Boy Scout pedigree Charlie presents, the omission of Leduc is interesting. It feels as if Leduc's name was too important, too personal, or too different to write down.

III. SHADOWS AND DISCREPANCIES

Since the early 2000s, the sexual abuse scandal has tended to shape popular expectations when it comes to stories about priests. Recorded practices of church evasion and secrecy (from the Vatican level down) have exacerbated trauma for victims. It is also true that the most salacious stories of priestly failure or crime evoke a kind of perverse narrative delight or *schadenfreude* when the "second Christ" has clay feet after all. The simplistic truism becomes an easy jeer at the end of an awful joke. For scholars of church history, for priests themselves, for the everyday faithful, the humanity of priests is no surprise. But any betrayal of a high calling is real; it taints everything—and the stakes happen to be high for those who benefit from an all-male religious monarchy.

In 2004, two years after the *Boston Globe* broke its Pulitzer Prize-winning story of massive cover-up by the Church hierarchy, the National Council of Catholic Bishops commissioned the John Jay Report to examine "the nature and scope of sexual abuse of minors by priests and deacons in the U.S. 1950-2002." The Report's calculation was that 3%-6% of all priests had been accused of sexual abuse during that period. Other estimates put the total number at 5.3% or even 9%, and individual dioceses report higher rates within narrower timeframes: more than 10% in Providence, RI (1971-2006), and 7.7% in Philadelphia (1967-2005).

But not all priestly troubles are criminal ones. After conducting a 25-year ethnographic study, psychotherapist and former priest, Richard Sipe, author of *A Secret World: Sexuality and the Search for Celibacy*, estimated that, despite their ordination vow to be chaste, only 50% of priests are practicing celibacy at any given time. Sipe distinguished his focus from other studies because he documented actual behaviors and practices rather than attitudes (such as "honoring" or being "satisfied" with the celibate state).

Violations of chastity need not be predatory; they could be solitary violations, through masturbation, or through consensual homosexual or heterosexual affairs. Moral and practical crises arise not only for a priest himself, but also for any romantic or sexual partners, for any children who result from secret unions, and for parishioners or fellow clerics who observe or become aware of a priest in a compromising position. Any priest who has grave problems and breaks his vows may have mentors that guide, advise, or reprimand him, but he may also find compatriots who merely enable him. As Sipe writes in his essay, "The Celibate Myth," "The efforts of those who honestly and consistently try to practice celibacy are not to be denigrated. But sexual patterns and practices cannot be discounted... Bishops and priests have honored celibacy in word and not deed."

Sipe points out how the privileged place of the priest in a group of other ordained men (who themselves may or may not be living according to their promises) creates opportunities for complicity, dishonesty, and extortion. In order to retain status within what Sipe calls "the celibate/sexual system," the façade must be preserved at all costs. This twisted dynamic has often been justified in the name of saving the faithful from "scandal." It also has contributed to reluctance on the part of some clergy to speak out about the criminal activity of others, because they are vulnerable to exposure for their own sexual activities—consensual if hypocritical violations of their vows.

McGinnis shared his perceptions about sexual behavior in Galveston-Houston during the 1960s: "There was an extreme amount of gay activity among the priests that was very well hidden—I discovered years later," he said. "I was naïve about all of this. There were a lot of priests who had been very active, even in seminary. There were priests I knew that later died of AIDS, and I couldn't believe it. It was an undercover subculture in those days."

I learned firsthand how the official church response to men who had adult relationships with women could be especially harsh—as if the brotherhood itself had been betrayed. One woman who married a priest spoke to me frankly about how her husband's former colleagues cast her as a villain. According to her, her husband was refused a Catholic burial.

I spoke at length with Joseph Coleman (SMSU 1951-1955) who shared that he was sent to a "house of affirmation" following a consensual affair in the early 1980s. He left the facility—and his diocese—without looking back, married the woman he loved, and never heard from his bishop again. ("To be fair," he added, "I wasn't reaching out to them, either.") He explained how he wished that his seminary education had more deeply encouraged him to examine his most secret and personal feelings, but also expressed that he was crushed when celibacy was not made optional after the Second Vatican Council.

I asked about his relationship to the church, and Coleman told me that he still attended mass and was studying scripture a great deal these days, with a regular Bible group. "I didn't ask to be released from my vows," he said. "I'll be a priest until I die. I'm just not in the Catholic Directory anymore." There was no pension for him, either—a financial factor that increased the stakes for anyone who considered leaving.

I talked to and read about many priests who, contrary to stereotypes about hedonism or failure, left their collars behind as an assertion of spiritual maturity, seeking a healthier identity and relationship to the church. This cost the faithful access to decent and conscientious men. Coleman's story contains a particularly apropos example. In March 1966, five months before Whitman's rampage, Coleman made national news when, serving as police chaplain in Providence, RI, he entered the second story of a building shot through by police with tear gas. He talked a gunman into releasing three hostages and giving himself up after a two-hour siege. No one was killed that day.

Coleman may have struggled with celibacy, but here was one powerful illustration of how he had taken the deepest lessons of seminary to heart during a violent and potentially fatal crisis with strangers who needed his service. "That was the Sulpician way," he told me later. "They always emphasized that our primary role was to be available, to ask 'how can I help?'" He was chaplain to police as well as college students in the 1960s, during a time fraught with conflict and heartache. By contrast, Leduc smiled and joked plenty but could seem remote or out-of-tune even among people he knew. Unlike Coleman and others (regardless of sexual orientation) who faced a crisis of vows, Leduc remained in the priesthood and was listed in the OCD until his death.

I had to engage, of course, the worst-case scenario. Leduc's name did not turn up in any current databases of credibly accused sexual abusers—either among priests or Boy Scouts of America— which means that there are no public records of accusation or litigation. To be fair, however, lack of criminal complaint is a low bar to measure the quality or depth of a man's commitment to ministry and does not preclude a spectrum of serious problems. Lack of public complaint cannot exclude, for example, the possibility that Leduc, like thousands of priests, struggled with (or occasionally dispensed with) his profession of celibacy.

Leduc died nearly twenty years before the Church-wide scandal broke in 2002, so he was essentially protected if anyone sought to complain posthumously. Texas also has a strict statute of limitations law that has insulated Catholic authorities from facing decades-old complaints. The Galveston-Houston diocese participated in the John Jay Study, and afterwards, a pastoral letter released in 2004 by then-Bishop Fiorenza stated that all priests and deacons "credibly accused" since 1994 had either resigned, died, or had been removed from active ministry. The report also stated that 80% of "credible" allegations by "known victims" involved incidents prior to 1980 and reported between 1994 and 2004—an important distinction, as it cannot account for complaints deemed "not credible" or brought forward under either of Fiorenza's ecclesiastical predecessors, Bishop Louis Morkovsky or Bishop Wendolin Nold, both long-deceased by the date of the statement. The diocese reported paying out $3.6 million dollars for settlements, counseling, and legal costs (a relatively small amount when compared to dioceses such as Los Angeles, Boston, or even Dallas).

The 2004 statement emphasized that the diocese received a commendation for "having a sexual misconduct policy for clergy and lay personnel since October 1, 1990." However, the chancery office has (to date) declined to release the names of the 22 priests and 4 permanent deacons "sustainably" accused, leaving us with an algebra problem rather than full disclosure. A few identities are discoverable through other sources. Four known men accused and officially suspended—before and after 2004—were contemporaries of Leduc who outlived him: Rev. Laurence Peguero (ord. 1947); Rev. Charles Schoppe (ord. 1949); Rev. Anthony Hernandez Gonzalez, an Oblate father (ordained 1957); and Rev. Jesse Linam (ordained 1961).

The time window in which Leduc lands is an uneasy one. I felt wary as I discovered that his combination of activities, problems, temperament, and assignment trajectory made him an outlier by an average measure. He spent the last decade of his priesthood on a combination of "leave" and "medical leave." But he appeared to retain some degree of protection, even when no longer in

Houston. He had former classmates, if not friends, in high places.

As research in cases of problem priests has revealed over and over again, diocesan officials would have been motivated less by concern for Leduc personally than by protecting the image of the church. This motivation would have been stronger if any chancery officials knew that one particularly troubled clergyman had ties to a man who committed mass murder. Who on earth could secure an answer to that question?

I had brief subterranean contact with an attorney who for five years defended the Galveston-Houston Archdiocese against complaints. He walked away from this job after publicly sharing how denial of his own sexual trauma at the hands of a priest years before had made him sickly complicit. Leduc's name was not one the attorney recognized, and he did not think he knew anyone from that generation who might be willing to talk. I had already crossed off names of potential contacts because they had died, had an illness or disability that severely limited communication, or simply wouldn't respond to requests to talk.

I put off an interview with one of those men until I thought I had reasonably exhausted willing clerical contacts still residing in or connected to the Archdiocese. Now retired with a status of Archbishop Emeritus, Joseph Fiorenza had been one year ahead of Leduc at SMH, and was appointed Bishop of San Angelo in 1979. He then served as Bishop, and eventually Archbishop, of Galveston-Houston from 1984 to 2006. Because of his sturdy placement in the hierarchy, I did not anticipate learning much, and I was inclined not to approach. But one source encouraged me when I asked whether to bother. Perhaps if Fiorenza understood that I was trying to put a human face on a priest with problems, he might talk to me not as an administrator or bishop, but as a former seminarian and colleague of Leduc's.

I had to reach out through the press office via email, and the spokesperson was always polite to me. Through all the formal cordiality, I still worried about being "handled" by proxies—that is, after all, any media officer's job. I sent my inquiry: Would former Archbishop Fiorenza share any memories he had of a priest I was writing about? I wasn't looking to ambush anyone. I wanted a human perspective. I had no complaint. The usual. When the spokesperson asked for the name (I had been prepared for this), I told her that I was uncomfortable sending it in an email to her; instead, I could send a photograph she could pass forward.

The polite but firm rejoinder came: "It's just that Archbishop"—she used his title as a formal name, no "the" in front—"Archbishop has specifically asked to know the name before agreeing to the interview."

I stated that I would be happy to communicate the name verbally to the archbishop's secretary, but I repeated my compromise of the photograph, this time actually sending a picture of Leduc (one I had captured from a wall during a visit to SMH). Six days passed with no answer.

I followed up, writing, "I absolutely understand if the interview is not going to be possible, but I would be remiss if I didn't make sure." The next day I received the answer that Archbishop would not return to the office until the following week, and would be unlikely able to participate in the interview. I thought the process had come to a clean conclusion.

However, the next day, the spokesperson sent me another email stating that if I could send my specific questions, Archbishop might have time to answer electronically.

Okay, I thought. I'll see what happens. I spent time crafting ten questions—many were situational and thematic: about seminary life and instruction at the time, seminarians who departed, the chaplaincy and Vietnam, parish priesthood during changes of the turbulent 1960s. My last questions were about Leduc and again included the photo. Since I included the document as an attached file, what the heck, I included his last name, too.

I waited four days, then inquired to confirm that the questions had been received. The spokesperson stated that she had forwarded them to the archbishop and would let me know if she heard anything. Another six days went by. This time, I emailed to ask whether it would be more accurate to report that Fiorenza "did not have time to address" any of my questions, or if he had "declined to answer" any of them. At first, the spokesperson said that she did not think he had time. The very next day, she sent me the answers.

The resulting material felt surreal and pointless. Most of the responses were so generic that I could have written them myself. The one answer—and the longest—where Fiorenza seemed to have spent the most time, described grim conditions at the old seminary in La Porte, emphasizing the lack of heat, AC, and modern plumbing. His emendations were indicated in a blue font. I had expended hours of effort across nearly three weeks to discover nothing new.

When it came to Leduc, sentences were crafted with almost absolute negation, displaying a lawyerly skill so familiar in official statements or even depositions: "I remember Gil Leduc as a seminarian but I do not remember much about him. I have no memory or knowledge about his reaction to the changes you have referred to above. I believe he died while I was serving as the

Bishop of San Angelo. I did not have a chance to speak to him before he died and I do not know anything about his final illness."

This response did reveal some knowledge, however: Fiorenza had used Leduc's familiar name—something I had not done—and he had remembered or checked on the year of his death. The gist of his message about Leduc seemed to be: I was never responsible for this guy.

It would be poetic to say that at this moment a cock crowed in the distance. Perhaps I should have imagined the Godfather theme instead. Biblical and mafia jokes aside, I had to speak up. I confessed in an email to the spokesperson that it was impossible to distinguish between the voice of Fiorenza as a person and the voice of the official institution in the responses I had received. Would he be able to answer any follow-up questions from me, whether on the phone or in person? (After all, I thought, now he had the name.) This time, the answer was no, he would be traveling.

Many Catholics had brought grievous complaints and much tougher requests to their own bishops in good faith, trusting their church fathers to do the right thing. But I had seen the documentaries and read the reports of how these same people were ignored, brushed off, or lied to by officials. The patterns of communication were sadly predictable. In response to long and excruciatingly detailed letters composed by women or men reporting molestations, bishops were often unable to muster empathy for anyone but the alleged offender, expressing only generic phrasing about "your concerns," or "your candid expression of opinion," or "the hardship." These letters often hit all the spiritual clichés: calling for "compassion," "the sake of the faithful," and "God's forgiveness," concluding with "every good wish" and "warm personal regards," and "devotedly/sincerely yours in Christ." Personal encounters were similarly nerve-wracking while simultaneously pacifying, including advice to "be very careful of slander." In the worst cases, those who approached chancery offices with serious questions were shamed, blamed, and accused of trying to profit from allegations of abuse.

Knowing all this on an intellectual level, recognizing that I had no complaint against Leduc personally, I experienced a physical reaction in the pit of my guts when the exchange concluded. I was exhausted and depleted in a way that felt technically out of proportion, yet was also deeply familiar and undeniable. Somehow the whole thing called up memories of priests I mistrusted—particularly one very "traditional" pastor who was happy to see my mother volunteer to teach catechism Sunday after Sunday for years at our parish, but who turned a deaf ear to her distress when my father left.

The questions I'd prepared were straightforward and open-ended, yet the official answers were closed-off, insulting to an average intelligence. How is it that I was actually ashamed of asking? That seemed to be the key. I believe now that it wouldn't have mattered what questions I asked, how I framed them, or in what order. Priests I interviewed had described their own depressing brush-offs in scenarios where they sought dialogue with superiors. One retired priest preferred to keep the content of his discouraging encounter with one of Fiorenza's predecessors to himself, but he said the meeting concluded abruptly when the bishop stood up at his desk, offered a handshake and only one comment: "Let us pray for each other." Another priest ordained in 1955 at SMSU, Msgr. John Brady, had told me flat out: "I'm amazed I'm still a Catholic. You can't trust bishops anymore. But

I made a promise that I'd never allow anybody to take my faith."

I had initiated this contact without a lawyer, without a media organization behind me, without any connection to the diocese, and my failure was predictable. I would not be asking Fiorenza or any other officials about Leduc's assignment record—nevermind Charles Whitman. What I received via email and printed out in my hands was an ordinary artifact of clerical non-conversation, a non-responsive response. I had expected a clear demurral, but the back-and-forth rigamarole was more unsettling than an outright refusal to engage, almost as if constructed to involve or implicate me more deeply in the shallow outcome.

Still, it was breathtaking how unequivocally Leduc was kept at arm's length in the response. I simultaneously felt pity and suspicion.

The encounter drove me to understand Fiorenza's career more thoroughly. Before being appointed as head of Galveston-Houston, Fiorenza was bishop of San Angelo, Texas, from 1979 to 1984. During that time, he accepted a Worcester, MA priest named Rev. David Holley into the diocese. Holley would eventually be sentenced in 1993 to 55-275 years imprisonment for raping boys in New Mexico. Correspondence between bishops published by the *Dallas Morning News* in 1997 indicated that after a trial period, Fiorenza was aware that Holley's "past problems" ... "had surfaced again." He did not report Holley to police but did ask him to leave in 1984, the year Fiorenza returned to Galveston-Houston as bishop.

Fiorenza went on to serve as President of the National Council (and eventually Conference) of Catholic Bishops from 1998 to 2001, just before the wave of abuse allegations crested in the U.S.

(He had served as Vice President from 1995-98, and continues to be part of the administrative board.) Although Fiorenza was serving at the helm when his diocese created the sexual misconduct policy in 1990, he was also named in a 2004 conspiracy lawsuit alleging that he and Msgr. William Pickard (ordained with Fiorenza in 1954) had failed to report abuse of three young men by a Colombian expatriate seminarian training to be a deacon in Galveston-Houston in the mid 1990s. That case was internationally notable because it named Cardinal Joseph Ratzinger as a co-defendant, though Ratzinger was eventually shielded from legal action upon his election as pope (a "head of state" exemption). The case was settled in 2008, and its terms are undisclosed.

There was no evidence that someone this long-invested in the clerical structure at such a high level could interact any differently with a layperson. My exchange did dramatize how the hierarchy could simultaneously insulate a priest and wash its hands of him. It also suggested that Leduc was not an inspiring subject for the chancery office, or for this former classmate.

Fiorenza, for his part, with the help of a highly trained team, was simply communicating as bishops had learned to do. Nothing about the encounter was personal. In theological terms, I suppose the conversation was ontologically impossible: I was not worthy of a frank exchange.

Perhaps that was why the whole experience bothered me. After all that had happened in the church, part of me wanted to believe that interaction with a bishop could be more than ceremonial. Maybe in his own frail way, Leduc had dreamed of that, too.

On the other hand, when a priest makes his way on thin ice for a long time, shallow waters are exactly what he counts on.

IV. Finding a Face

Here are the photographs I have seen of Joseph Leduc, in order of discovery.

1. On microfiche at a library in his hometown of Waterbury, CT: Dated June 5, 1955, the *Waterbury Republican-American* published an article announcing that Leduc would sing his first high mass at his childhood parish of St. Anne's. Preaching the homily was a visiting priest and a relative of Leduc's mother: Rev. Real Beauregard from St. Hyacinthe, Quebec. Interestingly, this article complicated the report (in one obituary) and a common reading of Leduc's FBI statement that his "very first" mass was offered in Lake Worth. Based on records now available, Leduc clearly had two first masses—perhaps one "high" and one "low"; or simply one for the people who knew him where he grew up, and one for his later parish in Florida.

   In any case, on the badly scarred film, Leduc's photo appears to have been taken in early seminary days (c. 1950). His large ears and toothy smile oddly evoke both Opie Taylor from *The Andy Griffith Show* and Alfred E. Neumann from the cover of *MAD Magazine*. His eyes are sloped and tired looking on a narrow face. The contrast was so sharply different from the Montgomery Clift fantasy I'd been harboring (see Hitchcock's *I Confess*) that I printed the image out with the article and stared at his face for long stretches at a time. There was a lack of depth or warmth in this smile, a kind of squirrelly quality about the image. Leduc didn't look like a future priest I would feel comfortable confiding in. Maybe he would be fun at a parish breakfast or a bingo game.

2. Located during an on-campus interview and guided tour

with the current rector of SMH, where Leduc was ordained despite a librarian's email to the contrary one year earlier. Photo discovered during an escorted tour across the grounds, through the cloister, the original dorms, and a classroom building: A portrait (c. 1955) of J. Leduc and the faces of the five other men in his ordination class, along with portraits of Bishop Wendolin Nold and the seminary rector, all inside a frame on wall of a second floor hallway. Here, Leduc's face looks much, much older: heavy eyelids, vacant eyes, a possible shadow of suntan from glasses across the bridge of his nose, the hint of acne scars. His lips are closed, a blend of frown and near smile that reads as a faint smirk. His head is tilted to the side and slightly forward. There is something smoldering about this photo, some underlying worldliness and sexuality. There is something attractive, sad, cold, and a bit smug about his expression. When I later showed this photo to Jack McGinnis, he said, "Oh wow. That's the face I remember. There was a lot going on that no one could touch."

3 & 4. Handed to me by an archivist during my brief visit to the Galveston-Houston Chancery Office: Xeroxed photographs dated 1969 and 1981 from reports in the *Texas Catholic Herald*—one announcing a new parish assignment, the other with his obituary. This stock photograph was taken at an odd angle, with Leduc's eyes (this time framed by black horn-rims) flicking off-center to the right, looking at someone or something other than the photographer, his mouth slightly open as if in mid-word or mid-sentence, a deadpan aside. The mood of this image is a blend of annoyance and exhaustion, even resignation, but his hair is tidily combed, his face clean-shaven.

5. Also handed to me by an archivist in the Chancery Office: Xeroxed and captioned photograph, undated and un-sourced

(likely from *Texas Catholic Herald* c. 1967), showing Leduc seated in partial profile among other men on duty at Elmendorf AFB, greeting wounded soldiers on aircraft en route from Vietnam to the lower 48 states. The close cut of his hair makes a clean line over his ear and along his neck, and one can just see the side frame of his glasses. He wears a flight jacket with a fur-lined hood that rests at his shoulders.

6. Discovered on a vestibule wall during visit to St. Dominic's Church, Sheldon Reservoir area on the outskirts of Houston: Larger version of picture #3, likely an original print, framed in light plywood, with a brass label attached to include his name "Rev. Gil Leduc" and his dates of service. His framed photograph is first in a line of framed photographs on that wall, a shrine to all the other pastors who served there. His name is also still listed as "founding pator" [sic] on the parish website.

7. Received electronically from the archives of St. Mary's Baltimore: Leduc's official photograph as a first-year seminarian. As in photo #1, he looks incredibly young—too young for a 22 year-old. Here, his broad smile of crowded teeth (with especially prominent canines) seems at once unserious and accommodating. The acne marks, even retouched, mottle his complexion in this photo, and his Adam's apple looks unusually sharp. Despite the youthful expression, he has deep creases and bags under his eyes. He looks virginal, open, uninitiated—simultaneously eager and dopey. I feel sorry for the face in this picture. The band of his white collar has not been attached properly, so one can actually see the skin of his throat above the cassock button, as if he had been in a hurry, or as if the collar did not fit him properly. (See photo, page 36)

8. Nearly a year later, received via mail by a classmate from

Assumption Preparatory School in Worcester, MA, following a telephone interview: a photocopied image of Leduc's senior portrait (c. 1947) originally published in the school yearbook. This is the only photograph I've seen where Leduc is not wearing a uniform. Instead, he wears a dressy houndstooth jacket, a loud tie. His expression here (steady gaze and the barest smile) most resembles his ordination portrait and thus forebodes a similar ambiguity, but it lacks the weariness captured later. Looking at this face, I imagined alternative lives—bachelorhood, marriage and kids, a career as a professor, insurance salesman, surveyor, shopkeeper, mailman.

Together and separately, the images are difficult to read. This difficulty coincides with impressions shared by people who knew him well. On the one hand, a cousin told me, "Gil always wanted to be a priest. Always." Yet her husband added what a riot Gil was, to the point where, "Sometimes he'd say things and you'd think: This guy's a priest?"

What had the handsome, blonde Charles Whitman seen in this face, in these expressions? I didn't know what I saw, exactly. But it didn't put me at ease.

In April 1929, six months before the Stock Market Crash and twelve years before Charles Whitman entered the world, Joseph Gilles ("Gil") Leduc was born in Waterbury, CT. In Catholic history, the city is also known as the hometown of Father Michael McGivney, founder of the Knights of Columbus. The most prominent landmark of "the brass city" remains the imposing clock tower at Union Station, modeled after the Torre del Mangia in Siena, Italy.

Originally from a family in French Canada, Leduc's father

had emigrated and worked as a clock adjuster at the Waterbury Clock Company. Leduc's mother also had French Canadian parents, though she had been born in Rhode Island. In addition to raising her son and keeping what her niece called an "immaculate home," she was at times employed as a toolmaker and a factory bench worker.

In the first two years of his life, according to census records and city directories, Leduc's parents shared space with his maternal grandparents and his uncle in clapboard tenements, first on Cherry and then on High Street. By the time Leduc was ten, he and his parents lived on their own in a Dover Street apartment one block behind the newly-built copper dome and grey stone spires of St. Anne's Church, a parish originally founded in 1886 to serve French-speaking immigrant families in the city.

He remained an only child. His lack of siblings, his name (pronounced like the feminine "Jill"), and small, wiry frame would have likely made him a prime target for teasing and for bullies, so one would expect him to cultivate attitudes and skills to help avert trouble and maneuver socially. Clownishness combined with external pieties could have secured Leduc a kind of camouflage as well as strategic adult allies. As a result, he would have cultivated adequate likeability to evade heavy scrutiny and to pass through.

As a child, Leduc could easily walk from home to church to the parish school, and he would have been among the first Boy Scouts in the original troop organized at St. Anne's in the mid 1930s. When he graduated from the eighth grade in 1943, he went away from home to an all-boys' boarding school, Assumption Prep in Worcester, MA, an institution run by the Augustinian Fathers and known for academic and social discipline. Next to his yearbook photograph (c. 1947) are descriptions: "Has hidden qualities of a leader...earnest worker...willing and reliable... minds his own business (rare quality here)...eagle-beaked nose...loves classical music...prefers manual to mental labor."

The yearbook caption lists Leduc as a member of the drama club as well as to the Cercle St. Jean, a group of more than forty young men interested in the priesthood. I later discovered that Leduc was not only a member of the Cercle, but was an officer who held three posts his senior year: Vice-President, Secretary, and Treasurer. His caption also does not mention his role as member of the yearbook editorial staff, as a photographer.

After graduation, Leduc enrolled at the University of Ottawa, where he majored in languages—an unsurprising choice, given his likely exposure to, and facility with, French at home, English in school, and Latin at church.

According to his cousin, Leduc's mother had back problems and wore a brace, so her doctor recommended life in a warmer climate. Just as Leduc left Ottawa and entered the seminary for the first time in 1950-51, his parents built a modest one-story house in Lake Worth, Florida, and moved there permanently. The couple eventually added a small extra room to accommodate their son on visits home. According to the cousin's husband, Leduc's father bought and ran a gas station not far from the ocean, near Route 1A. Advertisements from the period appear to confirm this.

Following ordination, Leduc's active priesthood in Houston can be divided into two phases: before military and after military. The first phase spans the decade from 1955-1965. In summer of 1955, Leduc served approximately one month at Sacred Heart Parish in Lake Worth. For the next ten years in Galveston-Houston, Leduc served at parishes spanning a wide geographical area criss-crossing the large diocese: first, in central Houston, at

Annunciation Church (1955), and then at Christ the King Parish (1956-1961). His third assignment was farther east, at St. Pius V Church in Pasadena, but he left this parish within a matter of months, before the end of 1961—a likely indication of problems. There is no official letter on file for Leduc's next assignment, on the south side of Houston, at the fledgling "split off" parish of St. Philip Neri (late 1961-Dec. 1964). For at least the first six years of his priesthood Leduc was active with the Boy Scouts, eventually serving as Catholic Area Chaplain into the early 1960s. In 1964, the bishop approved Leduc's pursuit of an Air Force chaplaincy. By 1965, during the transition period, Leduc was assigned even farther east, near the border of Louisiana, at St. Mary's Church in Port Arthur. That July, Leduc attended training at Maxwell AFB in Alabama, and by spring 1966, he accepted his temporary station at Lackland Air Force Base in San Antonio. Altogether, that totals seven known assignment locations in ten years—a great deal of movement before his relocation to Alaska.

Whitman arrived in Texas and renewed contact with Leduc in Fall 1961 (in his statement, Leduc says he "had close contact with him" at the time), coinciding with Leduc's move from Pius V to Philip Neri. Within only a few months, Leduc helped Whitman marry one of the first people he would murder.

It doesn't seem that Whitman was inspired by Leduc's example or guidance, if any, because sources suggest that he practiced his faith less and less. In his At-a-Glance Diary, the last self-recorded deposit to the collection plate at church was October 1, 1961, which seems to mark an end to, or at least interruption of, his regular mass attendance. Ironically, this occurs after renewed contact with his priest friend. Leduc also reported to the FBI his assessment that Whitman had become "a playboy" and was "losing his basic principles and faith," whatever that meant.

Leduc's language on the surface seems to ape Catholic code for disapproval of sexual activities, but it is worth noting that this was also high times for Hugh Hefner and James Bond. Ian Fleming had been serializing his Bond stories in *Playboy* since 1959, and by 1966 there had already been four feature length films about the debonair ladies' man, his spy toys, and his "girls" with risqué names. In that context, "playboy" in the popular vernacular can read as a backhanded compliment or a throwaway joke rather than profound concern. Unlike Whitman's other friend, A. J. Vincik, Leduc offered no specifics about questions Whitman was asking regarding morality, nor does he explore the content of their conversations about changing practices, experiments, or beliefs.

In summer 1962, following a one-month engagement period, Leduc expedited the mixed-marriage ceremony of Charlie to Kathleen Leissner, who would remain a practicing Methodist. Leduc later told the FBI that he had "objected" to Charlie's "pushing so hard to be an Eagle Scout" at a young age, but he reflected no similar caution or concern about the speed with which Charlie sought to be married—a much more significant and life-changing decision, as well as (for Catholics) a holy sacrament. In one premarital letter to his fiancée, Charlie suggested that they spend part of his twenty-first birthday weekend visiting Father Gil, presumably to introduce her. According to her brother, Nelson, Kathy was the first member of the family ever to marry a non-Protestant. He also shared his impression that the whole marriage felt "like a whirlwind."

There was no obvious incentive for such speed—Kathy was not pregnant, and Charlie was not heading to Vietnam. Letters between the mothers suggest that both were caught off guard but making the best of it. The two families met for the first time the day of the ceremony at St. Michael's Catholic Church in Kathy's hometown of Needville, a small farm community southwest of Houston.

Nelson recalled some surprise at Leduc's presence as the presiding clergyman. "I knew Father Pekar," he said, referring to the pastor of St. Michael's at the time. "I had no idea how Father Leduc came into it as the priest. He damn sure didn't act like it."

Despite the complex circumstances, especially for the time period, Leduc made only a passing mention of the marriage arrangements to the FBI and said that the date of the wedding was "now unrecalled." He also never referred to Charlie's wife by her correct name, calling her "Katherine" rather than "Kathleen" or even "Kathy." While he may have performed wedding ceremonies of passing strangers who blurred together, this was the wedding of someone he had known for ten years. His vague memory is striking in proportion to his recollections about the reasons for Charlie's haste to become an Eagle Scout a decade earlier—"at around the age of 12…at the time, the youngest boy" to achieve that status: "[Leduc] and the institution sponsoring the Boy Scout Troop objected…but [Whitman] continued his aggressiveness toward this goal because [his] father was so persistent in urging [him] towards this goal."

The lack of content in Leduc's recollection seems matched to the hasty ceremony. While not uncommon at the time, particularly in the South, mixed marriages between Catholics and Protestants were still officially discouraged and also monitored by church rules. A series of at least six catechetical instructions was technically required for any non-Catholic who did not convert, along with signatures from both parties indicating a promise to raise any children in the faith. All such couples had to receive special dispensation from the bishop. Unless express permission was granted, such ceremonies were also supposed to "look" different from weddings between Catholics: they were supposed to take place in the parish rectory rather than in the church itself, and (as severe as it sounds) even a bridal gown or floral decorations were officially forbidden. There was not supposed to be a nuptial mass or any service of communion.

We cannot know whether the expected information for the bride-to-be was provided by Leduc or another priest altogether, or if Leduc somehow waived or "signed off" certain rules to make the process easier. Regardless of ecclesiastical technicalities, the time crunch was extraordinary, not allowing for much depth of communication or soul-searching. It was already mid-July when Charlie wrote to his fiancée that Father Gil was "supposed to call" him—on August 1—about Kathy's religious "instructions."

The only indicator of "difference" was the lack of nuptial mass and the hour of the ceremony: the invitation records the time as 5:00 PM on a Friday, rather than a Saturday morning or afternoon. Photos show Whitman kissing his new bride in her white wedding dress at the altar rail, suggesting that permission for the church location was either attained or not even requested. In the background, wearing a white surplice rather than full vestments, Leduc smiles down at the couple. At a glance, he could pass for an altar boy.

One could interpret the apparent ease of Whitman's marriage as evidence of kind-hearted advocacy and indulgence on the part of Leduc, but the evidence rather supports a picture of Leduc less as fatherly ally and institutional skeptic than as playmate who simply understood how to game the official rules. Nelson recalled that Charles had assured his bride's family that the whole "Catholic thing" didn't matter to him anymore ("he was kind of over it"), and that the sole point of the ceremony was to show respect for, or avoid making waves with, his still-devout mother. In fact, the wedding ceremony was held on the anniversary of Charlie's parents, August 17. In a letter to Kathy a week before the ceremony, Charlie wrote that he needed to get his parents a card for the occasion.

Leduc's physical entrance on the scene of the wedding was not typical for a priest. Nelson described how Leduc seemed to come from nowhere, swooping through Needville in a blue Oldsmobile convertible, top down, and into the church parking lot. A nameless blonde woman in a low-cut dress seemed oddly "cozy" alongside Leduc in the front seat.

The nature of the relationship was impossible to assess, Nelson stressed, but he pointed out that he wasn't the only one to notice her. "Some of us were worried that Charlie's mother would see them and freak out, you know?" He didn't remember Leduc or the woman attending the reception hosted at the Leissner family home (photos do not show Leduc in attendance), and Nelson also had an impression that Leduc and his friend seemed in a hurry.

Nelson recalled that someone—Charlie, possibly—told Leduc to "cool it." He also had a memory of Mrs. Whitman thanking Leduc afterwards for the "beautiful ceremony." I wondered whether Charlie subsequently asked, or told, Leduc to be on his way.

Because of their interactions during the previous year, Charlie already would have known Leduc's proclivities, whether he considered them ironic, flamboyant, embarrassing, or bold. Perhaps

Leduc's attendance at the reception wasn't expected in the first place. Nelson's description of Leduc's odd presence suggests some kind of inside joke between friends.

Nelson remembered overhearing Leduc talking to some of the guys, saying how he and his guest were on their way for a weekend somewhere. "Going down to the Corpus, maybe?" Nelson recalled (regional shorthand for Corpus Christi). But, as I would discover, Leduc owned property along the Chocolate Bayou, which he and others referred to as his "bay home." It makes more sense that any comments signaled retreating there.

Four years later, after the groom killed his bride, Leduc would tell authorities that he observed "playboy" tendencies in college freshman Charles just months before assisting with his marriage. The disproportion between Leduc's casual disapproval and the sickening gravity of the murders makes me wonder whether he had heard similarly shallow speeches from a pastor somewhere, or from an official at the chancery office. Either way, Leduc seemed to be parroting only the most superficial concern.

As small and strange as he may have appeared, he was flashing the fancy car and the priestly magic powers that made him more like James Bond or Bruce Wayne than Francis of Assisi.

V. White, Washed Hands

Leduc's difficulties likely surfaced prior to his arrival in Texas. One clue is that his "transfer" from one seminary to another was not as seamless as presented in the FBI narrative, nor was it as simple as mentioned in obituaries in the *Texas Catholic Herald* and the *Palm Beach Post*. Unlike other college students, candidates for the priesthood are not simply entitled to enroll wherever they choose. They are also not entitled to complete seminary studies and be ordained just because they desire it. Seminary transfers for unclear reasons are considered a "red flag" by researchers who study formation histories of problem priests.

Candidates must first gain approval by a bishop (usually of their home diocese) in order to enter seminary. Some "lifers," as they were called in the 1940s and '50s, attended minor seminaries at high school/junior college age and then (if approved) matriculated forward to the appropriate major seminary where they would complete studies for ordination, for up to twelve years of study. Other students entered only after completing high school and college at separate and sometimes secular locations, reducing their total seminary time to eight or even four years. In this respect, Leduc had a distinct advantage over many other men in religious life: by the time he was ordained, he already had a Bachelor's Degree that would have afforded him professional alternatives to ministry.

The catalogs of St. Mary's Seminary Baltimore/Roland Park (SMSU) included expectations about how candidates were to be monitored by their pastors during vacation, to "render a full account of their mode of life." Pastors at the home parish of any seminarian were expected to observe and inquire about "habits of life both present and past." They were obliged to report either to the bishop or to the seminary superior any concerns about "the morals of their seminarians," "frequentation of the sacraments," "faithfulness in other religious duties," and "whether they have dressed as become students for the priesthood." All information was to be provided in the strictest confidence, under seal. Testimonial letters were expected at the end of each summer period from any pastor at locations where the candidate spent a considerable part of his time. Individual seminarians were also expected to prepare and turn in summer sermons on assigned subjects. How carefully these protocols were followed, of course, would depend on the candidate's pastor, bishop, and instructors.

If a seminarian withdrew or got expelled, he could not easily move over to another seminary the way a regular college student might be able to. He had no right to appeal the verdict. However, if he still wanted to be a priest, he might approach his sponsoring bishop, who had discretion about whether to accept an explanation and send the young man elsewhere for training and then bring him home to serve. If his home bishop accepted the decision of the original seminary, the candidate would have to locate an alternative pathway and find another bishop to take him in.

There's an extra factor. While a traditional academic institution might keep records of reasons for expulsion or removal from a program, precise explanations for "clipping" a seminarian were not written down. The secrecy of specifics was encoded with heavy implications, so that any bishop, seminary rector, or religious order who approved a transfer ran a risk of ordaining someone who was, at best, ill-suited for the vocation—or, at worst, posed a danger to himself or to others.

How did Leduc—who was born in Connecticut, studied as an undergraduate in Ottawa, then moved to Florida with his parents and enrolled at St. Mary's Baltimore—get ordained a priest for the diocese of Houston, Texas? I wasn't alone in wondering. "How he came to us, we never knew," one classmate from Houston told me.

Because I located an article showing that Leduc returned to celebrate his first high mass at St. Ann's parish in Waterbury, where he had attended Catholic school through the 8th grade,

I thought perhaps the diocese of Hartford had been his original sponsor for study. But they had no record of him. The archivist informed me that even if Leduc had moved, transferred, or left the priesthood, they would have kept a record that showed him as a seminary candidate. "We'd have a folder for him," she said.

Next I emailed archivists at the two institutions I knew Leduc had attended up to his early twenties: the University of Ottawa and SMSU. I discovered something interesting. Neither institution had any record of Joseph G. Leduc. Instead, they had records of Gilles Real Leduc—a man with the same birth date and birthplace. Photographs from the archivist at SMSU further confirmed that indeed I had located the right person. She also shared records that showed Leduc studying for the diocese of St. Augustine, Florida, starting in September 1950, but leaving November 13, 1951, the Tuesday after Veteran's Day.

Because his Florida obituary had identified this location as a "minor" seminary, I had to make sure: Was this the minor seminary? The archivist informed me that St. Charles Seminary was the only minor there at the time, and that Leduc definitely attended St. Mary's. My later visit and viewing of photographs confirmed this with another record: Leduc was listed as a First Year Theology student in the official catalogs from 1950-51, with an original expected ordination year of 1954. Identified as Gilles R. Leduc, he also stands smiling on the second-to-last step in the group photo of his class, published in The Voice of St. Mary's Seminary. The School of Theology calendar for Fall 1951 indicates that his departure fell three days before mid-semester exams.

After his departure, Leduc did not return to Baltimore. He also did not enter another seminary in January, which might have indicated a simple matriculation process, recovery from an illness, resolution of a technicality, or a swift change ordered by his bishop. But regardless of the reason, the bishop of his home diocese in Florida could have sent Leduc anywhere and brought him back as a priest if the transfer were a matter of accepted preference or procedure, or if Leduc had made a successful petition upon something as serious as "clipping" or expulsion. In fact, according to repeated public accounts in the past twenty years, many priests later convicted of serious crimes against children had been too easily approved for seminary transfers by their home bishop and simply brought back to serve.

Based on available records, Leduc appears to have been completely cut loose from the bishop who had sent him to be ordained in the first place. Of the five students sponsored by St. Augustine to begin theology studies in 1950, Leduc is one of two who did not finish there. Another classmate from the diocese, Martin O'Toole, departed two days after Leduc did, also before midterm exams. It is unclear whether he ever became a priest.

Leduc took approximately one year to make his transfer. When he finally enrolled at St. Mary's in Texas, in September 1952, he had spent ten months at home with his parents. Most importantly, when Leduc transferred to the second seminary, he no longer used the name he had used in Ottawa and in Baltimore. All references from Galveston-Houston forward list him as Joseph G. Leduc, J. Leduc, or J. G. Leduc, rather than Gilles Real. Use of name "Real" goes back further for Leduc. The record from Assumption Prep, where he attended high school from 1943 to 1947, also documents his use of the name "Gilles R. Leduc" next to his portrait.

I was not able to find a baptismal record or birth certificate. But considered altogether, the available information strongly suggests that after his seminary transfer, Leduc chose a different name officially than he had used up to that point. While he still went by "Gil" to those that knew him well, the name "Real" disappeared, suggesting some kind of separation from the past.

The only "Real" I could locate in Leduc's story stood out significantly. A Canadian priest relative on his mother's side named Real Beauregard, fifteen years older than Leduc, offered the homily at one of Leduc's two first masses after ordination, the "high mass" celebrated in Waterbury for a brief homecoming at the parish where Leduc had grown up. Traditionally, the priest who takes on this role is highly symbolic as a mentor. There are also documented accounts of new priests whose first-mass homilies were delivered by the clergymen who had sexually initiated—or even abused—them, often years before.

We will never know what kind of influence this priest had upon Leduc. Yet something interrupted his seminary training, and according to a cousin, Leduc was determined to become a priest, almost as if he were unable to conceive of an identity without that role. His inability to let go adds interesting context to an observation offered by McGinnis, that Leduc seemed "threatened" and "uncomfortable" around other priests.

Why would Leduc eliminate the name of a religious mentor from his own name, and then invite him take such a symbolic place at his first mass? Perhaps "Real" coincidentally referred to another relative, or there was no way to refuse the traditional expectation. Perhaps he simply did not inform family members about the adjustment, because the change was a cosmetic or technical appeasement for his new bishop—a means to an end.

As a priest, Leduc would be responsible for consecrating the bread into what Catholics identify as the Real Presence of Christ.

This act is considered a sacred mystery of faith. Who Leduc was, and how he presented himself, offers a worldlier problem. He seemed to evade a question about identity in this early shift of names, as if one name referred to the priest, the other to the man.

☦

When Leduc entered St. Mary's Baltimore in 1950, he was in the same cohort as Thomas Anglim, an Irish immigrant who became a highly popular and revered priest in Florida and who outlived Leduc by twenty-nine years to the exact day.

Anglim eventually served at Sacred Heart Parish and presided at the funeral mass of Charles Whitman and the mother he murdered. At the funeral and in a printed message to parishioners, Anglim made a highly controversial public statement virtually absolving Whitman of serious wrongdoing for the murder of his mother, his wife, and thirteen strangers, including an unborn child. Anglim's statement concluded, "We trust that God in his mercy does not hold him responsible for these last actions." Anglim made a "dog whistle" reference to Catholic doctrine about mortal sin, suggesting that Whitman's crimes would not have risen to that level.

Four decades after the shootings, Msgr. Anglim would be posthumously accused of sexual abuse by an African American man whose allegations seem eventually discredited. However, evidence emerged that at the time of the Whitman massacre and funeral, Anglim was supervising a priest at Sacred Heart Parish named Anthony Mercieca, who later admitted to sexual contact with one boy at the parish in the mid 1960s. That boy, Mark Foley, become a U.S. Representative who resigned in 2006 when allegations surfaced that he had sent explicit sexual messages to teenage Congressional pages.

Another in Leduc's cohort at Baltimore was Rev. Bryan O. Walsh, whose handsome face made the "centerfold" in an issue of the *Saturday Evening Post* documenting the first ever outdoor ordination ceremony of the class of 1954. Walsh was later the director of the Cuban Children's Program/Operation Pedro Pan, which brought 14,000 unaccompanied minors from Cuba to escape communism between 1960 and 1981. One of those minors later alleged ongoing sexual abuse in 1964 and filed a lawsuit after Walsh's death against the diocese for negligence. The case was thrown out based on the statute of limitations.

To be clear: Anglim had a straight pathway to ordination with his class at St. Mary's in Baltimore. Anglim became popular and charismatic, with people rushing to his defense when allegations of misconduct surfaced. The steeple of an old church was consecrated in his name.

To be clear: Walsh had a straight pathway to ordination with his class at St. Mary's in Baltimore. There is now an archive of his personal papers stored at the seminary. He is particularly beloved by the Cuban community in southern Florida, and was also a leader for Catholic Charities. Under Pope John Paul II, Walsh was designated chairman of a papal committee on migration and refugees.

Leduc, by contrast, was not able to finish with his original class of 123 men. He had to make another plan. One contact that could have aided him was a slightly older classmate from the diocese, Father Matthew Morgan, ordained at the end of Leduc's first year of study. Morgan's first parish assignment was Sacred Heart. When Leduc left the Baltimore seminary and returned to his parents' house, Fr. Morgan was assistant pastor. A 1952 newspaper report about a spaghetti dinner fundraiser at the parish named Morgan as "spiritual adviser" for Troop 119 and Leduc as "scoutmaster." Other reports later document that Morgan was active with Leduc's father in the Knights of Columbus.

Leduc must have seen Morgan as an ally: he was one of two priests Leduc mentioned to the FBI as a resource for more information about Whitman.

☦

One plausible explanation for Leduc's ability to maneuver and relocate might be his involvement in Catholic scouting. The vast Catholic scouting program was thriving in the Houston area in the early to mid-1950s, formally organized under the direction of Rev. Henry A. Drouilhet, listed as Director of Catholic Scouting for the entire diocese. By contrast, the diocese of St. Augustine had no such program yet in place.

There is also the reality of supply and demand. First, at the Baltimore institution, Leduc was one of 341 seminarians representing fifty-six dioceses—and the Sulpician order that ran the program could afford to be strict. (One alumnus suggested, however, that the faculty-student ratio unfortunately made it a good place for certain personalities to hide.) At the Texas seminary where Leduc transferred, by contrast, he was ordained in a total class of six. On one hand, it seems odd that whatever his troubles, Leduc would have been more likely to complete his studies at a larger institution where he would have a better chance at blending in. On the other hand, it is not surprising that an already-massive diocese with a steady demand for priests and a much smaller seminary would "not happen to see" any problems Leduc might have very well learned to conceal better, as long as he could help meet a specific diocesan need.

According to statistics in the OCD in 1950, the year Leduc began his studies for the diocese of St. Augustine, the number of Catholics there numbered just over 71 thousand, with 192 priests—roughly 2.7 priests for every 1 thousand Catholics. By 1952, the year Leduc left the area, the total Catholic population nearly doubled, jumping to 125 thousand, while the total number of priests increased only to 196—a reduction to 1.5 priests for every 1 thousand Catholics. These figures suggest incredible growth and regional demand that could incentivize flexibility in recruitment and retention of seminarians by any bishop willing to overlook problems.

But Houston was already much larger. The year Leduc transferred, there were 215,627 Catholics and 248 priests—a less dramatic increase from 205,148 Catholics and 227 priests in 1950, but still a meager ratio of 1.1 priests for every thousand. While the ratio in St. Augustine at first glance appears slightly better than the ratio in Houston, the drastic jump in southeastern Florida's Catholic population suggests a statistically more urgent need for priests to administer the sacraments necessary for active members of the faith. Yet even this urgent growth did not earn Leduc a "pass" from the diocese that originally sent him as a candidate for ordination.

My two inquiries to an archivist with the diocese of St. Augustine revealed no records of anyone with the last name Leduc ever serving there—neither as a seminary candidate nor as priest. I consulted with Rev. Msgr Peter Riani, ordained at St. Mary's Baltimore in 1955. He spent years of his priesthood as President at Wadhams Hall Seminary-College in Ogdensburg, New York, helping it to develop a library and meet accreditation standards. He shared his knowledge of situations where a seminary declined to move a candidate forward, but then discovered the man had gained admittance at another seminary and become a priest anyway. He described occasions where Seminary A made a phone call to Seminary B to mention a problem or complication, only to be asked: "But why did you ordain him?"

Another priest from Riani's class, Msgr. Joseph Showfety, served as Chancellor for the diocese of Charlotte from 1972-1979, and he provided an account nearly identical to Riani's: someone from another diocese called to complain about a priest they had ordained, leaving Showfety to respond, "I told you not to ordain him!" He went on, "If you ordain a jackass, he stays a jackass. Priesthood doesn't change human faults. Young men have to be prayerful, be faithful to the office. Some men you can't keep, and can't help."

In a subsequent consultation with Riani, I shared new information I found about Leduc's abrupt departure from Baltimore, the change of name, the apparently missing file at his sponsoring diocese, and the transfer to Texas. "I don't want to be prejudicial," he said, "but the transfer itself is not a good sign."

"The file could just be missing," I said.

"That's possible," he said. "It's also possible that whatever happened was so bad that they destroyed the file."

I asked whether he knew of uniform practices for records handling, and recounted the gist of what the archivist at Hartford had explained to me: that if a man was sent to become a priest for their diocese, even if he left, they would have his name in a folder somewhere. "It all seems too complicated," I said.

"Different dioceses might do things differently," he said. "But I have a little advice I tell myself when things get too complicated."

What was that? I asked.

"I tell myself to back off. You don't know what you're stepping into."

As a writer, of course, I couldn't accept this idea. But as a

Catholic, I knew exactly what he meant.

I finally located and communicated via email with Frank Briganti, one of Leduc's five ordination classmates at St. Mary's Houston. Now retired and married, having worked more than thirty years as a practicing clinical psychologist, Briganti recalled Leduc as a "very poor student" with a "pleasant personality," and as a person who "laughed easily." He could not recall Leduc ever raising a hand or asking a question during their "nearly ninety classes together." He also knew nothing of Leduc's family or socioeconomic status, his seminary transfer, his history or involvement with scouts.

Briganti said he couldn't understand how Leduc had been able to pass through to ordination, though he imagined that "perhaps the profs saw that he was a good person." Still, based on his training since that time, Briganti frankly volunteered to me that if it had been possible at the time, he would have had Leduc on probation and "wished him well as a layperson." Perhaps this is exactly what some wise instructor or spiritual director at Leduc's first seminary attempted to do.

Briganti shared one especially vivid memory. A few months before ordination, he asked Leduc why he wanted to be a priest: "He very openly said that one day he was talking with his local parish priest in Florida and noticed how soft and white his hands were." Leduc told Briganti that, in that brief experience, he decided he wanted the job of priest, because "it would allow him that 'softness.'" Briganti told me that the answer personally appalled him.

VI. Catholic Culture: Clerics, Confessionals, and the Social Milieu

In the Catholic Church there are two basic categories of priesthood: the diocesan (also called "secular") and the religious. The latter include Jesuits, Franciscans, Dominicans (and so forth), and all of them live in accountability to their particular communities, according to the vision or mission of a holy founder, and they take a vow of poverty. Some religious orders are highly secluded, dedicated to study and to prayer. Others are missionaries dedicated to helping those who are poor, ill, incarcerated, or lacking education. By contrast, diocesan priests are the guys who work among families in local parishes, as assigned by the bishops of a geographical region called a diocese, to administer sacraments for Catholics in the area.

On Leduc's mother's side, according to his cousin, there were many priests and nuns, and the examples Leduc observed inside his family would have normalized the choice to enter the seminary. Growing up in a French Catholic parish and attending Catholic schools also surrounded him with a variety of other men and women who had chosen religious life.

Ordination would both enable and require Leduc, like every other Father and Monsignor, to hear confessions of all varieties of petty and serious sins from average people, who would make their own assessments of his counsel during the sacrament (whether he was gentle or harsh, thoughtful, dismissive, or cold). It's a much smaller pool of priests who can say that they were personally acquainted with a former penitent who committed a televised and gruesome mass murder, and then was killed in the act. It is an even smaller pool that would know such a killer well enough to be considered worthy of an FBI interview. For the moment, it appears to be a pool of one.

There would be no record of whether Charlie as a young boy ever made confession to Rev. Leduc in those first few weeks he served at Sacred Heart Parish—nor on any occasion over the next eleven years. Even if Leduc had never heard confessions or one-on-one confidences to alert him about violent possibilities in the mind of a friend or mentee, it would be normal for the average priest to be deeply stricken in the wake of heinous acts committed by someone he recognized. Whitman's first two victims were his mother, Margaret, and his wife, Kathleen—women Leduc had met. And because Whitman himself was killed, Leduc never had the chance to talk with him again.

It's also likely, however, that Leduc had not been truly able to perceive what he may in fact have been told. Seminary instruction at the time would not have prepared him to face such intimate violence: "[Our teachers] never, ever taught us how to respond to people's pain," Father McGinnis told me. "We spent months on whether it was—I'm serious—mortal sin or venial sin. No one ever said, 'Well, what do you say when someone comes in and says that the husband has hit her four times? What do you say when someone comes in and says my son is on drugs?' Nothing. Absolutely zero."

Regardless of what warnings Leduc might or might not have been privy to, Whitman's horrific crimes could reasonably rock even the most cavalier personality into a state of permanent gravity. Some priests would have blamed themselves for not being able, or knowing how, to intervene. Some might have asked for approval to move to a more secluded place, or into a religious order. The most committed might have channeled reactions by writing or talking with others about details they were permitted to share, or by re-awakening their ministries to devote energy and time, both inside and outside their parishes, to avert such horrors: through outreach and counseling for newly married couples, college students, military veterans, or survivor-victims of crime or of abuse in families. Some priests might have chosen to leave the priesthood. Others would have simply broken down.

The timing of the shootings is significant when considering the range of possible reactions for a priest who personally knew people involved. This was a volatile decade, both before and after the murders: of civil rights marches, riots, anti-war demonstrations, brutal assassinations, and nuclear anxiety. With the conclusion of Vatican II, Catholic clergy and laity were questioning church hierarchy and even the government more openly. The church was asking its congregations and its clergy to participate more fully in an active faith—sharing the mass liturgy in vernacular languages rather than in Latin, abandoning (or at least re-examining) rote rituals, and applying the spirit of Christ's gospel to everyday life rather than complying with a list of technicalities learned from catechism. A spirit of civil disobedience inspired some priests and theologians to challenge what they saw as arbitrary or harsh rules that disregarded established research and knowledge of human sexuality and psychology. There were also steps towards ecumenism, symbolized by Pope Paul VI's visit to the United States in October 1965—the first pontiff ever to set foot on American soil—offering mass at Yankee Stadium, meeting with Lyndon Johnson, and addressing the United Nations.

For some, this period indicated only a "hip and groovy" shift, an excuse for self-indulgence. But many serious Catholics (both priests and laity) became publicly active not only in debates about papal infallibility, birth control, divorce, and clerical celibacy, but also about racial integration, voting rights, and Vietnam. Catholics were on the social radar: Thomas Merton, the poet; the radical, anti-war Berrigan Brothers. Even establishment figure Bishop Fulton J. Sheen—a friend of J. Edgar Hoover and as famous for his anti-communism as for his radio and TV programs—eventually took a public stand urging an end to violence in Vietnam.

It's a stark juxtaposition: The same week a former altar boy shot up the Texas capitol of Austin, President Lyndon Johnson's daughter, a famous convert to Catholicism, celebrated a very public wedding at the National Shrine of the Immaculate Conception. Issues of *Newsweek* and *Time* document the coincidence with dueling cover images—the radiant bride and her groom, the killer and his dog.

With so many visible options and models, how would Leduc respond?

A priest knows more than he may share. The Catholic layperson may over or underestimate this burden; non-Catholics may simply find it impossible to fathom, perceive it as sneakiness or dishonesty. The priest knows, then tries to forget, then remembers again: the voices that whisper in the confessional, how he can hear the rustle of coats or skirts or keys, the squeak or clack of shoe soles and heels, the faces he may have seen.

Because of the sacred seal of confession, the priest must not indicate if he recognizes anyone in the church vestibule, at the parish pancake breakfast table in the basement, at the dinner where he is a special guest, from the pulpit as he looks upon his people or—close, closer—across the pale wafer of bread between his thumb and forefinger before he places it on their tongues or in the palms of their hands.

Other confessional items, a primer:

Starting in the Middle Ages, Catholics were obliged to kneel before a priest and name their sins at least once a year. The confessional booth ("the dark box")—with its privacy screens and curtains or doors—was not used until the mid 16th century, following the Reformation.

During the late 1950s and early 1960s, a "spirit of permissiveness" among some priests began to blur traditional boundaries, so that social events with young people became occasions for "friendlier" or less intimidating confessions, as well as occasions for abuse.

Catholics now refer to confession as the Sacrament of Reconciliation, which can be administered either behind a traditional screen or face-to-face. In order to receive absolution, penitents name their sins, accept a penance, and express contrition stating "a firm purpose of amendment." There are two categories of contrition: "imperfect" (motivated by fear of punishment) and "perfect" (motivated by love of God). Imperfect contrition is sufficient.

No one can be absolved of sins confessed "in advance."

No one can be absolved by proxy. Confessions must be made in direct, live, spoken communication with a priest.

The two categories of sin are "mortal" and "venial." Mortal sins must be confessed prior to receiving communion, in order to prevent sacrilege, and prior to death, in order to save one's soul from damnation. Conditions and categories of "mortal sins" were much agonized about in the mid-century catechism, especially regarding sexual matters. See also *Youth and Chastity*, by Gerald Kelly, SJ.

Ideally, priests provide guidance along with absolution.

In some cases, a priest may withhold absolution if the sins are grave and the sincerity of the confessor is in question. (Aside: In the late 1960s and '70s, some priests withheld absolution from married Catholics who confessed using artificial birth control.)

A priest cannot absolve himself but must confess his sins to another priest.

A priest who sins sexually with another priest may not be absolved by his partner. He may not absolve a layperson with whom he has had sex. The Church teaches that it is a grave Canonical crime to exchange absolution for sexual favors of any kind, yet a layperson who reports such solicitation by a priest runs the risk of being excommunicated for false accusation.

Under the seal of confession, a priest may not reveal anything he has learned in the confessional. This does not preclude him from acting on information learned outside.

The seal does not bind the person who confesses to the priest, though the belief that the seal applied to them prevented many Catholics from reporting a priest's sexual invitations before, during, or immediately after the sacrament.

A priest is discouraged from confessing his sins to his supervising bishop, as this would effectively preclude the bishop from making administrative decisions regarding the priest's assignments and fitness to serve his vocation.

An illustration: In the confessional, a rectory housekeeper repents to her priest that she stole $25 from the jar he keeps in a cabinet above the refrigerator. Because of the sacred seal of confession, the priest may not fire the housekeeper, move the jar, or mention her behavior to anyone else. He may not treat her any differently when he sees her again.

So: when Leduc said to the FBI that he first became acquainted with the killer before he was a killer, between the ages of 9 and 11 years old, that he knows the killer's father was brought up in an orphanage, that the killer had two brothers, that the killer's father was "aggressive" and "very demanding," that the killer was a "nervous type of individual during the entire period of his acquaintance...and had the characteristic of doing things on the spur of the moment" (but that all "spur of the moment" activities "were towards the good"), that the killer's mother might have left her husband if not for the children and also for her Catholic faith, that the killer took the train to Parris Island to join the Marines, that at college the killer and two friends killed a deer and dragged it through the dorm to butcher in the shower, leaving a trail of blood on the floor—these are all bits of information that required open conversations or experiences not revealed during confession.

The priest may not disclose whether or not the killer as a child or as a young man ever confessed to him in the box, or face-to-face—about rubbing his private parts in the dark, or sneaking liquor from a friend's father's cabinet, or enjoying dirty pictures, or hitting his younger brothers, or missing mass, or complaining about his dinner in a scene that created an argument between his parents, with his mother's arm getting nearly yanked from its socket, for which he might have blamed himself.

This would not, however, preclude Leduc from expressing dismay or grief at the heinous acts committed by his friend, or indicating sympathy for the wife and mother who were murdered in the dark, hours before all the strangers, nor would it prevent him from expressing any understanding about how the children and their mother experienced paternal "demands" as violent or damaging, if he had seen evidence or heard complaints of such violence. Even in third person monotone, FBI narratives from other background witnesses included phrases such as "terrible thing" and "unbelievable" and "quite upset at his death and that he had performed the act [Whitman] had performed," as well as words such as "hard" and "harsh" even "crazy" to describe Whitman's father's treatment of his family.

Reverend Leduc's statement omitted any such language, commenting only that Whitman's father "was very strict in rearing his children and desired perfection from them," and that Whitman "always appeared to have resentment" of his father's "regimentation." Leduc's statement did not betray empathy or affection, and did not include idiosyncratic narrative detail about interactions or conversations. It did include, at both the beginning and at the end, a careful and explicit statement that he did not want "any publicity or disclosure of this information outside public authorities who have official interest," as if he himself were requesting a confessional seal for non-sacramental disclosures.

Not once did he refer to or react to his friend's crimes.

From the late 19th century to the 1960s, *The Baltimore Catechism* (also known as the "little blue book") was the standard instructional text for Catholics in the United States. Both Leduc and Whitman would have known the text well, whether they took it seriously or not. The book offers direct and simplistic answers to religious questions ("Who is God?" and "Why did God make you?") as well as clear-cut lessons on Catholic morality and practice.

An illustrated version, *The New St. Joseph's Baltimore Catechism*, was first published in 1962. Along with the traditional "blue book," this version continues to be used by more traditional

Catholics who find post-Vatican II catechisms too wishy-washy. The text remains straightforward. Artwork consists of black, grey, and red illustrations, and each one depicts a particular lesson—about the sacraments, the Ten Commandments, the mass, or a moral dilemma.

Images and captions reveal as much about the initial audience and the Cold War time period as about the instructional goals. One page illustrates four weapons available to the faithful to ensure the conversion of atheists/communists, non-Catholics, and "bad Catholics": a Gatling gun of "sufferings and sacrifice," a cannon of "prayer", the rifle of "good example," and the revolver of "encouragement." Violent metaphor was simply part of the wallpaper.

Another picture demonstrates the hierarchy of each person's place in the church. Eleven human figures are shown carrying individual crosses up the side of a mountain. At the front of the line walks Jesus, followed by his mother Mary, then St. Peter, the pope, a priest, a nun, a religious brother, a father, a mother, a little boy, and finally a little girl. Aside from the figures wearing garb appropriate to the religious life, there are no single adults depicted on the journey. There are also no married people without children, no divorcees, no former clergy, and no one meant to be identified as gay. Every face in the illustration is white.

Social messages were a powerful aspect of the "hidden curriculum" not only in Catholic catechism but also in daily parish life during the period. Class photographs at St. Mary's Baltimore during the early 1950s document a sea of white faces, a testament to the history of racial segregation in Catholic ministry. Priests I spoke with were highly aware of the problems. Msgr. Riani (SMSU class of 1955) described how classmates formed social cliques—a few "not so Christian," including one that expressed adamant racism: "These guys would say, 'The blacks don't have the same souls as we whites.' "

✠

The second of two priests Leduc mentioned in his FBI statement was a Southern Jesuit and former Navy chaplain named Rev. Samuel Hill Ray. He had been educated in Montreal and also spoke French. At the time of the shootings, Ray was assigned to El Paso, Texas, but he had been a parochial minister for three years at St. Ann's, the West Palm Beach high school Whitman attended in the mid 1950s. He also served as pastor of St. Ann's Parish.

When the Supreme Court ruled "separate but equal" unconstitutional in *Brown v. Board of Education* (1954), Ray had been working as a spiritual counselor at Loyola University in New Orleans. According to Professor Jerome Henry Neyrey, S.J., of the University of Notre Dame, Ray was not just an "eccentric" but also an "unabashed racist." He had spoken out for years against racial integration of colleges, churches, and public spaces, loudly contradicting the Jesuit leadership in letters as well as in wider social forums, such as presentations to the Exchange Club. Ray made statements about the dangers of "miscegenation" and also argued the "benefits" of segregation, expressing his fear that any discussion of racial equality could lead to Communism. In one notorious letter, he referred derisively to the "notorious 'Christian Conscience' about all the downtrodden jigaboos" (qtd. in Anderson 90).

Historians note that the Jesuits never formally reprimanded Ray; they simply re-assigned him in 1955, from Loyola University to St. Ann's High School in West Palm Beach. It was the beginning of Charles Whitman's freshman year there, as well as the summer of Leduc's one-month stint of service at Sacred Heart. Leduc had met Ray or heard about him through Charlie or others. Ray was the featured speaker at a Knights of Columbus breakfast in 1958 where both Leduc's father and his former classmate from St. Mary's Baltimore, Rev. Matthew Morgan, were initiated as third-degree knights for the Lake Worth Council.

While the transfer from university to high school may have looked or felt like a demotion, it is doubtful that Ray's attitudes would have been challenged much when interacting with impressionable adolescent white students at St. Ann's. He was not keeping a low profile, either, speaking to groups including Catholic Daughters, Mothers and Teachers, Rotary, and Kiwanis. His speeches mostly addressed the dangers of communist "infiltration," and his list of grievances included "federal interventions to guarantee civil rights of Negroes in the South."

Ray's presence as a figure in Whitman's story not only underscores one racist mindset of the time, both inside and outside the Catholic Church, but it reminds us that Whitman's identity was forged within the ugliest traditions of the White South—traditions not yet summarily rejected by all clergy.

In his strange comment to a fellow seminarian, Leduc said that memories of a priest's "soft, white" hands had sealed his motivation for entering religious life. Altar boys, seminarians, and priests were highly conscious of hands and hand gestures as fundamental aspects of the Latin rite at the time. What to touch, what not to touch, where to touch—the altar, the host, the chalice, even the people—were an obsessive focus. The ritual preparations before mass, as the priest dressed, emphasized hands. He would rinse them and pray, "O Lord, give my hands power to wash away all evil." Then, as he donned the white alb, he would say, "Make me white, O Lord, and purify my heart…"

That a priest's hands were literally "white" (clean, unblemished, pale, privileged) would have been visible, but "soft"? Was Leduc recalling the priest's touch on his forehead or cheek during a blessing? Had he shaken his hand after mass, or after altar service? Had there been other physical or even sexual contact? Whoever the priest was, Leduc mentions nothing of substance about him.

Softness evokes many things. To the child who grew up in a factory town, the priest's hands could indicate an ease of life, without the calluses developed by repetitive work or even injury. To a young boy who longed for warmth, softness could indicate affection or acceptance, a sparing of the rod. The desire to "be" soft could suggest a yearning not to prove one's manly temperament through toughness, or a desire to express culturally feminine traits. But softness also can connote an ease bordering on laziness or spiritual laxity, an un-Christian desire to avoid "taking up the cross"—one of the primary spiritual duties of the priest.

In Catholic tradition, some of the most powerful images of hands are both violent and sensual. Christ's hands, pierced by nails, embody the spirit of sacrifice and divine love. Thomas the Doubter is finally convinced of Christ's resurrection when he places his hands into the gaping wound under Christ's ribs. In the Song of Songs, an erotic ancient poem used in the Catholic apocrypha to analogize Christ's union with his bride, the Church, we find this passage: "My beloved put his hand by the hole of the door, and my bowels yearned for him."

Until the 1970s, when communion could be taken "in the hand" by members of the congregation, no one but a priest was allowed to touch consecrated bread. With his thumb and forefingers, the priest would place the consecrated host directly onto the tongue of any communicant. In the 1950s, Catholic schoolchildren were actually instructed about how to tilt their heads, open their mouths, and fold their hands to receive communion.

Despite a relaxation of certain external pieties, the teaching remains that only the hands of an ordained male may turn bread and wine into the body and blood of Christ.

☦

Although Rev. Leduc himself could have used a serious spiritual mentor, Charles Whitman attached himself at a very young age to the priest as guide. One of Whitman's friends said that when Leduc was available in Lake Worth, Charlie "could jump on his bike and zip over to the church and commiserate." Later, in Texas, Charlie "did trust [Leduc's] judgment" even though Leduc "wasn't there for him like he might have wanted."

Whitman's desire for guidance does not mean that he would be able to distinguish between healthy or unhealthy influences. Witnesses after the shootings talked about how his pregnant mother was hospitalized after a beating with a stick of wood. They also described how his father threatened to harm him as an infant, only to be rescued when his mother's dad, a policeman, stepped between the couple. A visit with relatives was interrupted by a fight that escalated when his father threatened his mother with a pistol. One witness wondered whether any brain abnormalities had resulted from early and repeated head trauma.

From the cracked lens of his earliest understandings, Whitman was psychologically as well as physically vulnerable, like any child in a family with a violent parent. He learned from infancy how to cultivate the external impression that "everything was fine," despite whatever realities he witnessed. Perceptiveness would not have been rewarded at home.

Jack McGinnis drew parallels between the dysfunctions in families ("nothing goes in, nothing comes out"; "triangulation") and the worst dynamics of clericalism. The stakes for both systems were high: "The fight or flight that gets developed out of childhood trauma is about staying alive. And denying it, not facing it, is often about staying alive." Similarly, he said, in the clergy culture of the time, "one of the deepest flaws was the inability to recognize and confront pathology... Nobody would say, 'We can't tolerate that kind of behavior.' Every single dynamic of the dysfunctional family is involved in the clergy system—or was, at that time."

To protect an image of the happy family, Charlie's father was particularly attuned to eliminating undermining influences as best he could, whether perceived or real. He restricted Whitman's contact with neighbors and classmates, and also attempted to prohibit participation in attractive group activities (statements to the FBI mention "rules" about the jazz band, the football team, even the military—until Whitman ran off to join).

Leduc's hunting trips with Charlie and his non-Catholic, not religious father—likely without the two younger brothers, who would have been under ten years old in the early 1950s—suggest that the seminarian posed no apparent threat to the father's authority. It is reasonable to infer that, unlike Whitman's biological father, Leduc did not "demand perfection." That contrast alone, especially coming from a candidate for priesthood, would have been highly attractive.

But even if Leduc seemed more relaxed than "regimented," he must have deferred to the status quo. Leduc's acceptance by

Whitman's father is not a great indicator of his value as a grounded person who represented a healthy, alternative adult reality. Whatever the basis for the bond between Leduc and Whitman, based on nearly four decades of recovery and his work as a counselor, McGinnis shared his view that the tragedy of both men had to share a common root: "The emotional underpinning always, always comes from childhood. Not maybe. Always. I'm more convinced of that than there's a God."

I discovered only the barest facts about Leduc's own family relationships, but his cousin twice corrected my word choice when I asked if the family was "private" or kept to themselves. "Secretive," she said. "They were secretive."

VII. Drinking, Driving, and Other Deeds

In my conversations with those who knew Leduc as a scoutmaster, priest, and relative, people described him as "jovial" or "a riot," simultaneously unusual and unremarkable. Parishioners and colleagues told me that Leduc was "difficult to get close to" or that they recalled speaking with him but couldn't remember any topics discussed. Altogether these descriptions tracked with the most striking elements of the caption next to Leduc's high school portrait: "hidden qualities," "leader," and "minds his own business."

One former Houston priest and now licensed clinical social worker, Felix Scardino, ordained at SMH in 1963, said that his mother frequently prepared meals at their family's home for Leduc and other priests serving at Annunciation Parish in 1955. At the time, Scardino was a teenager preparing to enter seminary that Fall, and while he remembered talking with Leduc, who was newly ordained, the two were "not chummy." There was, Scardino said, "a strangeness about him… a strange evasiveness."

McGinnis was in the same class as Scardino. A survivor of severe childhood trauma, McGinnis has been committed to his own sobriety for more than four decades and now works as a minister to high school students, helping them recognize and heal from abuse and family dysfunction. He entered SMH in 1955, and he worked the priest retreats when they were still hosted during summers at the seminary. McGinnis told me that he felt shocked and disappointed at these gatherings: "I thought this would be a spiritual experience and it was just a drunken orgy…They were drinking the whole time, bringing in cases of beer and other things. I had never seen anything like that."

McGinnis recalled seeing Leduc as a young priest for the first time in this setting. He said Leduc's heavy drinking was noticeable ("I remember how much he drank"), and yet compared to the habits of others, it wasn't exactly unique: "It was part of the pattern." He observed that it was hard to read Leduc or get a sense of what he really thought—even about topics debated among clergy. "My heart always went out to Gil because he always seemed uncomfortable, threatened," McGinnis said. "We never sat down and had a heart-to-heart, but I observed that early he always seemed kind of hyper-vigilant around other priests…He was so disconnected from life somehow, from people, that he might make comments like 'This was absurd,' but it wasn't like this was a conviction, something he felt really strong about. It was more like he had a quiet desperation. Here's another day. It's going to be this way again."

Heavy alcohol use was not out-of-step for the clerical culture at the time, McGinnis said. Priests did not confront each other about drinking because there was a lot of it going on. "Every rectory had a closet full of whiskey you could get to at any time," McGinnis said. He also described an indelible memory of Leduc almost fifteen years later, at Leduc's final parish assignment where the two men crossed paths for a time. One morning, Leduc poured two whole cruets of sacramental wine into the chalice at mass. "So he could get a buzz. That's how bad it was for him. It was really sad."

McGinnis shared his own isolation as an alcoholic until he entered recovery in 1970 ("It was extremely lonely"), including a suicide attempt that went unnoticed at his parish. But he did have friends. By contrast, he said: "I never saw Gil with a group that he seemed to belong to. There were priests who would travel together, or go out to dinner together. I never saw him with anyone."

Leduc's troubles were not relegated to drinking, though they at times seemed to be difficult to put into words. Another retired priest paused abruptly when I mentioned Leduc's name. I remember the catch in my own breath when he stopped talking. Up to this point in our two-hour conversation about seminary life and his own experiences in the priesthood, he had been incredibly relaxed and loquacious, sharing about his family, his love for God, and even his personal limitations ("I've never been very good at rules," he offered). When I pressed after his pause for clarification about Leduc, he said, "A lot of problems there. I think we better leave it at that."

The OCD lists their names together at one parish, but when I asked if they'd worked together, the priest said that no, he never did. Perhaps when their paths intersected, Leduc was barely interacting with anyone. In any case, this priest clearly wanted to maintain a distance. We went on to other subjects.

This is how it went, mostly. I wasn't sure I would find anyone who expressed fond memories of Father Leduc, much less described Leduc as a "confidant" or close friend, as the FBI documents stated he had been to Charles Whitman. But then someone who knew both men found the family tree I had built for Leduc on a genealogy website. His name was Francis J. Schuck.

I had tried and failed to contact Schuck (who also identified as Joseph K. Shook) multiple times nearly a year earlier but had received no response. He was important because he had befriended Charles Whitman during a mutual period of military instruction at the U.S. Naval Training Center in Bainbridge in July 1961, continuing the friendship when both enrolled at UT Austin. When the young military students came to Texas on scholarships in Fall 1961 as part of the Naval Enlisted Scientific Education Program (NESEP), Schuck was introduced to the priest Charlie had talked about. During their freshman year at UT in 1961-1962, Schuck also introduced Charlie to the young woman he would marry that summer. Our contact began on the genealogy website under profile names, but quickly migrated to email, phone, and eventually several in-person visits when I traveled again to Texas.

Despite a fairly narrow timeframe of acquaintance with Leduc (Schuck left UT to return to active duty in Fall 1962), he recalled the priest with affection and told me that he loved him like a brother. He volunteered that, not being Catholic, he "wasn't too appalled" by anything Leduc did. His first recollection of meeting Father Leduc was when he, Charlie, and another friend made the nearly three-hour drive from the university to St. Philip Neri parish in south Houston. At the time, the parish consisted of a house not far from where the diocese had purchased land to construct a church. The pastor supervising Leduc at Philip Neri was Rev. Ernest ("Ernie") Michalka, who also served as a judge for the ecclesiastical court of the diocese during the early 1960s.

To Schuck's recollection, the pastor wasn't home during their visit, and so the three young men stayed up and drank "probably half a gallon of whiskey" in the rectory that night with Leduc. (Schuck said that Charlie didn't drink much, if at all.) The next morning, the young men were impressed when they watched hungover Father Leduc put on his vestments to say mass in the makeshift sanctuary set up in the garage. None of the young men attended the service.

Schuck said that around this time, Leduc was being told by Michalka or another senior priest that he would need to join the military in order to avoid "defrocking," and that Leduc eventually complied because he "loved the priesthood" almost as much as drinking. I had suspected that the timing of Leduc's entrance into the military (combined with his relatively short-lived period as a chaplain) signaled trouble. Schuck volunteered his own perception without being asked.

During Fall 1961 and Spring 1962, Leduc occasionally met Schuck, Whitman, and a crew of friends for parties or what Schuck referred to as "scout events" at a resort property one hour south of the parish. When I remarked that it must have been difficult for Leduc to afford a property expense on his limited income, Schuck said that he thought the diocese itself was probably the "discrete" owner of this property and that Leduc was more like a caretaker.

Schuck recalled two full-size whaleboats that had been donated by the Coast Guard, and which Leduc docked in the canal behind the house, for scout training. Not many girls visited the location, to Schuck's recollection, because it was a "pretty heavy drinking crowd." In addition to gathering for talk and "toddies," Whitman and his friends also helped maintain and clean up the property before or after other guests arrived. During drinks around the campfires outside after a day of mowing, painting, and perhaps a barbecue, the guys would call him "Gileus Leduc de la Prieste." Though he never shared details about his family, "his name alone suggested French Canadian ancestry," and Leduc "let everyone believe" he had been born in Canada. Sometimes, Schuck said, Leduc loaned access to friends to visit on their own: "Keys were under the flowerpot. Once he got to know you, he trusted you with anything."

Schuck recalled problems when some guests borrowed the house for "private getaways." Though he never saw those people in person, "that whole business really was weird," he said. Schuck described cleaning up on one occasion after these other visitors had left the cupboards, fridge, and liquor stock bare, the residence a mess: "These people were higher levels of the clergy, who didn't feel obligated," he stated. "Yet they had the wherewithal more than anybody else who went down there, and the biggest opportunity, too."

This perception is impossible to verify now. However, Father McGinnis had recalled that the drunken "priest retreats" he witnessed in the mid-1950s stopped being held at the seminary some time in the early 1960s, and it occurred to me that Leduc's property might have been one new location used for some of these parties. The timing is right. But it is equally plausible that Leduc merely vaguely attributed any mess to clerics he didn't like, adding an air of importance or legitimacy to the property, covering up his own habits or problem status, and enlisting the sympathy—and labor—of impressionable college kids.

Another incident Schuck shared allegedly followed an evening pig roast. After a late night of eating and drinking with Schuck and other visitors at the resort, Leduc got up to make an early drive back to St. Philip Neri to say mass, and the guests woke to prepare breakfast and clean up. When Leduc returned a few hours later to inspect and approve, Schuck and the remaining friends headed north, towards Houston, in two cars. Leduc followed slightly later, overtaking and passing them at a very high speed in his blue convertible Oldsmobile.

Schuck reported that he and the others watched as Leduc was pulled over by a police car. In his Poncie Ponce hat, Aloha shirt, and Bermuda shorts, Leduc supposedly tried to talk his way out of trouble with the officer by offering a lame, overdramatic excuse. Schuck joked that he must have flashed some of his chaplain cards or urged that he was in a rush to administer the Last Rites. The young friends pulled over and tried to intervene, but Schuck said that the policeman insisted on arresting Leduc and taking him to jail, adding that he and his friends drove Leduc's convertible back to the rectory, and the pastor from St. Philip Neri made the journey to post bail. Whether drinking was a factor in the alleged arrest, Schuck could not confirm (although he described the incident initially as a DWI), but he said he was certain about the speeding.

Schuck shared that Leduc said he was not very fond of one supervising priest, perhaps the very person who had bailed him out of jail and warned him about defrocking, but who also seemed to know about his bayou getaway: "He often did comment that [the pastor] was just waiting around for his Bishop's ring." Leduc allegedly considered the other assistant at the parish "a phony" that was always "kissing butt" with the pastor. Schuck added that Leduc admitted "every now and then, he did regret his vow of chastity."

What was Leduc like, then, in "serious" mode? Schuck offered no substantive details. All he said was that Leduc was "priestly" and had taken a vow of "charity," and also that he was easygoing and popular with his flock because he seemed to be part of a "new wave" of Catholics who wanted more "chilling out" by the church. When I pressed more about charity, he only repeated Leduc's devotion to the Boy Scouts and Sea Scouts, although even on this subject he described scout activities as Leduc's "easy excuse to leave parish chores to his fellow parish priests and seminarians."

Schuck also stressed that he only remembered seeing Leduc in clerical garb (including a simple collar) on two occasions: the hangover mass and Charlie's wedding, where Schuck recalled that Leduc drank whiskey with some men in the wedding party in the priest's office before the ceremony. Schuck insisted that when among Whitman and friends, Leduc mostly represented himself as a layman.

To be fair: at the time, Schuck was a fellow drinker and occasional weekend visitor, not a member of any parish, so he would not have had firsthand knowledge about Leduc's everyday interactions when there was more at stake. Schuck's impressions overall suggested that Leduc did not care much for his regular duties at the growing new church, and yet he seemed able to secure people to clean up or do landscaping for him at the extra property: "Gil had a way of getting other people to do those menial tasks," Schuck stated. "If it could be done by somebody else, and he could talk them into it, that was what was done."

What did Charlie Whitman think about all this at the time? If he had anticipated being closer to Leduc based on a much younger and idealistic impression, could he at least rely on the priest for mentor's advice when it counted? Schuck had described Leduc as a "wise little man" whom "Charlie was blessed with [as] someone he could really become absorbed in." In the context of so much heavy drinking, this claim seemed especially important. When I asked how Whitman reacted, Schuck's response surprised me. "I don't believe he ever saw Gil drunk, and I know he didn't know about the arrest. If he did, he put it out of his mind." Denial was clearly a theme of the time, as "no one really recognized that [Leduc] had a drinking problem…He just drank more than the average person and more often."

Most statements provided after the shootings describe Whitman as a relatively light drinker, though he did use prescription drugs and self-medicate with amphetamines. One of the most traumatic accounts of physical abuse by his father followed an early adolescent experiment with drinking gin around his eighteenth birthday. There are also significant expressions in Whitman's diaries that he was ambivalent and anxious about the subject of alcohol and/or the act of drinking it.

Schuck clearly liked Leduc and enjoyed his company enough to assume the best, and it was good to hear that position enthusiastically expressed, even with likely embellishments. But it bears noting that Schuck needed absolutely nothing from Leduc: not a decent homily at Sunday mass, not a sober, late-night bedside visit for a sick parent or child, not baptism for a new baby, not thoughtful counsel during confession. In a story that ended so violently, with crimes committed by someone Schuck knew (or thought he knew), his emphasis of positive impressions was understandable.

I found it hard, however, to buy that all these guys were gathering at the secluded cabin for entirely "wholesome" fun.

Schuck did share another impression that fascinated me: he was "ticked off" by how Leduc represented Charlie as a lapsed Catholic in his statement to the FBI ("most unpriestly, in my opinion," he said). I asked if he ever confronted the priest. But by the time the statement was available and unredacted for the public, Leduc had already died. Schuck was never able to confront him about the statement, or about anything else.

By Schuck's own admission, there was plenty he didn't know about Leduc's life, largely due to the fact that Leduc didn't share much about himself: "We were like a sabbatical for him. Some young guys who were older who had seen the world and maybe he could learn from us." There was also a dual persona of immaturity and presence of mind in Leduc's character that connected to other descriptions I had heard. On the one hand, Schuck said, "Gil was like a child. He'd dress up, put on a show, sign papers." But on the other hand, he added, "I see auras, ok? There was an aura about Gil that just presented itself, that manifest itself of him being in control. Sometimes people look to that in a leader." I asked about Leduc's hands, given all the time he seemed to spend outdoors. "It almost looked liked he had his fingernails done professionally, like with clear polish men sometimes use," Schuck said. "I used to ask him, 'Did they have a manicurist there at the parish?'"

Considered altogether, Schuck's stories and impressions

indicated that Whitman had spent plenty of time with Leduc in Houston and had introduced him to friends. But there were important facts about Leduc's "resort" that Schuck did not know—or disclose knowing—until the week I met with him in Texas. Leduc's personal signature appeared on deeds for the resort property, indicating him as the official owner rather than "caretaker." Eight months after the purchase, he borrowed a substantial sum of money against the property in a promissory note, and a few years later defaulted on the loan. His default occurred in May 1966, not long before his first official base assignment to Anchorage, Alaska, and eleven weeks before the murders.

Nearly one year before my contact with Schuck, I made an odd discovery in a newspaper search. In January 1962, the *Brazosport Facts* reported that the Liverpool, Texas, "resort home" of a priest named J. G. Leduc was burglarized. According to the newspaper, Leduc told investigators that the gun cabinet at the house was emptied of rifles, pistols, ammunition, and a Sam Browne belt. Nothing else was reported stolen. The sheriff's officer could not estimate the value of loss but stated how it appeared the burglar had climbed onto the garage or used a ladder to let himself into the sliding glass doors from a balcony.

This article yielded interesting material: Leduc wasn't just a reluctant or occasional hunter who understood shooting and perhaps owned a rifle; he was a guy who collected guns or perhaps stored guns for guests. He also owned or rented a weekend getaway, apart from the parish base where he would live most of the time. When I requested a copy of the original burglary report (under the Texas Public Information Act), I was not surprised to discover that after fifty years the record had not been retained. I scoured newspapers for any follow-up report or article, but was unable to locate any closure to the case. Whether the guns were recovered or anyone was prosecuted will probably remain a mystery.

I have to say: because this incident took place in the middle of Whitman's freshman year at UT Austin, it occurred to me that this had all the marks of the notorious "pranks" Whitman became infamous for in the wake of the shootings: from killing a deer and dragging its carcass through the dorm hallways, to grabbing a classmate in a headlock until he passed out, to returning to a poker game after a car accident, leg bloodied and pretending that a friend had died in the wreck. I could imagine Whitman returning to Leduc's resort house after a party or a hunting/fishing excursion and then clearing out the guns only to return them later: *Gotcha, Father. That's why you shouldn't drink so much.* But I don't think this is what really happened.

If Whitman's attachment to Leduc was half as loyal as Schuck suggested, it is more likely that someone else who'd visited or been entrusted with Leduc's hideaway had slipped in and taken what he knew was there. I can imagine this taking place whether Leduc was off the premises and back at the parish, or perhaps sleeping heavily at the resort after a night of drinking. The house was secluded enough that it would be easy for drifters or curious kids from nearby Alvin to stumble upon the place when it looked vacant.

The affinity for firearms and military paraphernalia in Charles Whitman's story is documented well. The guns in Leduc's story, and this burglary itself, would have provided an obvious area for bonding. Ironically, Schuck insisted that he had never seen Leduc hunt or shoot: "[One of our friends] was awful proud of a

.44 Magnum he had got, and he showed it to Gil, and Gil kinda took it like: 'Yeah, that's really nice, Bill.' He didn't hand it back the way you would typically hand back a weapon to anybody."

In such a gun-friendly crowd, why would Leduc play "dumb" or keep his weapons locker out of sight? Leduc's FBI statement echoes this discrepancy, where he mentioned Whitman's garage "arsenal" and pointed out that Whitman was "very proud of his weapons" but that he (Leduc) "did not pay attention to the number of weapons." Why try so hard to appear disinterested?

Understanding that this is Texas, after all, I sought feedback about the place of guns in clerical culture at the time and was not surprised to discover that occasionally a priest would keep a rifle or a pistol. McGinnis even recalled the legend of one pastor actually taking a shot at a guy who broke into his rectory at night. Still, he emphasized that guns didn't take up that much physical or psychological space for the average priest: "The availability of guns was different, and there wasn't the culture of 'protection' yet," he said. "I don't remember gun cabinets full of guns." (I hadn't mentioned the stash at Leduc's property.)

Leduc's Sam Browne belt—a belt including an extra strap worn diagonally from the shoulder across the chest—is also a kind of fetish item, indicating a knowledge and interest beyond the norm, possibly a gift or trophy from a war veteran. I also had to wonder: Did Leduc report everything that had been stolen?

While diocesan priests do not take a vow of poverty, Leduc had no ostensible reason to buy private property. At the time, any diocese would cover all basic lodging expenses—housing, housekeeping, and food—not to mention medical treatment. Leduc would have occupied the rectory of any parish where he worked;

he did not need to spend money on a place to live. Then there is the issue of time. Beyond daily duties, Leduc would have had weekend obligations as well (hearing confessions, saying at least one mass on Sunday). Most priests describe their work as being "on call" 24 hours a day—and, unless Leduc was on some kind of probation, there would have been plenty of work for him at a fledgling parish such as St. Philip Neri. On top of all that, during this window of time, Leduc's obligations were already divided by activities as regional scout chaplain for the Sam Houston Area Council, a massive geographical region. Finally, as a highly-trained scoutmaster, Leduc had the ability to hunt, fish, start a fire, pop up a simple shelter, and drink beer or whiskey anywhere he wanted to without major capital outlay.

To balance priestly obligations while tending and visiting property would have required not only financial means, but a bit of a manic, distracted personality. But it also could indicate that Leduc was kept on a long leash at the time, either because someone in authority liked him or because he had leverage. Schuck shared his impression that Leduc received "special treatment." He also believed that there might have been discrete financial or other support for Leduc's property from those who "enjoyed occasional 'sabbaticals' and 'synods' there."

While intriguing, this sounds more like a yarn that Leduc, or his young guests, could have easily strung out to deflect questions about how the property was used. The bottom line was that, as his pastoral role took a backseat to more secular activities, Leduc could play St. Peter in the bayou: he was officially keeper of the keys.

Brazoria county records revealed that two years before the

burglary, Leduc purchased land in the tiny hamlet of Liverpool Texas, south of Houston, nearly an hour's drive away from his parish base at the time. (Liverpool's population was below 200 people then, and still hovers around 500.) The two deeds that include his signatures do not record the actual purchase prices; they simply document a "real" property exchange of $10 each for adjacent parcels from two different individuals, Elmer E. Carey and L. G. Gaines. Together, the parcels sit on one side of a dead-end lane, tucked behind a cemetery that dates back to the 1800s. The lane sits on a short promontory bordered by thickets and surrounded by the dark, brackish waters of the Chocolate Bayou.

The average parish priest would not have the funds to buy property on his own. (In 1960, Leduc's base income per month would have been roughly $80 to $100, supplemented by fees for baptisms and weddings.) Occasionally, I was told that clergymen could pool resources and share the expense of an apartment or condo for vacations at a beach or on a lake. Most commonly, the few who made permanent investments either came from affluent families or had received an inheritance of money or property upon the death of a relative. One priest I interviewed had this opportunity but chose not to pursue it, stating that he believed it would pose too much of a distraction from parish duties. Leduc obviously felt differently.

How had he really been able to afford the purchase? Although his parents were alive, still residing in Florida and not apparently wealthy, it is possible that Leduc inherited money from a distant relative or received extra funds as a gift, perhaps upon ordination five years prior. Unless he literally paid $20 for the land, he would have needed extra cash. Schuck's suggestion that someone in the diocese had bankrolled the property "discretely" gave me pause.

It would have explained how Leduc had been able to afford the transaction, but it raised another serious question: why would "discretion" be necessary for a legitimate purchase of a property used for ordinary purposes?

Leduc went a step further. In summer 1961, just two months before Whitman arrived in Texas, a Deed of Trust shows that Leduc was granted a promissory note in the amount of $13,000 (adjusted for inflation, that is roughly $100,000 in today's dollars) using the purchased lots as collateral. An influential, well-connected local attorney named A. Guy Crouch II signed as his trustee. In essence, this transaction resembled a modern home equity line of credit, with the difference being that if Leduc defaulted on his payments to the savings and loan, Crouch had the power to auction off the land without going to court. Monthly payments were set at slightly more than $100—maxing out Leduc's whole salary.

If he had already received a windfall, why did he borrow so much money? The most reasonable conclusions would be that he used it to build and/or enhance the "resort home" that was burglarized only six months later. But I could locate no building permits from 1960-61 to verify construction, and when I inquired about the appearance and nature of the house he visited, Schuck replied, "It looked like it had been there a while...We'd get up there and scrape the old paint off, sand the wood. It didn't feel like upkeep on a house that had been built in the past six months."

Leduc could have used cash if needed to settle his seminary tuition (an obligation new priests had to navigate), with leftover funds to keep paying on the promissory note. It also would have made it easy for him to buy his nice car. What else did he need or want money for? For one thing, he could have financed a lot of social events. For another, it could have served as start-up cash if he lost his collar and had to find another way to live. If Leduc had "silent" partners on the investment, perhaps the money had been split up. If Leduc took payments to sublet the property for use by other clergy, he could have covered and made a slight profit—gaining access to information (perhaps quite valuable) about the men who used his place. Leduc could have easily viewed the cash and/or the property as a kind of insurance policy if he was not sure what the future held for him.

Regardless of how he used the money, unless the original equity invested in the property had come from his own cash, Leduc's withdrawal of any amount appears dodgy, fraudulent, or baldly capitalizing—depending upon the nature of his relationship to any benefactor and exactly how any funds were bequeathed. As the official owner whose name appeared on the deeds, Leduc had all the rights of a signatory. If he had been "asked" to serve in this capacity by someone who wanted to remain anonymous, he might have resented that position and felt entitled to break free.

In 1964, Leduc borrowed again. The same year he officially was approved to begin the process to become an Air Force chaplain, a mechanic's lien for $1,360.20 appeared on the property for construction "within 15 days" of a patio cover and screen. As a result, Leduc was obligated to an additional monthly set of payments scheduled over five years, at $22 each. By now, his total monthly payments would have far exceeded his guaranteed monthly base income as a priest.

Two years later, on May 16, 1966, Leduc defaulted on his promissory note. At the time, he was on temporary duty at San Antonio's Lackland Air Force Base as a new chaplain. Around this time, Leduc described in his FBI statement how Whitman, along with his wife and mother, all visited Leduc and that he "took them to dinner at the Officers Club." There were no indications of financial stress. He had moved on.

On June 14, trustee Crouch auctioned off the property for slightly more than $13,000 to the bank—no great profit was made, suggesting no notable improvements or losses on the land. There is no record of Leduc ever filing bankruptcy, meaning he simply walked away from land and a dwelling he had tended to, and to some degree shared, for more than five years. Perhaps the space had been contaminated in some way, physically or psychologically, or more simply: the property had fulfilled its temporary purpose.

Still, if someone else had bankrolled the initial purchase, then Leduc's borrowing and default on the promissory note (and walking away with cash) looks either like a payoff on the part of his sponsor—or as a "screw you" on the part of Leduc. Nevermind that this was 1966, long before foreclosure, short-sales, and "flip this house" were everyday terminology. The situation made Leduc a financial anomaly for the time, not exactly an average example of money management or responsibility.

However he had afforded the property and whatever he may have been mixed up in, Leduc seemed a capable trickster: a guy who could bargain, trade, scramble, and pivot to keep as many privileges as he could, including his status as a clergyman.

His strategies for self-preservation could have equally impressed and depressed Charles Whitman, who was facing and also avoiding interior and domestic turmoil of his own: at school, in the military, in his mind, and in his marriage. When it came to managing troubles of that variety, Leduc's capabilities were limited.

VIII. LEAVE NO TRACE

If Leduc found his place in one area of life, it seems to have been scouting. In his statement to the FBI, Leduc referred to his "instrumental" role in founding Whitman's Troop 119 in Lake Worth (1951-52), while he was biding time between seminaries. Leduc's cousin, who had little to no contact with him the last decade he was alive, stated her memory of a younger Leduc volunteering to be a scouting chaplain whenever he was needed. We now also know that Leduc received an Eagle Scout award from Troop 119 within weeks of making his seminary transfer to Texas.

At some point early on, Leduc was inducted into the Order of the Arrow (OA), a scouting honor society that recognized leaders who went above and beyond the call of duty. Importantly, as emphasized to me in more than one conversation with longtime scouts, OA differs from Eagle Scout achievement in that there's no way to "earn" it: the OA depends entirely upon the perceptions of other people. The OA is a prerequisite for the Vigil Honor, which Leduc received in Houston his first year as a brand-new priest. The requirements state that he had to have been put forward for the honor by another Vigil member, and I have located no document that reveals who that might have been.

If the Order of the Arrow status depends upon cultivating a positive perception among others, it means Leduc was able to make himself popular with Boy Scout peers, and with youths in general. Perhaps Leduc's superiors thought scout activities were the best way to manage or motivate a priest with Leduc's problems and kidlike appearance. Or maybe Leduc's advantage was that no one else wanted the job.

⊕

Only five months after ordination, in November 1955, Leduc's level of scout contribution was notable enough that he received the Vigil Honor. I spoke with Lamar Evans, a man who participated in the vigil ceremony at age 21 the same night Leduc did at age 25. The night, he said, was extraordinarily cold ("16 degrees"). While he remembered Leduc as a priest due to his clerical collar and his relatively young age (most Vigil members were in their 40s at the time), he had no interaction with Leduc before the ritual that night, when all the men were separated and left in the woods to build and tend their own fires until the morning: "When you get there, you wait for orders; you come for the vigil, then you leave," he told me. Communal breakfast the next day was quiet by tradition, and he didn't interact with Leduc there, either. "I can tell you there was nothing unusual about him," he said.

Leduc's Vigil Honor is significant, however. After combing the online database for the Sam Houston Area Council Colonneh Lodge, which lists names from 1923 through the present, I only found one "Rev." in the list ever to achieve the distinction, and that was Joseph G. Leduc. It was common for new priests to work with parish scout troops and youth groups, so the rarity of Leduc's status surprised me at first. But two regional scout historians I spoke with—Nelson Block and Marvin Smith—both emphasized to me that most parish priests would be so consumed by duties at their assigned church sites (including parish-based scout activities) that they would have to be extraordinarily committed and have special support from a bishop or other church leader in order to dedicate so much additional time away from their home-base congregations.

Considering his high level of involvement, Leduc seems to have left very little lasting impression. Msgr. John Brady (SMSU class of 1955) embodied the contrast. For years a nationally respected leader in Catholic scouting, he described to me how one priest chaplain made the difference in choice of vocation. "I went to Georgetown. My father was a patent attorney, and I was going to accept a commission in the Army after college. I didn't much like priests, and I didn't have much to do with them," he told me. "Bawling us kids out all the time, blaming us for stuff we didn't do. These Irish guys would even bawl people out in confession: 'You're going to hell.' I didn't want to be that. It turned me off really bad." As a young adult, inspired by a meeting with a good priest at a jamboree, Brady decided to change his direction. He wanted to leave a kinder, more compassionate legacy than most of the parish priests he had known as a young kid. When I spoke with him, scouting had been part of his ministry for nearly fifty years, and he received the Silver St. George Award in 2006.

By the early 1960s, at the height of his activity as regional chaplain for Catholic scouts, Leduc has a mixed presence as a clergyman. Yet two articles published during this period, also around the time he purchased his property, describe him as presiding over a public investiture ceremony held in Baytown for the purpose of scouts "re-dedicating themselves to Christ."

Because Leduc's name appeared in newspaper articles about scout activities in the area between 1960 and 1963, I sent multiple inquires including Leduc's name (and eventually a photograph) to a Houston native who has been active in Catholic scouting regionally since the 1950s. He himself received the St. George Emblem for Catholic Scouting in the early 2000s. The man had no memory of Leduc but said he would share the photograph with other scout leaders at meetings. After several months, he stopped returning my emails.

Again using newspaper reports, I located and contacted two former Baytown residents who remembered Leduc as their chaplain. Neither of the scouts I talked to ever visited Leduc's Liverpool "retreat" property. One, a former Eagle Scout named Robert Comeaux, did describe Leduc as having a good sense of humor (he was "very, very jovial"), though he couldn't recall any specific illustrations. He didn't remember anyone ever going to Leduc for guidance. He did have one vivid memory, however, from serving daily mass for Leduc during the weeklong National Jamboree in Colorado Springs in 1960: "He was the chaplain that went with us. We had mass there every morning—the fastest mass you could ever imagine. I would pick up the kit from his tent and then about five minutes later he would show up. It gave me just enough time to get the wine and the chalice, and the cruets. In about ten or eleven minutes, the mass was over."

At this time, the Latin rite of the mass was still the standard, which meant that Leduc could speed up or slow down the prayers as he pleased, as long as the altar boy could follow his cues. What decent kid would call any priest out on slip-ups or omissions? This was also a time before both bread and wine were shared with worshippers at services, which meant that the priest would be the only one drinking from the chalice. Perhaps Leduc just wanted to take his drink faster.

The details and recollections here—intersecting with Schuck's stories about Leduc's antics in the rectory, at the resort, and on the road—together suggest that Leduc's difficulties would emerge when it came to relationships with superiors, with adults who got wind of behavior they didn't like, or with older kids who were wising up. Younger boys would be less apt to judge him when he could build a fire, tie a knot, tell a joke, or even appear not to

PART II: TWO MEN IN BRITCHES

take Catholic "mumbo jumbo" too seriously. In other words, if he were not perceived as too severe as a priest, he would have been attractive during generations when priests could still be highly intimidating. Doing one's own thing was a sign of the growing antiestablishment ethos of the 1960s. Plus, Leduc drove a cool car and owned a bayou property, his own special place.

However Leduc may have managed or concealed his drinking over time, the mix of alcoholism, "jovial" personality, and contact with kids would cultivate opportunities for embarrassment, accidents, or complaint—even if no legal boundaries were ever violated. It is remarkable that in a social organization where he was clearly invested and had achieved recognition very early, Leduc seems to have left such a fuzzy impression. Lamar Evans reported only that he saw Leduc "a number of times" following the Vigil ordeal, but was not sure when he left the area. Leduc looked like a priest when necessary; maybe that was all anyone needed to know.

By 1968, approximately two years after Charles Whitman's tower rampage, Leduc returned to the Houston area when his active duty Air Force assignment in Alaska concluded and his reserve phase began. I found no continuing record of any work with scouts. No historian could find any record for me, either.

The only clue, perhaps a symbolic nod to his service—or a "carrot" to encourage sobriety and an adjustment of priorities—is that Leduc was awarded the St. George Emblem for Catholic Scouting in 1969, the same year of a short-lived assignment as a parish administrator, and just months before he was reassigned to live "in residence" at his last official parish in Houston. He is one of the first two priests ever to receive the award in the diocese.

In the end, neither the obituary from the *Texas Catholic Herald* nor the *Palm Beach Post* makes any reference to Leduc's work as a scout chaplain. While Leduc appears to be the only priest in the Houston area to receive the Vigil Honor in six whole decades prior to his death, neither this distinction, nor the Eagle Scout award, nor the St. George Emblem is mentioned in either obituary. Since scouting appears to be the most sustained accomplishment of his work as a priest, the omissions call attention to themselves.

It is interesting that, in adulthood, Charles Whitman himself withdrew from the Boy Scouts—an activity to which he was particularly suited as a former Eagle Scout and Marine—and this odd turn mirrors Leduc's fade from scout memory despite his deep involvement. After some time back home in Austin following his release from active duty, Whitman did re-enter the scouting world, spending several months as a scoutmaster in 1965 and demonstrating particular skill instructing boys about firearms. But by the end of the year, he quit.

The summer of that year, Whitman accepted a temporary residential internship with NASA and moved away from his wife to the Houston area, where Leduc was still awaiting his USAF chaplaincy training. Kathy joined Charlie temporarily, and the couple rented an apartment in League City. One friend reported that Kathy returned from a visit upset and talking about divorce, a subject that abated upon Charlie's return to Austin in the Fall.

In his FBI statement, Leduc does not mention seeing or hearing from Whitman during this time, even though this was the closest geographically the two friends had lived since Lake Worth in 1951-52. NASA's campus is situated on the route between Leduc's 1965 parish assignment in Port Arthur (an hour and a half away) and the resort property he still owned in

Liverpool (thirty minutes away). League City is even closer—only forty minutes from the resort. In correspondence with his in-laws in June, Charlie reported that he enrolled in Monday, Tuesday, Thursday, and Friday classes during the summer session at nearby Alvin Community College, a mere fifteen-minute drive from Leduc's cabin.

It would be surprising if the former scout and his onetime scoutmaster did not meet up before Leduc reported to Maxwell AFB for chaplaincy training on July 13, 1965.

Leduc's transfer into the military intrigued me from the beginning, as he did not have a long career in the service. The puzzle of how religious denominations "used" the military chaplaincy has been a subject for conversation since at least 1976, and not just among Catholics.

In an extensive interview dated July that year, Brigadier General Thomas Groome, Jr., then deputy chief of chaplains in the USAF who had served at Elmendorf AFB in Alaska from 1952 to 1954, described the problems that arose when various church officials sent clergy into chaplain assignments without really knowing anything about the men they were sending: "All too often we discover when we have some difficulty with a person becoming a chaplain that nobody had really known him when he was endorsed…We find that a number of the denominations are conscientious, well-organized and know what they are doing, and handle the programs well; others seem to be just very casual about the people they send in to be chaplains." Without identifying any churches by name, he went on to state that some clerical leaders seemed disinterested in screening the men they sent into the chaplaincy, underestimating military assignments as if they were "ministering the boys out to camp." The military, Groome stressed, wasn't "camp" on any level, especially during wartime.

Elsewhere Groome described the environment that would not be ideal for any priest who was struggling with drinking or his promise of celibacy: "[T]he model of the fighter pilot is one who can outdrink and out-fornicate and outfight anybody else... [I]t is the image of the military man as proving his manhood by drinking." Considered within the drastic Alaskan frontier, not to mention the Vietnam War, none of the bravado and dysfunction Groome describes here would add up to a "soft" environment for Chaplain Leduc, unless he was planning to fit right in or blow it off entirely.

Besides that, a chaplain's first duty was not supposed to be his own private therapy; it was to provide pastoral care and direction for men whose lives were on the line. Leduc's job at least part of the time in Alaska, in fact, was to meet with wounded soldiers en route home from the war, a duty he would have been ill-prepared to fulfill.

☦

Now that the U.S. has an all-volunteer military, even during wartime, we tend to treat service to Uncle Sam as a means for young men to "shape up," "get serious," or "find themselves." Inside all the marketing materials, the realities of combat and carnage seem secondary. Indeed, when Charles Whitman first enlisted in the Marines just out of high school in 1959, he sought to escape his father and his family problems, yet he readily accepted an NESEP scholarship to study at UT Austin.

Whitman returned to active duty in early 1963, only six months after he married Kathy, when his grades fell below acceptable levels and he lost his scholarship. By November that year he was referring to the Marines as a "waste." Ironically, this was after he got himself arrested and court-martialed, sentenced to hard labor, and demoted—for gambling, threatening another serviceman, carrying an unauthorized firearm, and lending money at usurious rates of interest. The record suggests that Whitman's "honorable" discharge in late 1964 was achieved because his father lobbied heavily through a lawyer on his behalf.

Leduc's commission was much different. In the mid-1960s, the U.S. did have a draft, but there was no law to compel any priest to enter the military. Still, pressure or encouragement from superiors could have been a strong motivator. Leduc enjoyed more privileges from the get-go than Whitman or other enlisted men because he had already earned a bachelor's degree and was an ordained cleric. He entered the military not only as a chaplain but as an officer with the rank of captain—the latter, in Schuck's words, "rather a stretch of the imagination."

The record also indicates lax supervision during his transition into the service. I located a newspaper article from March 1965, announcing a talk that "J. C. Leduc" (yet another mistake with his middle initial) was scheduled to present at a meeting of the Serra Club in Port Arthur. According to the announcement, Leduc was going to outline the "duties of chaplains in military service." But he had not even attended official chaplaincy training yet—his USAF records document that he wouldn't do so until five months later, in July. During this period, Leduc's pastor was Msgr. Henry Drouilhet, who had also been his supervisor as Director of the Catholic Boy Scouts for the diocese. Given his activities during the period leading up to commission, it seems that Leduc either sought an escape or was sent off to regain focus and discipline. It is also plausible that he viewed his military involvement simply as distraction and adventure, an outgrowth of a Boy Scout's notion that military service would be just like a round of "capture the flag."

What did Whitman think of Vietnam? More than that: what did he think of Leduc's entrance into the military? I located only one published account where the topic of the war comes up. Just hours before the first two murders, Whitman's friends Larry and Elaine Fuess stopped by the house for a spontaneous visit with Whitman, and Larry was quoted saying that Whitman "didn't understand why boys from the United States had to go over there and die for something they didn't have anything to do with." Fuess later told other reporters that he did not recall any discussion about Vietnam. While disputed, the account remains interesting in context: Leduc had been in Alaska for only seven days, and there was no way for Whitman (or anyone, for that matter) to know yet that Leduc would never be deployed to the killing fields.

Because chaplains were subsumed under a separate Catholic jurisdiction called the Military Ordinariate (now the Archdiocese for Military Services), bishops have been accused of using the chaplaincy corps as a dumping ground for problem priests.

One of the most notorious cases is that of a Dallas priest, Fr. Robert Peebles. In 1981, after being approved for the inactive military reserves, Peebles was promoted to diocesan Director of Boy Scouts in his diocese, despite known concerns about heavy drinking, allegations of indecency with a young boy, and sexual counseling. He was endorsed the following year for active military duty, and as a chaplain on assignment was apprehended for attempted rape at Fort Benning. He confessed to the crime but was permitted to resign from the military and was assigned to a parish in his home diocese two years later.

The remote Alaskan location itself has had a history of scandals related to troubled clergy. The Jesuits have been sharply criticized for not monitoring or intervening with abusive priests working among native peoples in Fairbanks. The director of Catholic Youth Organization and Superintendent of Catholic Schools for the Anchorage diocese in 1966 and 1967, when Leduc was assigned to Elmendorf, was Rev. Francis ("Frank") Murphy, a troubled priest transplanted "for alcoholism" from Boston. He was later accused of abusing five boys and amassing a disturbing collection of pornography during his time in Alaska. The allegations spanned a period of 21 years (starting in 1966). The case was settled in 2006 for nearly $1.4 million.

Keeping track of chaplain movements is a challenge, even under benign circumstances. While all priest chaplain names are indexed in the OCD as serving in specific branches, their actual assignment records have to be secured one by one, through the National Personnel Records archive. Even though military men, like priests, take assignments as they come, Leduc's relocation to Anchorage, Alaska struck me as extreme. Like another chaplain candidate I interviewed, he might have been presented with options and selected Alaska for the adventure of it, but he may have had no say in the matter. Elmendorf Air Force Base had existed since 1942, but the state did not join the union until 1959, and the Catholic Diocese of Anchorage itself had just been founded in 1966, the same year Leduc arrived. It truly was the last American frontier, not unlike southeastern Florida a generation earlier.

If Leduc had indicated a personal preference for this remote location, it dramatizes his own desire for a drastic geographical break. His "send off" into another male-only group (with plenty of alcohol and weapons) doesn't indicate in any way a coherent approach for redirection of a priest whose vocation had drifted off the path. I do not believe the assignment was entirely random.

Leduc's statement after the murders offers no clues regarding the content of his military experience, only his rank as a Captain, with an activity code (FV) and a serial number. A mistake (perhaps a transposition error) in his *Palm Beach Post* obituary said that he "accepted a commission" not in 1965 but in 1956—the second year after his ordination!—suggesting, erroneously, that he had been quickly sought-after by the Air Force. Until I had accurate information, this date eliminated a whole decade of assignments in Houston.

I made a FOIA request for Leduc's releasable information as a deceased veteran, and discovered that his active duty period was only about two years, from the time he spent in chaplaincy school in July 1965 to his release from active duty at Elmendorf with the Alaskan Air Command in late 1967. He subsequently continued Reserve duties from 1968 through 1969, at the same time he was based back in Houston and monitored again by the diocese. Much information on the records form is blank, but there were intriguing finds. Leduc's receipt of the Small Arms Expert Marksmanship ribbon provided an early indicator that he was no stranger to handling guns. He also received the National Defense Service Medal (awarded to all servicemen who served honorably during a time of national crisis) and the Air Force Outstanding Unit Award (not an individual merit).

During the years Leduc served, the Air Force provided a code when men were released from duty. After a lawsuit in the early

1970s, these numbers were abolished because they were deemed to be potentially prejudicial for future employers. Some of the codes (called SDN or Separation Designation Numbers) are unambiguous: "Completion of Active Duty Service Commitment" or "Recipients of Medal of Honor" or "To attend school" or "Unfitness—unacceptable conduct" or "Homosexuality" or "Conscientious Objectors." Even the apparently obvious category of "Upon established date of separation" had an official code. But Leduc's SDN is 614 P. 62, AFR 36-12: "Release for other miscellaneous reasons." Leduc is listed as "discharged," not "honorably discharged" or "dishonorably discharged." (Even Whitman, as noted before, received an honorable discharge from the Marines.) In the box labeled "Transcript of Court-Martial Trial," rather than indicating N/A (as in other places on the document), the report stated "Not in File." My FOIA request and subsequent appeal to the Military Justice Division of the U.S. Air Force for any transcript of Leduc's court martial trial, if applicable, yielded a "no records" determination.

So how had Leduc performed during his service—and why did he leave? I spent months scrapping to locate records that could provide names of living chaplains who might have memories of Leduc, either from his training at Maxwell AFB, his active duty period at Elmendorf, or during his reserve duties at several other bases. This was challenging for several reasons. The OCD lists priests assigned to different military branches, including ranks but not bases. The OCD entry for the diocese of Anchorage does not include base personnel in its listings.

Most irritating of all, my inquiry for military records supervised by the Catholic Church revealed that the Military Ordinariate did not keep any lists during this time, and also that military assignments were at the time supervised by the Archdiocese of New York. My contact with an archivist there at first simply yielded a suggestion that I return to the OCD. Upon follow up, I was passed onto a Catholic historian for the military archdiocese, who replied this way in an email: "Unfortunately, I have no idea where those archives are. In fact, I have asked the Archdiocese of New York—the Cardinal included—where they are, and no one seems to know. If I find them, I'll let you know." I responded with a question: Was he really referring to Cardinal Timothy Dolan?

His silence made the initial response read like a joke.

Meanwhile, I had sent a blind inquiry to Elmendorf AFB seeking advice from a site historian. An incredibly helpful and thorough officer named Joe Orr sent me all the records he had, including a narrative document titled Chaplain History Alaska Air Command (1956-1968), a batch of captioned photographs from the period, and a list of all available names of chaplains from 1965 through 1970. He said that all records from 1967 appeared to be missing or lost. Leduc's name appeared nowhere in any surviving documents, narratives, or lists, despite his arrival in July 1966. I forwarded Leduc's photograph with a name and asked for a final check, but Orr reported that he could locate no record of anyone named Leduc having been anywhere on the base. Upon his advice, I contacted Maxwell AFB, which houses all surviving Air Force records, with even worse results: they had no listings for any chaplains at Elmendorf at all.

Returning to the long list of chaplain names Orr provided me, I was able to locate and contact only two men. One was a Jewish rabbi, Azriel Fellner, who had served not only as a chaplain at Elmendorf for over a year but also as the sole itinerant rabbi for the entire state of Alaska during his assignment. The other was an Episcopalian priest, William Rhett, who had served at the remote radar location of Shemya. Fellner arrived slightly after Leduc departed, and had no memory of anyone by that name. Rhett's time overlapped with Leduc's, but he only briefly passed through Elmendorf en route to his island assignment. I sent him a photo of Leduc, and Rhett did not recognize him.

Rabbi Fellner's experience provided insights about the cultural and geographical environment as Leduc would have experienced it. In his role, Fellner did a great deal of traveling with his wife across the Alaskan tundra with its stunted flowers and trees, beautiful views of the Chugach mountain range. He described how the land at the time was "pristine, pure, and untouched" by the ravages of oil drilling. Anchorage was a "hamlet" and Elmendorf Base was small. Fellner noted the lack of warmth among chaplains at the time during his training and assignment period, across denominations. He said that Catholic and Jewish chaplains, in particular, didn't fit in well with the more Protestant culture of the military. Fellner, who was married at the time and also kept his Sabbath on Friday, reported that his commander was displeased that he wouldn't hang out for happy hour drinks at the officer's club. ("It was his Protestant privilege to ignore the Sabbath thing.")

By contrast, Leduc as a drinker had the social currency to blend with non-Catholics and macho military men. But how would he have handled darker moments? This was wartime after all—never mind the fact that a friend in Texas had just committed the most highly visible public massacre in recent history, and FBI officers showed up less than one month after Leduc's arrival to ask questions.

Add to these stressors the wartime reality of the chaplain's calling. Fellner recalled: "The black underside of the experience was dealing with casualties from Vietnam. Aircraft would arrive at 2 or 3 AM en route to the lower states. We'd greet them, they'd wait for refueling. Encounters? Most men didn't want to talk. They wanted a cigarette, or couldn't talk, or were sedated. We would say, 'Hello' and 'Is there anything I can do?' It was a sad, empty experience. The cases were varied: amputees, shellshock, blindness, limbs destroyed. Most were very young."

How crazy it felt: two government documents showed that Leduc had served in this exact location, and yet the actual site retained no evidence that he had ever set foot there. Again, Leduc had faded into the woodwork, as if he took the Boy Scout Motto, "Leave No Trace," to a level of existential achievement.

IX. A PRIEST IN THE GAPS

Based on the content of his personal papers, here are the things we know Charles Whitman took pride or pleasure in at various times: his Eagle Scout rank; his paper route; his Catholic Scouting award; his abilities with Latin as an altar server; his penmanship; his cleanliness; his shooting skills; his journal-keeping (for a few months); his father's financial generosity; his ability to turn down the proposition of a slut; his disdain for the Marine Corps; his wife, Kathy, also referred to as his "most precious possession."

Here are things we know Charles Whitman thought about based on additional sources: making money; staying awake; whether he was big enough; keeping a blackjack in his military locker; whether his penis was "a queer"; whether people would know he was only kidding; whether his brother's homosexuality could be cured; his wife's fear of him; his fear of sterility; his fear that he might assault her again; the safety of his mother; his grades; holding off a whole army from the top of the Texas tower; whether people would understand what happened to the dog.

Here are concerns that would have crossed Whitman's mind even though they are not stored in the written record: the first time he saw his father lay hands on his mother; what his father's hands or fists felt like; the color of his father's belt; which person his father would strike when there were options; if his mother fought back; where he could hide to avoid a beating; whether he raised or did not raise his hand or his fist to his father in self-defense; what it was like the day after a beating, at the breakfast table or the bathroom sink; what he said in the locker room when a classmate saw the welts on his back; what he thought of his grandmother living next door; whether his father teased him about the injury to his testicles; the first time he killed an animal; who had told him about "the birds and the bees"; the exact time and location of his first sexual experience; whether he could satisfy any woman sexually; how often he met with the priest in the first year of college; which college friends met the priest, and doing what and how many times; whether he met the priest's friends, if he had friends; when exactly he stopped praying, and why; what memories caused him to wake with fists cocked, ready for a fight; what his wife did to indicate when she was more or less afraid of him; exactly how he assaulted her and when it took place; what exactly prompted him to turn a rifle on his father when his father threatened his brother on a hunting trip; what he admired or did not admire about the priest; what his wife thought about the priest; whether he worried to the priest about his mother's safety; whether he told the priest that he wanted to die or harm himself; whether he needed or tried to contact the priest but could not, and what he felt about that; whether the priest's calls ever came, unsolicited and incoherent; whether the priest occasionally failed to return his calls; when and how the priest said goodbye, see-you-later-pal, that's-all-folks, sayonara.

☦

Experienced writers know that a journal can be a performance, even a lie. It takes practice and training to master the art of self-scrutiny in words. It's also serious Catholic discipline to develop a true and honest "examination of conscience." In seminaries Leduc attended, one intense practice was called *particular examen.* Neither was a skill Whitman ever demonstrated—in fact, he was a master of denial.

After the shootings, a UT Austin composition professor, Dr. Billie Jo Inman, shared her recollections of Whitman as a student in her freshman course during spring 1962. When Whitman received a "D" on an essay, he unsuccessfully appealed his grade with the chairman of the department. Inman held extra conferences with Whitman during that semester, and he still struggled to earn only a "C." (His high school English course grades—in contrast with his high grades in catechism—had been similarly marginal.) Inman suggested that Whitman struggled to develop his thinking fully, and that his most successful efforts came when regurgitating other people's ideas. She described him as "panicky" about grades, "pleasant…as long as things were going his way," and "someone that had to be handled very carefully."

None of his college essays have been archived, but a good sampling of Whitman's personal writing has survived. He did not discover the pleasures of actual journal keeping until November

1963 at Camp Lejeune, four months into his newlywed separation from Kathy, in a Memoranda notebook he began after his arrest. This journal period is relatively short-lived: in the canvas-bound *Daily Record of CJ Whitman*, begun in the early weeks of 1964, three quarters of the lined pages were left blank.

The tendencies described by his UT professor are observable in the range of entries, notes, and poems. Whitman's writing often contains a great deal of detail but reflects an enforced shallowness, a frustrating lack of empathy and self-awareness, an inability to make connections, and a reliance on repetition and cliché. "Enough of that" is one tag Whitman uses to back away from serious topics related to his own identity and family (his father's demands, his concerns about employment and his future). If he had never committed murder, we would say these artifacts indicate a lack of emotional maturity, perhaps some underlying fear of self-exposure.

One of the darkest gaps in Whitman's papers occurs in the first letter composed the night he killed his mother, Margaret, and wife, Kathy, before going to the tower the next morning. Whitman began the letter using a typewriter. He scans through reflections without specifying or deepening them, setting up a litany of generic excuses: "I don't really understand myself these days"; "I have been a victim of many unusual and irrational thoughts... it requires tremendous mental effort to concentrate on useful and progressive tasks"; "After my death I wish that an autopsy would be performed on me to see if there is any visible physical disorder"; "I decided to kill my wife after I pick her up from the telephone company"; "I truly do not consider this world worth living in"; "Similar reasons provoked me to take my mother's life also."

Because Larry and Elaine Fuess knocked on the door early that evening, some accounts or recreations depict Whitman literally interrupted midsentence, even though the Fuesses subsequently described seeing papers next to, rather than inside, the typewriter. Whitman himself wrote the phrase "friends interrupted" in the left margin at the place the typing ends, but the idea of a perfectly-timed interruption seems absolutely too "on the nose." As a writer, I believe it makes more sense that he had stopped writing for some time before the interruption, and decided (in Whitman's fashion) to "account for" the break—probably when he started writing again.

When we look exactly at what he was typing, we can see that he was about to finish one thought that he would have spent much of his life avoiding. It invited a long pause: a stare into space, a convenient trip to the refrigerator, a quick tug of the paper from the machine. The hesitation is common enough for writers examining difficult subjects, and no less surprising for a young undergraduate who had trouble getting a grip on his life. Add into this context a childhood of domestic trauma, mixed with Catholic and military notions about privilege and obedience, and stereotypes about strong, silent, or brash Southern manliness, and you have a lot of reality stuck in the throat. What did he think about "all his life" as a boy? How would he express a reflection that troubled him?

During the time between the typed and the handwritten clauses, Charles visited with Larry and Elaine, ate ice cream from a truck that passed by, said goodbye to his friends, and then committed his most intimate murders—first Margaret, and then Kathy. Even using a clinical instructor's eye, reading past misspellings due to violence, grief, and stress, the canyon of lost insight is horrifying:

TYPED opening:

> All my life as a boy until I ran away from home to join the Marine Corps

Handwritten (cursive) ending (roughly 8 hours later):

> I was a witness to her [my mother] being beat at least one [sic] a month. Then when she took [sic] enough my father wanted to fight to bring her below her usual standard of living. I imagine it appears that I bruttaly [sic] kill [sic] both of my loved ones. I was only trying to do a quick through [sic] job.

Whitman finished the letter with hasty and jumbled references to his mother's abuse and his father's behavior, along with superficial explanations for his own brutality ("I was only trying…"). Murdering his wife and his mother had substituted for self-reflection. Whitman marked the spot: "8-1- 66 Mon. 3:00 A.M. Both Dead."

He expresses no contrition here or elsewhere, only rationalizations. The autopsy Whitman requested in the typed opening before the first two murders captures an ultimate desire for some final, external assessment that could absolve him from responsibility. The lapsed Catholic was also making a transparent effort to lay down track that might mitigate any "mortal sins" he clearly planned and committed, one after the other, over many hours. He called himself a "victim," but as usual he was selective in his supporting details.

We must also visualize what was necessary before Whitman

could finish this and other letters. Each time, he performed a version of the *lavabo* he had witnessed at every mass as an altar boy. Except on these occasions, he washed and dried his own hands rather than the priest's. On these occasions, he washed away the blood of his own family members.

The four months leading up to the murders were especially stressful for Whitman and his wife. In March 1966, he received a phone call from his mother, Margaret, in Florida following a conflict that brought the police to his parents' home. She insisted that she was in fear for her life and asked her eldest son to pick her up. That month, Whitman made the long drive to Florida, packed his mother and her suitcases in his car, and drove her to Texas.

Whitman was still a struggling college student, newly married, without a full-time job and renting an apartment nearly 1,100 miles away from his parents' home. His mother had contacts of independent means living closer, but the complexities of her relationships to those friends and family members are not publicly known. Her desire to be as far away as possible from her husband speaks to his ability to dominate. She never could have imagined that death would come at the hands of the son who rescued her.

At first glance, Margaret's stand against abuse suggests not trauma but a pathway to health and a "new start" for both her and her sons. But the break was a powerful disruption of all the compartments Whitman had grown used to. Margaret's resolve, as a wife and mother—and as a Catholic woman—to break from a cycle established for twenty-five years is remarkable. In hindsight, we can also recognize both the doomed chivalry and melodrama of Whitman's role. He had lost his scholarship and was living on his wife's salary. He cobbled jobs together. He likely missed a few classes of his own to rescue her during a semester when he was already carrying a heavier-than-average course load.

Upon return to Texas, the calls from his father began—long calls at all hours, roughly every two days or so, repeating arguments, lectures, pleas and promises if Whitman would just convince his mother to return. Whitman's wife would have overheard many of these calls while she was trying to grade papers and prepare for classes and manage hospitality to her mother-in-law. Whitman's father began sending money to help support her, and within a short time Margaret moved into a separate apartment and secured a cafeteria job. By accounts, she was relieved to be away from her husband and was proud of her new employment.

During this time, there is evidence that Whitman was acting out to solicit guidance, directly or not. He apparently no longer saw religion as helpful (one story describes him leaving his apartment when Kathy's Methodist minister came to visit), and his wife advised him to seek psychological help. Whitman made a single visit to the university psychiatrist at the end of March 1966 but did not make any follow-up appointment. In an odd incident around this time, he showed up abruptly one night at the house of Barton Riley, a beloved UT professor. Stepping into the house, Whitman dropped a batch of papers onto the floor, declared a desire to kill his father, then played a manic rendition of Debussy's "Clair de Lune" on the piano. Somehow his professor talked him down.

Also that spring, a friend came by his apartment to find Whitman packing up books and rambling about how he was dropping out of college and leaving his wife because she'd be better off without him and that he had to leave because he had "something personal to settle." Witnesses reported that his wife, among friends, confronted him with "But why? Why?" Within a few days, Professor Riley heard of Whitman's plan and ordered him not to go through with it. So he didn't.

What was this "personal" thing to settle? What was the source of anxiety about whether he was good enough for his wife, and how he should just flee the scene? Other than his wife, who were his real allies?

By Spring 1966, Father Leduc had completed his chaplaincy training and taken up his temporary duty station at Lackland Air Force Base in San Antonio. To the FBI, he described two in-person visits with Charlie in May and June. The last visit would include both Charlie's wife and mother, near the date of Charlie's 25th birthday. Leduc was saying goodbye for the second time in eleven years—and this time, his destiny was much less certain.

☦

Catholic teaching about divorce has caused grief for generations, particularly for women who have been the heart of religious practice in their homes. This is especially difficult for children to witness, whether they are active in their faith or not, because it appears on the surface to penalize the church's most faithful (and usually female) members. It was not much of a choice: stay with your abusing partner and suffer, or leave and be cut off from your church.

Even now the church does not recognize divorce, but there is more clarity than half a century ago about the needs for separation under conditions of abuse or addiction. A man or woman who is living under violent or otherwise untenable circumstances can separate or even seek divorce from a spouse without being excommunicated. It is not considered their "sin." The problem remains that, no matter the reason, unless the person seeks and is granted an annulment, she cannot marry again as a Catholic. If she does marry outside the church as a divorcée, she will be excommunicated, which means that she will be barred from receiving communion.

If Whitman's mother, Margaret, had any desires for romantic companionship in her future, she would face an agonizing choice: my sex life or my sacraments. Whitman's father faced no such dilemma. The investigation suggested that despite his demands for his wife to return home, he was already courting other women. The November after his son's rampage and his wife's murder, he married again. Margaret's move towards divorce in spring 1966 must be understood as a radical act with high stakes for a devout Catholic. There is one account in the FBI records that during a visit to Florida in May to secure her own lawyer, she stayed with a friend or family member and attended mass, but her husband stalked her to the service and made such a vociferous scene that she had to leave.

A thoughtful and compassionate priest would have made a huge difference to Margaret. We do not know if she was finally acting under some pastoral encouragement, or despite years of counsel to the contrary. We must also remember that she been just seventeen years old when she married her husband in August 1940.

Joe Schuck shared that Leduc was "a very important aspect of Whitman's existence" during the stressful days of his parents' separation. Father Leduc, for his part, appears to have been utterly tone-deaf—as a "family friend" and as a Catholic priest—regarding the marital circumstances exploding in Charlie's family. In his statement to the FBI, he describes taking Charlie, Kathy, and Mrs. Whitman to dinner at the officer's club at Lackland sometime during June, approximately one month before all three would be dead. "Everything appeared normal" between Charlie and Kathy, he said, although Mrs. Whitman "was disturbed concerning divorce proceedings against subject Whitman's father." No kidding. Leduc made no direct reference to implications of a divorce, stating only that during an earlier visit in May, Charles was "in a turmoil concerning religion." Leduc also presented domestic violence as a matter of hearsay, stating that Mrs. Whitman "had previously told [Charlie] that her husband was continually beating her."

These are not the empathetic statements of a longtime friend or pastor; at best, they sound oblivious. Then again, they come from the same priest who brought a nameless woman (as his guest? as his date?) to a very quickly arranged wedding, supposedly performed in church "to honor" Charlie's mother and her faith. Leduc's detachment from the realities of actual women and families paralleled his troubled relationship to his own bride, Holy Mother Church.

During spring 1966, Whitman and his wife moved to a small house across the river in Austin, allowing some distance from his mother's new rooms at the Penthouse Apartments downtown. He filled the garage at the new house with weapons. When he saw the psychiatrist at UT, he admitted to assaulting his wife on two occasions but said that he thought she had "less fear of him now than in the past." On the self-assessment form prior to his appointment, there was a place to indicate which parent he spoke to when discussing his problems. He wrote, "NEITHER." He did not indicate any confidant at all: not his wife, not one of his brothers, not a friend, roommate or classmate, and not Father Leduc.

Whitman's mother's departure called the entire family system, with its agreed upon silences and secrets, into question. But a potential new family alliance was forming around her. His brother, Patrick, brought his wife for a time to Austin. Johnnie Mike also brought a friend during a vacation. By the time the shootings occurred, Johnnie had gotten into trouble with the law but told the judge he would rather pay a fine than return home to his father.

Ironically, it was not so many years of abuse that caused the crisis, but his mother's finally articulated fear, her desire for divorce and a new life. Like the other members of his family, Whitman had spent years adjusting to, accommodating, and even imitating violence. Until his mother left, Whitman had mostly functioned by keeping pieces of his life in separate boxes. Rather than inspiring him, his mother's choice was disorienting. Leaving her husband was the ultimate rejection of a submissive "woman's role." What, then, was the role of the eldest son?

In compartmentalizing to survive, Whitman was not so different from many of us, but the strategy was becoming less and less easy to sustain. The campus doctor described Whitman's acute distress at this time during his one and only visit: "The youth could talk for long periods of time and develop overt hostility while talking, and then during the same narration may show signs of weeping."

As a priest, Leduc had mastered a different survival strategy: slipping from one place to another. The move to Alaska must have looked like a clear solution to whatever problems he had in Houston. I imagine Whitman envying his friend's easy, officially sanctioned escape route.

⚕

Five years earlier, as a freshman in college, not long after he met up with Leduc for the first time in Texas, Charles Whitman recorded the purchase of a book titled *Love without Fear* for fifty-one cents. The subtitle of the book, which Whitman did not write down, is "How to Achieve Sex Happiness in Marriage." The book cover describes Eustace Chesser, M.D., the author, as "the foremost authority on sex technique." Originally published in 1947, Chesser's text strikes a minor chord inside the milieu of sexual research during the mid-20th century, from Kinsey through Masters and Johnson.

Throughout Whitman's life, "love" and "fear" had been tangled, even synonymous, so the title itself was understandably attractive. The book reads as a relatively progressive and unsentimental information manual about sexual technique and response, but it also preserves a male-centered and definitely traditional discussion of marriage, gender, and family roles. Chesser plays to a default male reader: "Every normal woman wants to be 'possessed.' She expects her husband to 'take' her"; "[W]omen want to be led step by step through the various stages of sexual intercourse." There is a soft and familiar misogyny about the book, and it would suit the imagination of a sexually curious, Catholic military scholarship kid who had just arrived at university. It would have been welcome compared to the usual cautionary fare for Catholic adolescents of his generation, such as Gerald Kelly's *Modern Youth and Chastity.*

In Whitman's hands, Chesser's text would provide perspective on a healthier partnership than what he had seen in his own parents or heard about in locker rooms. The book would demystify sex and compensate for gaps in his knowledge, while also providing titillating (if intellectualized) genital details and tips for sexual expertise—on paper, at least. It was more "serious" than *Swank* or *Nugget* or *Men's Adventure*. There weren't any pictures.

Under the surface, Whitman was seeking a way to reconcile his psychological and sexual questions, and it makes sense that Whitman sought to marry quickly, before he began his sophomore year. In the Catholic tradition, marriage—like baptism and the Eucharist as well as ordination (holy orders)—is considered a sacrament. Unfortunately, this also means that, without guidance and self-reflection, marriage can be treated as an almost magic ritual solution that resolves all contradicting tendencies, reconciling "high church" theology with the most venial (or most serious) personal shortcomings. It is not surprising that Whitman fixated on a wedding as a way to legitimize sexual feelings and transform himself into an adult by complying, externally, with Catholic teaching. But given the milieu of his violent family background, his enabling male peers, and his extremely stunted capacity for empathy and mutuality, this fixation did not bode well.

Whitman's correspondence with Kathy as his fiancée gives us a window into his self-serving agenda and technically moral thinking. He was invested in posing as a "good Catholic boy," yet he also reportedly assured Kathy's family that Catholicism wasn't that important to him. Any of the required pre-marriage instructions with a priest were so rushed (within just 10 days of the ceremony) as to seem more tactical than sincere, yet Whitman also informed Kathy that she needed to decide whether she would attend mass with him the morning before the wedding. His sexual comments are reductive, emphasizing both body parts and homophobic rules (and anxiety), as when he writes that his penis, "Walter," is "not a queer," like the poet Walt Whitman—"at least let's hope not." He also performs a dubious outrage when he hears that Kathy's father has suggested Whitman should not sleep at the house on a visit: "having relations…it's the last thing I want to do." Most of the sign-offs of his letters to Kathy and to her family from this period forward repeat a religious reference, "May God Bless You," that feels stilted and affected for a young man under twenty-five years old.

Marriage did not make Whitman a good partner, and there was little, if any, blissful honeymoon for Kathy. A lengthy letter her mother sent to Whitman following a troubling phone conversation in January identified his "desire to dominate Kathy" as a destructive force. She also urged the couple to seek counseling, both individually and together. But rather than heed his mother-in-law's counsel, Whitman dropped out of school and returned to active duty at Camp Lejeune in North Carolina, taking Kathy away from Texas—and her family—for about six months. By July 1963, she returned to Texas again, and Whitman remained on duty.

When Whitman wrote about Kathy in his diary during their long separation, he described how her lack of sexual experience was the key to her "success" as his wife, adding that he had "taught her how to please [him]," and stressing that their compatibility was "to his own credit." During this time, clearly lonely for her husband and also deeply aware of his insecurities, Kathy complimented him often. She also sent him gentle "food for thought," including a lengthy article titled "Sexual Communication." She shared stories from a "Marriage and Family" class at UT, a course she wanted him to take. At one point she shared a professor's theory that she thought was especially intelligent: how women's self-protection and lack of sexual response can be blamed on a history of aggression and "force" from men.

Whitman could not hear or understand what his wife was telling him. His self-image continued to contradict the physical reality: he lived halfway across the country from his wife for one and a half of their first two and a half years married. Whatever Whitman told himself about his skills as a husband or lover, his ideas of sex and love appeared depersonalized, and probably had been for a very long time. Distance was safer than intimacy, and much easier than daily partnership.

After the murders, an Austin shopkeeper came forward to allege that a clean-cut Marine matching Whitman's description had tried to sell off some pornographic pictures at his store sometime during 1962-63. The original story published in *Texas Observer* did not include any descriptions of the nature of the images the young man took from his pocket. However, the unnamed shopkeeper described how blasé the young man was about selling them off, and added that, when inquired about the market for these pictures—say, college students?—the young man said no, "grade school and high school kids." At this point, the shopkeeper maintained, he threw the young man out of the store.

While some historians have dismissed the account, it seems plausible for multiple reasons. The most important is that Whitman had a two-dimensional sexual imagination. I don't mean that he simply liked to look at pictures depicting nudity or sexual acts, but that he had a profound inability to see most people—especially women—as thinking, complex human beings with agency and desires of their own. His mother-in-law called this problem by name in her letter appealing for the couple to get counseling: "I know you think no woman can think logically," she wrote. "But I shall try."

In his journals, Kathy's body and sexual "abilities" were things to describe as his "possessions" to critique, shape, and remold. Other women were "wenches" or "whores", "girls" or occasionally "wives." A letter from Kathy to her mother after the second night of her honeymoon reported that Whitman took her to a striptease show on Bourbon Street as well as to a female impersonation club on the wharf at Lake Ponchetrain—suggesting that he was familiar with sexual entertainment and knew where to find it.

Whitman's demands and desires were consistently self-congratulatory. Even after he had lost his scholarship and landed himself a court martial, Whitman wrote in January 1964 of his frustration that his wife would not meet some unspecified expectation: "I wish Kathy would do the small things I ask her when I ask her...I put myself out of the way to do things for her...But it doesn't seem to be a 2-way process." Whitman's ultimate idea of "saving" both his mother and his wife from "suffering" was to objectify them in the most final and gruesome way—in their beds.

After leaving home, former altar server and Eagle Scout Whitman found himself embedded in guy cultures where soft-core pornography and live shows were part of the post-WWII milieu, even if retaining the seedy connotation to preserve the "illicit" thrill. If Whitman had not already been exposed to such material by adolescence, he would have been exposed once he left home. He was a Marine with enlisted status living in a barracks, then a male college student at a time when men's "stag" magazines flourished and Russ Meyer was just beginning to make his "naughty," campy films.

The fact that no pornographic photographs or publications turned up in the 1966 FBI investigation does not necessarily undermine the shopkeeper's story about three to four years earlier. A person who depersonalizes sex and eventually commits crimes doesn't necessarily keep a trove of gruesome images brimming under the floorboards as in some murder mystery cliché. He can easily indulge and be appalled by sexual material, compartmentalizing activities at different times, perhaps even condemning other people for their sexual attitudes or behavior, as Whitman did, especially in some of his final journal entries.

Perhaps pornography was merely a temporary ingredient of curiosity or experimentation. In 1962, he owned a Polaroid camera, a device that enabled the sixties equivalent of sexting. Correspondence from 1964 refers to one friend detained at the Mexico border for transporting "obscene images" along with Dexedrine, an amphetamine Whitman was known to be taking in 1966.

Soft-core porn was not as graphic as the images of our electronic era, but it was more mainstream than in the generation before the war. While it may have offended middle class sensibilities, it aligned perfectly with the prevailing paradigm that a man's sexual desire was the standard, and a woman was his conquest. In Catholic schools, young people were taught that the clothing and behavior of girls could cause a man's "fall." Any debate about pornography—never mind sexuality—that included women's voices, desires, and choices did not yet exist.

If certain images bothered a woman he desired to "possess" through marriage, then the "good Catholic" would have known exactly how to negotiate a new front. Why not try to sell them if he was going to dispose of them anyway? Whitman loved gambling; he worked the angles, and he flashed his toys, guns, and his money (even when he didn't have much—or when he was borrowing from his dad). Selling or otherwise getting rid of "dirty pictures" would not require a profound adjustment in his assumptions about women or sex. It would have given him another opportunity to show off.

In a police interview after the shootings, John Morgan (who had known Whitman for four years) recalled how his friend at times "talked openly about [his] sex life in the presence of Kathleen." Morgan also used the term "oversexed" to describe Whitman, which suggests Morgan's discomfort with his friend's apparently casual violations of marital privacy and embarrassing (perhaps sad) overcompensation for sexual insecurities.

Morgan's description relates to disturbing accounts about Whitman's father. Following an operation Kathy had for an ovarian cyst, he openly "raised question" about Whitman's "sexual relationship," which according to the doctor embarrassed Whitman (and one would imagine Kathleen, if she were present). Kathy's brother, Nelson, also stated that one of the final, upsetting phone calls to the couple from Charlie's father included a brag that he was having an affair with a woman Kathy's age.

Whitman internalized and projected sexual distortions along with very brittle measures of gendered "success." In the note he laid upon his mother's brutalized dead body, he described his parents in sexually insulting terms that reflect the Madonna/whore mindset he used to justify both "intense hatred" for his father and the need "to relieve [his mother's] sufferings": "He has chosen to treat her like a slut that you would bed down with, accept her favors and then throw a pitance [sic] in return." In the most gruesome moment possible, he rationalized his own violence by describing a degraded economics of sexual exchange within his parents' marriage.

We also have years of Catholic training, with its messages about sexual morality, confession, and secrecy—never mind Whitman's attachment to Father Leduc through more than a decade of formative years. The shopkeeper's story is alleged to have taken place during those months of renewed contact with Leduc in Texas, overlapping with the engagement and early months of marriage. Had pornography—or other "adult" entertainments—been brought to Leduc's cabin? Whitman had such acute anxiety during Christmas break that year, his doctor gave him a prescription for five milligrams of Librium three times a day.

Both Charlie's brothers suffered sexual disturbance and distress. Like so many young men of their generation, Patrick did not discover the safety or permission to identify as gay for years. Following a rough period after leaving minor seminary, Patrick spent several weeks with Charlie and Kathy during the first months they were married. Later the next year, he ran away from home and got in a car crash. His family reportedly worried about how to "cure" him, and he married the year after graduating from high school. After he came out to his wife and children in the 1970s, he left for California and eventually died of complications due to AIDS. Johnnie Mike, the youngest brother, had trouble with drugs and alcohol but also with girls, and the FBI recorded a complaint that he was a "peeper" in the mid 1960s.

From the most male-centered and superficial point of view, women were mostly veiled, visible to Catholic boys only as mothers, virgins, temptresses, or martyrs. If deemed holy enough by the fathers of the church, likenesses of women's bodies were crafted into statues and placed at side altars for veneration, with candles and flowers. Nuns who had taken a vow of chastity served as teachers. Even though the church identified itself as both "mother" and "bride," individual women had no voice of authority in the institution. Their labors as all-nurturing, self-sacrificing beings were simply expected. In the Whitman family, the woman Leduc identified as faithful to her church had endured beatings for twenty-five years: she was both mother and martyr, long before her son murdered her.

Considering all these layers, Whitman's experimentation with pornography would have been more predictable, and more average, than shocking. Any matter-of-fact assertion that children or young adults would make ideal customers for such images may have simply provided one shopkeeper with an unguarded glimpse into in Whitman's troubled and shallow sexual development. The only evidence we have of Leduc's "help," unfortunately, was his willingness to get Whitman married in a hurry. This hasty wedding—held on the date of his parents' anniversary—was itself a foreboding of the horrible ending. Kathy had been treated as a sacramental solution for deep-seated trouble she neither could have anticipated nor "cured."

In a newly discovered letter Whitman wrote to Kathy's parents after he killed her, we find narcissistic rationalizations for violence, insisting that Kathy's murder was "a favor" to end her "unnecessary suffering." But even more horrifying is the casual, dehumanizing association Whitman makes between sex and brutality, followed by his demeaning assessment of how Kathy fought for her life: "Tonight after she talked with you we shared a last interlude together, she has always been a fine lover. Then I tried my best to kill her as painlessly as possible, however, I have my doubts about how painless it was. She was a very strong girl."

By 3:00 a.m. the morning of August 1, Whitman had used the bodies of two women to prove that his will would be done.

In those dark and awful hours, he ordained himself high priest over life and death itself.

X. IF YOU LEAVE—OR IF YOU DON'T

Different types of mobility, inactivity, or leave for priests are identified annually in the OCD. Generally speaking, priests' names are included in the directory as long as the diocese considers them in good standing.

"Sick Leave" refers to sustained absence due to a medical problem.

"On Leave" refers to sustained absence for an unidentified cause. A priest can request leave for personal reasons, ranging from spiritual retreat to bereavement, to facing a crisis of faith or vocation. Leave can also be imposed administratively by a bishop as a means of disciplining a priest for grave cause. However, leave is not equivalent to laicization or "defrocking."

"Active outside diocese" can refer to military service, missionary work, post-seminary degree study, or other religious duties that absent a priest from his home diocese temporarily. Some dioceses list these activities separately.

Definitions and distinctions are not always easy to read. The terms blur together and sometimes operate as code for problems. The OCD contains no public listings for "suspensions" or limitation of faculties. Depending on the diocese, the bishop, and the nature of behaviors, alcoholism or other substance addictions could be treated as a medical or an administrative problem.

Allegations of sexual behaviors (ranging from consensual affairs to predatory abuse) have also been treated under both categories of leave. Priests might be moved around or promoted to leadership in a misguided effort to avoid, appease, or control unaddressed problems, whatever their nature.

In the Diocese of Galveston-Houston, Leduc's first two years of leave, 1972 and 1973, appear to be an administrative "house-cleaning" or priestly rebellion period. According to the OCD, 1972 lists seven priests "absent on leave" and only one on sick leave; 1973 lists nine priests "absent on leave" and only two on sick leave. This is a significant peak for "leaves" through 1982, the year Leduc's death is listed. One priest listed on Sick Leave for 1972 married the following year. Out of five priests on either form of leave for both years consecutively, all but Leduc appear to have married and/or left the priesthood.

One priest on leave starting in 1971 was Arthur Gagne, who at age 18 had come to St. Mary's Seminary in Texas around 1953, the end of Leduc's first year there. Six years younger than Leduc, Gagne also came from Waterbury and had attended St. Anne's parish. Gagne was ordained at St. Mary's Houston in 1961, and by 1974 he asked to be released from his vows. Soon after he partnered with a man named Jeffrey Meadows, who had divorced his wife. Among priests, the rumor was that Gagne later died of AIDS in 1985, but Meadows reported to me in emails that Gagne died of pancreatic cancer. His gravestone bears a single sad, wry message: "I told you I was sick."

When I asked about Leduc, Meadows said he did not recall the names of any priests his former partner had served with. If the two priests had any kind of relationship, Gagne had decided to separate himself.

In late 1967/early 1968, Leduc returned from Alaska to Houston for a temporary assignment one block from the chancery office at Sacred Heart Co-Cathedral, where he would have been closely supervised. There was no resort cabin. Charles Whitman was dead. During the first year of this re-entry period, according to his USAF personnel record forms, he also reported for Reserve assignments in New Mexico and Colorado. Newspaper records document that he said mass occasionally on the outskirts of Houston, at St. Joseph's Baytown.

He took one significant step to get his affairs in order. Not yet forty years old, Leduc made out his will in November 1968, witnessed by the then-librarian at St. Joseph's parish school, Josefa A. York, and a Franciscan priest, Thaddeus Palmieri. Leduc asked that fifty masses be offered for the repose of his soul upon his death, and allotted $100 as an offering for that purpose. He also appointed a layman and "beloved friend" Charles F. Ashy (now deceased), of Pearland, Texas, as his executor, and stated a clear desire for "no interference by the clergy" in the handling of his estate. He bequeathed the travel mass kit that he'd inherited from a priest who died in a small plane crash to whomever was scout chaplain for the diocese at the time of his own death. He bequeathed his personal chalice to the Catholic Near East Welfare Association, to be used "in the missionary fields."

That Christmas, Leduc had something to look forward to. In January 1969, he was to begin serving at the newly-formed parish of St. Dominic's, a former "mission" church in the Sheldon Reservoir area northeast of downtown Houston. The post was announced with his photograph in *The Texas Catholic Herald*. There was much work to be done at the church, where facilities consisted of a trailer for the priest's residence and a makeshift church space made from metal siding on a cement slab. As the first parish administrator, Leduc had the sacramental, liturgical, financial, and community obligations of a pastor without the security of that title and role. If he proved himself in good faith to the satisfaction of the congregation and the bishop, he would have become the pastor. It was more responsibility than he had ever been granted before, and the weight itself might have doomed him—"special treatment" didn't help anymore.

In August the same year, after not quite eight months, Leduc was removed. He had missed his last chance to start over in Houston.

✜

The OCD lists Leduc's final assignment after St. Dominic's as "in residence" at Assumption Parish. Father McGinnis told me that "in residence" could signal many things, including "if you can wake up in the morning, you do; if you can't, you can't." One parishioner at Assumption from that time could recall Leduc physically ("He was a very small man"), but otherwise he didn't remember much, only that Leduc "worked with the youth a lot" and pretty much "just lived there." Another man said, "He had a problem. If he took a drink, he couldn't stop. I don't like to say this," he went on, "but I think they sent him to dry out."

The longtime pastor at Assumption when Leduc arrived was Rev. John Perusina who, McGinnis told me, was the first pastor in Houston to create a parish council of laypeople, a move considered too progressive for some of the old-guard clerics, even after Vatican II. "I heard other priests criticize him with no mercy," McGinnis said. "'Who does he think he is? What is he doing? We can't do that yet.'" But the chancery office also viewed Perusina as an asset in difficult situations, McGinnis added. "He was famous for taking in priests that were having a problem. The leadership knew that he was very sensitive, very forgiving, very supportive. They sent me to him before I sobered up...He was kind of like the treatment center for priests who were having a hard time. He was loving, pastoral, caring."

Perusina's gentle approach had serious blind spots. When McGinnis entered Alcoholics Anonymous in 1970 after having what he describes now as a spiritual experience, he shared this new direction with his pastor: "Perusina even said to me, 'I never knew that you were alcoholic.' And I said, 'Come on.' He said, 'No. I didn't notice it.' I said, 'You had to notice it, how much I was drinking.'"

In May 1970, during Leduc's first year in residence at Assumption, The Houston Knights of Columbus (KC) Credit Union sued him for defaulting on a loan he had taken out two years earlier, on November 30, 1968 (only a few days after he made out his will). The amount cited in the Plaintiff's Original Petition and attached "Exhibit A" is $1,585.80 (roughly $10,000 in today's dollars), an amount so specific that it suggests payoff of another debt, perhaps credit cards or a car loan. According to the Petition, Leduc made a single payment in January 1969 (his first month as administrator at St. Dominic's), but made no payments afterwards. Despite the evidence attached to the petition, including his own signature on the note and payment schedule, the Defendant's Original Answer states tersely that Leduc "denies generally and specially each and all of the allegations... and demands strict proof thereof." The picture of a priest and former Boy Scout blowing off a loan from a Catholic institution such as the local Knights of Columbus suggests a mix of desperation and entitlement. By

1974, the case was dismissed for want of prosecution.

Although the citation form indicates Leduc's address at Assumption Parish, that is not the address written on the proof of service form completed by the deputy. Next to Leduc's name, time, and date of service, is another location: 301 San Jacinto. At that time, this was the jail in downtown Houston.

It's possible that, barring an outright error on the form, Leduc was at the jail providing some service to prisoners or to police that day. But this is not Leduc's most highly functional period. The lawsuit begins roughly one year before he goes "on leave." By two accounts, Leduc is drinking heavily during this time. Taking the official documents at face value, the simplest explanation is also a plausible one: Leduc was already detained for another reason when the deputy came to notify him about the lawsuit. There was no way he could evade this complaint.

By 1972, Leduc went on leave from Assumption and did not have another parish assignment. Perusina moved the same year to take the helm at another parish, and the priest who took his place at Assumption also happened to be Vice-Chancellor of the entire Diocese: future Archbishop Joseph Fiorenza.

The archivist for the Galveston-Houston diocese informed me that there are no accessible records of any addresses for Leduc after 1972 (except for his parents' home, near the time of his death). Thus there is no way yet to document whether he spent time in a house of recovery for alcoholism, emotional distress, or psychiatric problems.

While Leduc had no official assignment from this time forward, there is no record that he was laicized, and no accessible records

PART II: TWO MEN IN BRITCHES

reveal whether certain of his priestly faculties (for preaching, for saying mass, or hearing confessions) were limited. On the official rosters at least, even after leaving the area, Leduc appeared to be a priest in good standing for the diocese of Galveston-Houston—which meant that the official church "family," his bishop, would have remained financially responsible for his basic welfare according to Canon Law. Where would the chancery send his monthly stipends?

A search of available Houston city directories revealed no "Leduc" with his initials at an address in the area. However, a search of Harris County Clerk records showed that a Houston dentist named E. A. Serabia sued Leduc in 1975 for failing to complete payments on a large bill for serious dental work at the beginning of his "on leave" period: "Defendant promised to pay Plaintiff for same but although often requested to do so has failed and refused, and still fails and refuses to pay amount, all to Plaintiff's damages in the sum of $1,800." Procedures included full mouth X-rays, impressions for a partial, extractions of four lower front teeth, removal of a bridge, and then insertion of prophylactic caps, partials, ceramic crowns, and a 10-unit bridge.

The attached account statement from dental appointments in April through July 1972 shows Leduc's address at a house on Cottage Street in Houston. The plaintiff's petition also states that Leduc could be found at St. Edward's Church in Spring, Texas (neither address was accessible via chancery archives, nor does the OCD list his name at St. Edwards). The 1975 court citation includes a deputy's handwritten note: "Repeatedly unable to contact subject for service."

Three years after the initial filing, documents show an order to serve Leduc as a "non-resident defendant" in Florida, listing an address at Church of the Assumption in Pompano Beach. The proof of service form this time is not signed at all. A few months later, apparently following another failure to serve Leduc, the case was dismissed.

In that day and age, it couldn't have been exactly easy to sue a priest—assuming that the dentist knew Leduc was a priest. Wondering about that, I sought contact with Dr. Serabia. He responded by phone, leaving a message that he didn't remember much about it, also adding: "You can contact me by letter if you like, but I'd rather not talk about it." He did not respond to further contact.

By the time he stopped paying his dental bill, Leduc appears to have been living in a state of suspended clerical animation. Either he was refusing medical supports available to him through the diocese, or he had been cut off. Either way, Leduc effectively disappeared or had been allowed to make himself invisible when called to account for his debt, even though we know where he ended up.

⊕

At some point in the early to mid 1970s, approaching his mid-forties, Leduc likely returned to southeastern Florida to live with or near his parents in Lake Worth, the middle class town where he had first met Charlie Whitman as a toe-headed kid. In more ways than one, Leduc made his way back to the first chapter of this story—to his transition between seminaries, his introduction to the Whitman family, the church where he first served, his parents and the small house that was supposed to be a new beginning. Leduc's prodigal journey did not include the reconciliation or the feasting of the biblical parable.

According to the archivist for Galveston-Houston,

correspondence in his file suggests that Leduc did seek a parish assignment in the diocese of Miami, which had split off from the formerly giant diocese of St. Augustine, the original sponsor for his seminary studies. After all these years, he was not embraced again. This reprise of his limbo state had to have been distressing and depressing for him personally, and likely a source of embarrassment and shame for his parents. I combed newspapers for any mention of Leduc during this decade and came up empty—not even a mass announcement.

Despite the dentist's complaint identifying the church in Pompano Beach, my inquiries confirmed no record of any official assignment in Miami, or in any then-nearby dioceses in Florida. Leduc was never "excardinated" (formally released) from his home diocese in Texas, nor was he "incardinated" (formally accepted) into any diocese in Florida. This finding is significant, as the default practice among bishops at the time often accommodated movement of clergy—even in cases where they were fugitives from criminal complaint. Reasons of health or a desire to be closer to family were two of the most standard and common justifications for priestly movement, even under egregious legal circumstances. Getting an assignment or "residence" should have been fairly easy.

Other priests on leave for much shorter periods asked for ecclesiastical release or simply walked away, motivated by prospects of a different life. If Leduc had simply gone AWOL, he should not be listed as a priest in the OCD. If Leduc were truly in good standing or in severely ill health, why are there no there any chancery or directory records of any addresses or assignments? The Houston archivist informed me that there is no official record that Leduc had "retired." He was also too young to claim Social Security. It was maddening. He appeared, from a practical standpoint, to have had some of his faculties limited; perhaps he had, unofficially, discarded them all by himself.

✛

Because of Leduc's return to Florida, I wondered if he had any contact with Charles Whitman's surviving family members. If he was attempting any twelve-step program during his early leave years, perhaps he desired or needed to make contact with the Whitman family for some part of his recovery process. Since he had not been able to attend any of the funerals, it would not have been unusual to pay respects or visit graves.

Based on the final payment of $50 posted in April 1973 to his outstanding dental bill, I hypothesized that Leduc left the Houston area around this time. Without money or another place to go, home in Florida would have been the most ready alternative. Three months later, Charlie's youngest and most overtly troubled brother, Johnnie Mike, was shot outside Big Daddy's bar in Lake Worth. He died in the early morning hours of July 4, reportedly a few days before he was scheduled to take his plumber's exam. This is important because, according to reports, Johnnie was finally getting his life together after years of personal and legal troubles, including drugs. Some time after Johnnie Mike was killed, Charlie's other brother, Patrick came out to his wife and two daughters as gay and departed for California.

Had either brother met with Leduc or encountered him by accident at a market or liquor store, or heard from others that he returned to the area? Did he attend Johnnie Mike's funeral at Sacred Heart or his burial—at the same site where Charlie and Margaret were interred? Did Leduc pay condolences to the patriarch of the family? A Florida newspaper report in 1976, marking the tenth anniversary of the shootings, placed Patrick in the Lake

Worth area, stating he no longer worked with his father's business and that the two were no longer close.

I located Patrick's surviving spouse and one of his daughters, but neither responded to my requests for any memories of Leduc. Johnnie Mike's wife has been dead many years, and his surviving daughter fiercely protects her privacy.

✚

In the civil case eventually dropped against Leduc for failing to pay dental bills back in Houston, a last address on a subpoena placed him at Assumption Parish in Pompano Beach, Florida, in 1978. No official record confirms Leduc spent time there, and proof of service forms for the court are blank. But the pastor at that time (and for twenty-one years) was Rev. Rowan Rastatter (known as "Rasty"), by public accounts a no-nonsense, cigar-chomping priest who spent half a century of his active service dedicated to troubled boys, unwed mothers, and Spanish-speaking migrant workers in southeast Florida. When he died, his funeral was attended by bishops and archbishops from his own and surrounding dioceses.

Rasty had another characteristic that would have been more relevant to Leduc, whether comforting or not will remain undetermined. Between 1959 and 1964, Rasty had served as an assistant at Sacred Heart Parish in Lake Worth. Charles Whitman had reportedly served as his altar boy, too, and Rasty presided along with Revs. Thomas Anglim and Eugene Quinlan at Whitman's funeral.

I picture a court deputy with a fold of subpoena papers walking up to Rasty's parish office in 1978, and the stocky pastor with a wet cigar at the corner of his mouth merely shrugging shoulders from behind the screen door and shaking his head. Then later, elbows propped on a kitchen table or at his desk in the rectory, or perhaps growling into a phone with its cord hanging slack, the priest told Leduc to stop being a jackass and take responsibility.

Perhaps he sighed wearily and sent him on his way: You weren't straight with me, Gil.

Perhaps he called the chancery office, flabbergasted: Who is this guy, and why did he tell anybody he lived here?

Leduc's life was almost over.

☩

On January 19, 1981, after ten years of leave from his home diocese, Leduc died at the age of 51, predeceasing his father by four years, his mother by fifteen. Despite the length of his absence from Texas, the *Palm Beach Post* referred to his "recent" illness. By contrast, the *Texas Catholic Herald* called Leduc's entire absence (over more than a decade) "sick leave." He is included in the official necrology of priests in the diocese of Galveston-Houston.

The Texas Catholic Herald reported that Monsignor James Madden (now deceased), a priest from Leduc's small ordination class in Houston, travelled to Florida to offer two funeral masses. This fulfilled a specific request in Leduc's will, though whether he reached out to Madden himself, or whether his parents or another clergyman did so, is unclear. The local obituary announced that Leduc lay in state at Sacred Heart Church, where his funeral was also held. His coffin occupied the same space as Whitman and his murdered mother.

What of Leduc's chalice, his vestments, or any other personal effects? According to his cousin, Leduc's parents did not keep any items that had belonged to him. One has to wonder what he actually had left. His cousin provided me with a copy of the memorial card from the funeral mass. The concluding lines from the prayer of St. Francis Assisi are printed inside, under a plain black cross. Leduc's body was buried in the priests' section of Queen of Peace Cemetery in West Palm Beach, marked by a flecked granite stone with a bronze cross that included his ordination date. The local Knights of Columbus assisted at the burial.

Leduc's friend from Sacred Heart, Fr. Matthew Morgan, was buried two decades later in the same section. Leduc's parents' graves lie fifty paces away.

✛

Leduc as a person, and as a priest, was physically and metaphorically buried in his own story. Despite the easy smiles and laughter described by others, much indicated a double, closeted, miserable life.

Only active as a priest for about sixteen years, Leduc had been able to mask his alcoholism through superficial sociability for nearly two decades, yet somehow he also stretched the bounds of what was appropriate or even minimally functional in ministry— even during decades when priests were granted a great deal of inappropriate latitude. This suggests that he managed to alienate parishioners and significant superiors, who struggled with how to "handle" him and ultimately let him drift and disintegrate at a distance. Minimizing, ignoring, or hiding his relationship with a man who killed so many people would not have helped, either. I wonder whether he had any soul to confide in.

As Father McGinnis put it, pausing during one of our longest conversations, "The system allowed Leduc to experience a very slow death. Just watched him and didn't do anything about it… Who knows why, but I think that's true. One diocese to the other, parish to parish. He died a long time before he died."

In Leduc's worst and loneliest silences—in the secrets he was supposed to keep and the secrets he may have denied knowing—where was Charles Whitman? In *A Chorus of Stones*, a book that examines the generational accretions of warfare and domestic violence upon individual people, Susan Griffin likens the effects of deep and perhaps suppressed memories to the effect of radiation upon the body. "No detail that enters the mind, nor the smallest instance of memory, ever really leaves it," she writes, "and things we had thought forgotten will arise suddenly to consciousness years later, or, undetected, shape the course of our lives." Leduc seems to have thought that surfaces would suffice, that they could protect him.

Once he returned to Florida, Leduc became a priest without an official parish, a single man drifting during a decade of sex, drugs, and rock and roll, sleeping at a bed in his parents' house when he had nowhere else to go. If he wore no collar, he would have passed for any other short, aging single guy on the streets and shores of West Palm Beach or Miami. Who were his friends? When (and where) did he say mass, ever? Schuck's jolly "Aloha shirt and Bermuda shorts" image of Leduc from more than a decade earlier now looked tattered and pathetic, depleted and used up.

At some point, Leduc contracted an illness. His cousin told me that she offered to come down from New England to help, but Leduc's mother told her not to. When I asked about cause of death, the cousin said she remembered her aunt talking about people wearing masks when he was in the hospital. She also used the word "quarantine," but with a question mark in her voice. AIDS did cross my mind, but data suggests it was still too early for that.

Her husband reassured her out loud that Leduc's illness had to be related to liver damage: "You have to understand," he said, turning to me. "Priests—they get up at five a.m., they drink wine at mass every morning. And he really could put them away." He smiled a little.

He added another detail that neither one of them could explain: how, in the end, all of Leduc's teeth turned black. Neither one knew which hospital had treated him.

✟

Leduc died as an inpatient not at St. Mary's, the only Catholic hospital in Palm Beach County, but at the secular Doctors Hospital (now defunct, and a location for residential development). This seems odd for a man identified as "priest" on his death certificate and gravestone. At St. Mary's, he would have had pastoral visits daily; at Doctors Hospital, he would have needed to make a request. According to probate documents, Leduc left a debt to Carte Blanche credit card ($661.86 dated September 1977) as well as bills to two physicians (including one for "unpaid pathology services" just two days before he died). A judge issued an order striking all claims from Leduc's estate ten years later.

I discovered one final strangeness and dramatic public display of initiative: a complaint Leduc himself filed on April 21, 1980—two weeks after his fifty-first birthday—against a man named Craig Stanley Gregory and Allstate Insurance Company. The surviving docket suggests a car accident, with damages in excess of $2,500. The chronology preserved by the docket (the only remaining public document) is fascinating. The court was unable to serve Gregory, who seemed to disappear. There is no countersuit, which suggests that no one alleged that Leduc was at fault. Leduc responded to interrogatories from defense attorneys on November 17, and only eight weeks later, he died. After his death, Allstate continued to depose doctors from Doctors Hospital, the VA Outpatient Clinic, and the VA Medical Center, also retrieving records about Leduc's health. Court filings show that a judge voluntarily dismissed the case at the request of Leduc's own attorney, with prejudice. Both sides agreed to pay their own legal fees.

The pending litigation perhaps explains the four-day delay in the signing of Leduc's death certificate, suggesting that hospital pathologists might have spent extra time examining his body. His official death certificate states that no autopsy was requested. There is no way to know what the pathologists would have been looking for, or whether the accident accelerated his death. Florida does not disclose cause of death as a matter of public record until fifty years afterwards.

There was something extra sad as well as disturbing, in the end. After Leduc died, according to his cousin, his mother used to repeat: God should have taken her son as a little sickly baby.

Concluding Rite

I made a final January pilgrimage to Houston. I spent many hours talking with Schuck at his home north of the sprawling metropolis, and even rode along with him one afternoon to confirm the route to, and location of, the Liverpool house where he had hung out more than fifty years earlier with Whitman, Leduc, and other friends. That day, Schuck wore a blue and yellow Hawaiian shirt and khaki Bermudas, "in honor of Gil."

His wife joined us for the exploratory mission about an hour south of the city.

As we drew closer and wound the roads towards Leduc's hideaway, we passed an erratic mix of shacks, abandoned or boarded-up structures, small pastures, trailers, middle class and occasionally extravagant houses. From the mostly deserted marina, we could see a few boats and yachts down the bayou: some tidily docked by owners, others ostentatiously capsized years ago, left for someone else to drag away. The surface of the brackish waters rippled and churned. A houseboat could look abandoned until a person stepped onto the deck, disembarked, and disappeared up a pathway on the shore.

Schuck's wife seemed to anticipate my questions. "There's no zoning," she emphasized. As we rounded a corner towards the wooded road and the graveyard, she leaned forward between the front seats: "Well," she said, "this isn't exactly a resort area here."

Schuck disagreed, but I was somewhat relieved to hear his wife say so. I had visited the place before and had thought the same: the location felt odd, less like an idyllic retreat than "the boonies." It would have felt even more tucked away fifty years ago.

We idled for a few minutes in front of the spot, three parcels of land on one side of the cul-de-sac. A two-story house from the 1970s stands there now. Leduc's structure no longer remains, but a slab transformed into a platform for a standing garden seemed to mark the most likely spot. "Did you ever play around across the canal?" I asked, indicating an island-like thicket across the water, behind where the house would have stood.

"We didn't play," he said. He sounded solemn, but then he delivered the punch line. "You have to understand: we were serious drinkers." He handed me a paper-clipped sheaf of real estate records for the lots on the cul-de-sac. Based on his penciled-in construction dates, only two or three other structures had been here when Schuck and Charlie joined Leduc, or else came down to take the keys from under the flowerpot and let themselves in.

There are still no lights along the county road. It seemed like it would've been a hard place to locate in 1961, especially without GPS. When I mentioned this, Schuck said Leduc kept a compass on his car's dashboard. Of course I also remembered: they were all Boy Scouts.

Using body memory, Schuck navigated another forty minutes south, and we stopped at Red's Seven Seas Grocery, located along the beach in Galveston. Originally a bay-style house with an open porch stocked with cans of beer and bottles of wine and liquor, according to Schuck, this was a spot where Leduc and his guests secured their alcohol if they ran out during blue law hours. Liverpool, after all, was located in a partially dry county.

"It's sure a long way to drive," I said.

He smiled. "If only you're sober at the wheel."

My last day in Houston—the Martin Luther King, Jr. holiday and, coincidentally, the anniversary of Leduc's death—I visited St. Mary's Seminary one more time. The broad gates stood open and the long driveway and sprawling lawns felt at once inviting and intimidating. At the chapel, I had missed a late morning mass, and the room was dark, deserted, and cool. The sanctuary apse—gold mosaic that sparkled like a crown when illuminated—now cast a grey hood over the tabernacle and altar. I walked down the narrow nave, between tiers of pews stacked choir-style along the walls. Perfect bands of green marble marked the floor leading towards the sanctuary. Stained glass motifs glinted against the sunlight: young seminarians wearing the white surplice and holding missals, flat-faced priests in red robes. The glowing lamp near the sanctuary told my Catholic self: Christ is really here.

Since 1955, six decades of men have passed through this space—have filed through the doors, have knelt and stood in pews, held open books of prayer and sung hymns. Looked at each other. Lowered their eyes. Some disappeared from their places like ghosts and went on to other lives. Some slammed the door behind them. Sixty years ago, Leduc prostrated his small body on the floor in front of the altar, waiting for the bishop's hands to transform him into a brand-new being. He remained a man.

I genuflected on two knees instead of one, bending forward and pressing the flats of both my hands into the cold surface, more from curiosity than piety. The marble felt as unforgiving as it looked. When I sat in a front pew, I tried to imagine where Leduc found himself during those three years—and where Briganti sat, Fiorenza and Pickard, Gagne, McGinnis, Tarte, Scardino. So many others. The station of the cross on the wall in front of me was sculpted entirely of Latin words: *Jesus condemnatur ad mortem.* I had to crane my neck to study the altar and its large wooden crucifix above the tabernacle, the tortured Christ's skeletal ribs in sharp relief giving away part of the end of the story.

I wanted a conclusion, but I was in the wrong place for that. According to teachings I learned long ago, any mass celebrated at this altar with its white cloth continues a perpetually redeeming sacrifice—Christ's offering of his innocent body to save mankind. The difference, we are taught, is that the act was transformed into a bloodless banquet of bread and wine, a celebration not of murder and death, but of mercy and resurrection. There is no greater love than this, we are told, than when a man lays down his life for his friends—especially the ones who sleep as he sweats and prays in the dark garden, who pretend not to know him after he's unjustly convicted, who betray him with their smiles or kisses even before he is arrested, with their toasts at dinner, their Hosannas and high-fives in the streets of an unfamiliar city.

A Marine Corps training film from the 1960s documents the competing gospel Whitman had been taught in preparation for his own ordination as a member of an exclusive branch of the American military: "Eight weeks," says a man's voice, "to fuse you and your rifle into one perfectly working unit." In the footage, one uniformed man after another takes the rifle assigned to him at the armory, and the voice-over recites part of the Marine creed: "This is my rifle…My rifle is my best friend. It is my life. I will master it as I master my life." What about the man who could not master his life, who used his gun to master it for him?

Leaving Texas the next morning, I read—and saw report after report—about *American Sniper* exceeding all box office records, earning $105 million over the long weekend. On a holiday to honor a pacifist civil rights leader killed by a sniper, droves of Americans celebrated the story of the lone gunman we sent to another country, his record number of "good kills" through a riflescope, the crusader's cross tattooed on his arm. The mash-up of imagery made me ill. Warped by privileges of election and Empire, the gospel of offering and self-sacrifice wasn't the good news anymore. Maybe we say Jesus was a cool guy, but we spend more time at the foot of the lone gunman than the foot of the cross.

Until, of course, he turns his weapon on us.

PART II: TWO MEN IN BRITCHES

Commentators often say that Whitman introduced Americans to the fear of violence in public spaces. Perhaps that is true for white people. But the crimes marked something else: a high point of mass marketing and production during the first televised war in our history, the collision of Swanson TV dinners, polyester carpeting, Howard Johnson's, Brachs candy, air rifles and cap guns, men's adventure magazines, and scenes from massacres.

In a way he could not have fully understood, Whitman brought our war system home—to his family, to his bed, to the top of the landmark tower—the same week B-52s emptied their bellies to carpet bomb Vietnam's Demilitarized Zone. It wasn't just the former Boy Scout and discharged Marine who prepared so carefully in the dark morning hours. It was also the disillusioned altar boy who didn't pray anymore, the abused son who severed his marital ties and apron strings with a knife, the violent husband who feared he might be sterile. His father's demands and ranting phone calls and sexual insults could be drowned out permanently. Bruises could heal, bones could knit, scars could be covered, but Whitman had learned that the vernacular of singular violence could be louder than anything, perhaps even ordnance paid for by taxpayers. Men got away with so much in the privacy of their homes and churches, so much could be hidden.

If he could not make life, he could fire bullet after bullet until the end of the world. There would be no way, he must have thought, to ignore him now.

When Leduc received word at the base in Alaska—via special phone call, or upon hearing the delayed broadcast—I picture him pouring several fingers of whiskey and thinking that his friend was a famous individual now, practically a legend, and that this bizarre and godless act had nothing whatsoever to do with the church that so explicitly instructed them to be good. When FBI agents arrived, he had to wonder (didn't he?) which superiors had been informed. How did he see it all? What hurt? What was already fading?

✠

Imagine beginning moments, like smudges on a beige wall:

The summer before his freshman year of high school, Charlie was beginning to stand taller than adults, though he was still slender, like a boy. He could not help this. Perhaps he wore a Timex watch. He did not yet own a motorcycle. During this period, he first served mass for Father Gil, the scoutmaster who returned to Florida with special powers and a new title.

Who knows how many Sunday or daily masses he served for him? Perhaps Charlie pedaled his Schwinn down "L" Street well ahead of his mother and two brothers, locked the bike to the racks on the school sidewalk. There would be humid breezes from the nearby lagoon and the ocean, where the sun would either pull itself from the water or hang back beyond the haze. He would enter the side door to the sacristy with its hardwood closets and cabinets, the kneeler and folding chairs that creaked. He rustled the black or red cassock over his clothes, as usual, and put on the white surplice. He would place the cruets properly, making sure to wipe their outsides clean, filling one with water and the other with unconsecrated yellow wine. On a small table, he would fold the fresh finger linen, placing it with the glass basin for ritual hand rinsing during mass. At the appointed time, he would stride onto the altar and genuflect with the long-neck candle-lighter before touching it to each sacred wick. He would be afraid to do anything wrong.

Perhaps the priest was late to the sacristy—only a few minutes at first—which made the boy feel necessary and helpful, perhaps slightly superior. The priest rushed and smiled, knowing well that the boy would square it all away. The usual silences observed by other priests would be broken during preparations. This is the drawer where we keep it, Father. Don't forget the ciborium. It's ordinary time, Father, so here is the green chasuble, not the purple one. The priest must have reciprocated as he donned his vestments. Father Matt got a new car, you see that? You don't have to be so serious all the time. You really can touch the chalice if you want to. The boy might not have been so sure.

Father Gil was not intimidating like the others. There was something loose about him, as if he knew and did not know what he was doing. Charlie could bring his own order, and he could relax because he knew there would be no reprimands. That first mass, perhaps Charlie was struck by the heavy scent of aftershave—Aqua Velva?—so preferable to the smoke smell lingering on other priests, on the parents. Before mass, there might have been his priest friend's mother, kneeling in the front row, glass rosary beads dangling from her small hands. What if she seemed to see but did not smile at him? Perhaps Charlie wondered whether her back brace felt uncomfortable against the wooden pew, or maybe he did not know about it.

At the end of mass, the people sang. In the courtyard, they would call Gil "Father" for the first time and shake his hand. He would smile and laugh and say little. The people would congratulate his parents. There was a luncheon at the parish hall,

Madonna Hall, perhaps with pressed sugar cookies and coffee in a large percolator, small square sandwiches and crudités fanning out together on an oblong tray. Another priest may have raised a paper cup to share a toast and gripped Leduc's small shoulder.

Something was broken or not quite right, and it would be business as usual. Parishioners filed onto the sidewalks for an afternoon rosary procession, then returned to church for a solemn benediction. Charlie could picture his Daddy at home—rolling up his sleeves after a nap in the La-Z-Boy, digging in the side-yard, gouging bushes with clippers, emptying a mouse trap—and he knew where he did not want to be.

Imagine the surprise: a weekday when Father Gil arrived early. Perhaps another boy already in the sacristy when Charlie entered—someone smaller and younger, already in his cassock and looking tired or sulky, sitting on his hands. A kid who probably got lots of nosebleeds. Whose shoes were scuffed or muddy. So did you sleep in today, Charlie? You remember that I leave in a week? The priest might have said something similar, sharing a look with the smaller boy, who would shrug or roll his eyes—a disjointed, unlikely conspiracy.

Such amusement that excluded him would feel alien, catching in Charlie's stomach or the back of his neck, but he would be taking a cassock from a hanger in the cabinet. Sorry, Father. Charlie would not mention the priest's tardiness on other occasions, or how the priest had flubbed the Latin during the Last Gospel and skipped other parts entirely. The priest would wink at him or laugh and muss his hair—of course, there was no problem.

But perhaps Charlie saw that the cruets on the side table had not yet been filled, so he filled them. He wiped them with a cloth. After mass, what if he saw the smaller boy alone in a corner of the courtyard, cramming his mouth with Milk Duds as if he had never been hungrier in his life.

☦

Eleven years later, Whitman performed a televised ritual that imprinted itself onto our American psyche—not only of blood, but denial and silence, toxic elements of the dark new sacrament: a mass shooting.

Early that morning, there were epistles he had written and sent, the journal texts he had re-read silently before dawn broke, his wife's body in the other room. He had scratched a new note on his favorite page: "I still mean it." For vestments, he put blue nylon coveralls over his plaid shirt and denim britches, so that he could pass for a university janitor when he parked in the wrong place. He prepared the trunk of supplies and an extra bundle carefully: there was a large knife with his name on it, and a hunting knife, and a pocket knife; there were all the boxes of ammunition; the shotgun he bought at Sears and sawed off in his garage, and the 6 mm Remington rifle with its extra scope; there was the Channel Master 14 transistor radio, and the ear plugs, the grey gloves, a white jug filled with water, a jug of gasoline, a box of kitchen matches, cans of food, a jar of honey, and a package of sweet rolls. He used a new dolly to haul and then roll it all into the elevator, and then bumped up the last remaining stairs. Only the faithful could enter the final level, the place where he built his barricade in a doorway. That's what the shotgun was for.

The vestibule chamber for the observation deck would have felt less like a closet than the sacristy did—the door had window panels, after all. There were no candles to light. He had brought all the necessary elements himself. And when he pushed through the door and onto the deck, he took his place on an altar three hundred and seven feet above the streets, as if he had walked onto the ledge of a world made of air, far above the sidewalks where shapes that barely looked like people seemed to move. It was not enough to be anointed, to be chosen. He wanted to touch the people with a blaze of deadly fire and remain almost invisible. He could have them, the masses, all to himself. There would be no sanctuary—not anywhere.

There were cracks overhead in the hot air. The first woman hit the searing pavement. A windowpane shattered. The boys on a bike teetered and fell. A puff of smoke rose from the distant tower ledge, a mystery under the high noon heat and the piercing blue sky. The people ran or ducked into offices and shops, and they also lifted their faces and shielded their eyes and pointed cameras upwards because they didn't understand what was happening, or that what was happening here would happen again and again, and that his face had been in front of them all the time.

Part III

Father's Rules

Let your family present a united front to the world.... Don't discuss family problems with outsiders.

Kay Toy Fenner, *American Catholic Etiquette* (1961)

When his parents saw him they were astonished, and his mother said to him, "Son why have you done this to us? You see that your father and I have been searching for you in sorrow." He said to them, "Why did you search for me? Did you not know I had to be in my Father's house?" But they did not grasp what he said to them.

Luke 2:49, *New American Bible*

Charles Whitman's father, C.A. Whitman (center), with Charles's mother, Margaret (right), and wife, Kathy (left), 23 November 1963. *Credit: Courtesy of Nelson Leissner*

THE Boy Scout Handbook was meticulous. The Baltimore Catechism and the altar boy handbooks were meticulous. His father's rules for the household and for behavior were meticulous, although they were not written down and could not be checked for consistency. To entertain any notion that they should be checked or should be consistent was to invite the belt or the back of the hand. Four people lived in the house with the father and his rules about bedtime, and good neighbors, and television, and haircuts, and the Democratic Party, and black people, and copper pipe, and bare feet, and the value of a dollar, and what was considered private and what was his business, and what wasn't funny and what must be considered a joke.

For twenty-five years, four people would learn not to talk about it. Outside the house, the heat would be woozy. Picture banana palms that swayed wet shadows across the small pool. Picture the father's plumbing truck churning up the driveway and past the house, into the slot near the garage, where the engine would stop. His expectations upon crossing the driveway and opening the screen door and entering the house could not be

read in advance, yet had to be calculated. The father's expectations might not exactly complement the odor on his body after work: sweat and grease, standing water and sour mud. The four people knew they were dependent for their livelihoods and should consider themselves lucky, and so they would pretend there was no smell.

The father's expectations tended to be retroactive, but not always. He would take a shower before dinner, but not always. He would change his shirt, but not always. Why hadn't you left the windows open, to ventilate the house? Why had you left the windows open, to draw all this filth and humidity? Where is that American history homework? Why are you showing me this American history homework? Why can't you smile, boy? Wipe that smile off your face, boy. Why are you touching my rifle? How can you learn to shoot if you don't hold this gun?

The rules could not be gamed. If the children tried to game them, they would lose. If the woman tried to game them, she would lose. She was the keeper of the books and ledgers, and the father profited in part because she was meticulous, too. She lost anyway. Eventually she would be called unsophisticated and simple, a perfectly good mother, a gracious woman, a good Catholic. She would be called awful stubborn. She would be compared to a slut from whom one took favors in bed and then tossed in the street with a pittance. But that would come after she was dead.

So the table would have plates on linens in the parallel places, with glasses of milk for the children, and a perspiring pitcher of water or lemonade. This time, when she heard the truck door creak open and shut, she spooned the meat onto the plates. Or: She left the meat to warm in the skillet. Her boys had already eaten dinner and she had cleared their dishes and they were just closing the doors to their rooms. Or: Her boys were bathed and seated with the plates and the milk, waiting with their hands under the table, and not like young ruffians. The boys could see the dilemma, which was also their own. Their napkins remained on the table, under forks. Or: Their napkins lay in their laps. Or: Their napkins were tucked into their collars.

There were his boot-steps. She could crush a cigarette into a teacup, and narrow threads of smoke would rise. It was all the same. It was all not the same.

Yesterday nothing. Tonight the edge of her left eye and the top of her cheekbone. Two weeks before, an ache under her dress. Now it was the dog yelping. Before that, her jaw against the corner of a cabinet. Then it was the crick of his neck inside the sticky bend of his father's elbow. Tomorrow perhaps nothing again. Why not her neck this time? Why not the brother who sat in the corner on the floor with his mouth hanging open? Why the small of the back instead of the wrist? Why the fist instead of the boot? Why the finger in his face, instead of the belt, and then the belt anyway? Why the bullied brother yanked off the tricycle while the other brother laughed with a stick? Why his arm instead of his ear? Why her face and not his? Why his face and not his?

The woman would powder her bruise, which was like making a circle over it. Perhaps she smudged Vaseline into the swollen pink split where her lips made a corner. Sometimes there was a wad of frozen meat from the icebox. Her sons buttoned up their shirts. Welts would heal. Sometimes a bone could knit itself and so a doctor (the father's friend, also mayor of the town) would not always need to be notified. Sometimes the neighbors would catch glimpses—from across hedges, from the sidewalk across the street. When nothing happened, it was almost worse, because something would.

The oldest boy watched and tried not to, and understood yet also did not. Perhaps the father would bring home a pot of purple orchids or a silver bracelet and kiss the woman in the bend of her neck, under an ear, or give the boy dollar bills for the baseball mitt or the air rifle. His mother would buy Oreos, or would put chocolate-covered bridge mix or perhaps a sticky pile of orange circus peanuts in a glass dish on a side table. The father would grab one son by the chin and wrestle the baby brother and say what a proud man he was, how his family was the best at everything.

Like mirrors in a park for someone else's amusement, the rules did not match up. Their funny shapes did not make the boy laugh. It was best to look at his toes and feet against the floor, or to watch the ceiling, and to move forward or backward or to the side as he concentrated on other thoughts in the hallway. Had he folded the newspapers for his paper route? Had he counted his wages? The boy learned to amuse himself. He could count the guns mounted on the walls.

He served mass according to the rules. He would heap the unconsecrated hosts—like little discs of white paper—in the gold ciborium and wash the glass cruets and dry them, and also try to keep them from clinking together. In the sacristy, he helped the priest with his sacred vestments, slippery taffeta or heavy tapestry layered over humble linen or cotton, sometimes in silence and sometimes with talking. The priest was supposed to pray.

During the ceremonies, the boy knew when to chime the sacred bells, and when to bow, when to strike his breast, and when to lift the back hem of the priest's chasuble in the most sacred moments. There was even a comic book, *Know Your Mass,* which showed clearly how the ritual would guide him step by step on an ascending pathway from prayer, through instruction and the Credo, to the top of a moving staircase, where only the faithful were allowed to enter the final chamber.

He learned Latin according to the rules and won a prize for

doing it best. The boy would get lost anyway. Perhaps one should say: Also. He would practice the piano because his father laid a belt across the music stand. Or: He would practice the piano because he loved to play. Regardless, he performed on display from a young age, sometimes in duets ("Russian Picnic") and sometimes solo ("The Joyous Waltz"). After the atrocities, his father would say that people had to understand: this boy was sick.

The mother and the boys broke the rules intentionally and by accident, and they all went to confession. Some of the rules were God's and some of the rules were the father's. It was hard to tell them apart. The church taught that there were mortal sins and venial sins. Mortal sins killed the soul, and any person who died without confessing them went to hell. Some mortal sins were easy to commit, such as missing Sunday mass on purpose or touching yourself inside your sleeping bag. It wasn't like a person had to commit murder.

The mother and the boys were expected to confess, according to the teachings of the church for baptized Catholics—teachings that were not followed by the father, who did not confess because he had no religion except plumbing, and septic tanks, and how to make money. He was already a priest in his home, because he expected his family to do the right things, and he gave absolution to his customers, because he cleared their shit away.

The father could not have worried about what his children or wife might happen to tell any priest in the dark box or in the rectory. He would understand that exceptions could be made because he approved checks for the church school and for piano lessons, because he wanted them to have everything he didn't have, because he had a long day, because his ulcers were flaring up again, because he wanted to be proud of them, because he did so much for them already and because he was man of the house. Mostly, because he was a man.

The father considered himself demanding, but not violent. He had spent part of his childhood as an inmate in a boys' orphanage and learned to be tough and to endure. Here is your milk for the morning. Here is a bandage for your skinned knuckles. Here is a bowl of grits, a spoonful of oatmeal. No one will respect you unless you fight back when a boy shoves his arm against your throat. Beware the mud on the path outside the latrine when it is dark. The headmaster keeps a rawhide strap because God loves you. Bow your heads. Didn't I tell you this is for your own good?

There is no record that the father complained about the orphanage or about the conditions of his childhood. Once he married, he bought his mother the house next door to the one where his family lived. She was living there when he told reporters on the front lawn how his wife's awful stubbornness led to clashes and his temper made him knock his wife around. He also said he was not ashamed of spanking his children, that he should have punished them more. After the awful events, neighbors said the father always had given his sons too much permission and too little freedom.

After a time, the man's wife would have gone to confession mostly by herself, since her sons were becoming men too.

The boy became impulsive about rule-keeping as well as rule-breaking. (Later, to a close friend, he would explain that each group he belonged to had given him a different set of expectations.) He was considered polite and mischievous, as well as noisy. In the first grade, he scored 138.9 on an IQ test, indicating "very superior" intelligence. Of the three sons he would become a man first. He would die first.

When he was in high school, Sister Marie Loretta reported that he was very capable, also intelligent. In his personal qualities he fell into the N for Normal range. He was purposeful and sought additional work, though he was slightly less self-reliant. He earned A's in Catholic Morality and Catholic Doctrine, but a D in English III. In four years he had fourteen, then zero, then twenty-six, then twelve absences. (The records said: an emergency appendectomy, an operation to remove a blood clot from one of his testicles following a motorcycle accident. There are also complaints of dizziness, resulting in no diagnosis of cause.) Upon graduation, he ranked seventh in a class of seventy-two.

But before that, he had learned to be handsome in pictures and popular with classmates and not to demand explanations he might have wanted at a much earlier age, and also how to excuse himself. His penmanship was perfect. He completed all the necessary tasks to gather merit badges so that he became an Eagle Scout by the age of twelve. Achieving this rank seemed rushed, according to a scoutmaster who was also a seminarian, who saw that the father appeared very demanding and in a hurry.

At some point, the boy began calling his penis by an old man's name (perhaps a poet's name?): Walter. Someone took a photo of the boy standing with cupped, praying hands at the foot of the altar rail, several steps below the altar and its tall candles. He wore the Boy Scout uniform with the sash displaying all his badges in parallel rows, buttery hair combed away from his forehead. The smile was practiced and slightly pained-looking, as if he had held his face that way many times, or for a while. Behind him, above his head, a pale Christ hung on the cross.

The boy would pedal his Schwinn—and eventually drive his motorcycle, until he crashed it—up and down the straight streets named for letters of the alphabet, then across the avenues named for numbers. In the tidy order arranged by city planners, the letters did not spell anything. The numbers did not add up.

⊕

The seminarian was twenty-two, then twenty-three, then twenty-four, then twenty-five while visiting his parents on breaks from studies. Thus, during his early twenties, he somehow became friends with the boy who at first was nine, then ten, then eleven, and twelve years old. Or: He became the boy's mentor through weekly gatherings of the Boy Scouts. Or: the seminarian felt some pity for the boy, perhaps because (or instead of) a pity he felt for himself. Or: he plainly attached himself to the boy during visits home because the boy was beautiful and blonde and growing tall (while the seminarian had dark hair and acne scars, also glasses and a frail build). Perhaps the seminarian and the boy saw something in each other that they could not articulate.

In any case, one cannot declare that the seminarian was a family friend in the same sense that one uses this phrase speaking of average families who mingle for picnics and bingo tournaments and block parties and Knights of Columbus pancake breakfasts. The boy's family did not mix casually and easily with other people. According to his father's rules, there were restrictions on who was a worthy association and who could be let into the house. A neighbor, for example, would say that she played with the boys outside, but there was no way to get past the front door. (Then again, she was not studying for ordination to the priesthood.)

Somehow the boy, the father, and the seminarian took hunting trips, which suggested that the father did not see the seminarian as any threat or challenge to his authority and his practices. The seminarian knew rules, too, and how to respect or at least to manage them. Or when they did not apply.

The foundation and depth of the relationship was not straightforward, yet the boy and the seminarian maintained a connection until shortly before the boy committed his crimes and was killed. Perhaps the boy's turmoil became the priest's turmoil, or they had always shared a kind of turmoil they could not talk about, alone or together. Perhaps they were equally incapable of experiencing and recognizing turmoil as it took place. Some habits could become rules. There was no happy ending for either of them.

One night before turning eighteen, the boy broke a rule by drinking gin on a dare with a friend. We are not sure if this was his first time experimenting with alcohol, or merely the first time he was intoxicated. The friend drove him home after midnight, but the boy yelled out at a policeman they passed on the street. The policeman stopped them and drove them the rest of the way. At the boy's house, the father yanked him from the car in the middle of the street and knocked him around. Then the father dragged him across the property to the pool behind the house (picture a large, square spa sunk into the ground). The friend said he heard yelling, then a heavy splash. The boy's two younger brothers had to be somewhere in the house, and their mother.

Reportedly, the father later called the boy's friend and said Do Not Talk About It. One account says that the mother called with the same request, though it is possible this is a typo in the transcription. The boy later told the priest, though the priest does not say whether this conversation occurred by phone, by letter, or in person. To the priest, the boy said he thought he could have drowned. Despite the father's warnings to keep quiet, the friend from the car, and other classmates, talked and even joked about the incident at school. One person recalled people teasing the boy on another occasion about whether he was going to celebrate his birthday the same way again.

In the boy's medical files dated around this time, there is a record of fracture on the first metacarpal bone of his left hand. We don't know whether his father bent back the thumb or if the boy fell on all his weight and snapped it against the edge of the pool. We do not know if this injury was incurred in a separate incident. No exact treatment is recorded, and we do not know how long it took the bone to heal. But for a while, the boy would have had difficulty grasping things. Or he would have grasped, and it would have hurt.

✚

To get away from his father, the boy took a train to Parris Island and enlisted in the Marines, who kept their rules in a code. The boy put on a uniform and posed with his mother. His shoulders were thickening and he was starting to look like a man. He earned a sharpshooter's badge.

The Marines gave him a scholarship so he went to college in Texas, approximately three hours from where the priest held his permanent assignment. The first semester, he kept a day planner faithfully, at least until Thanksgiving. During the first week on campus, he logged in the cost of his phone call to the priest—his other father at a home away from home.

For a time, the college boy recorded his daily expenses and activities and tried to add things up. He would warn himself: Spending Too Much. Watch It. He would console himself: Dinner was expensive, but I was hungry. He failed an English placement test. He met a girl. He went to Sunday mass and recorded the money he put in the basket. He bought a book called *Love without Fear*, which included sections titled "The Technique of Love Play," and "How to Manage the Sex Act," and "First Intercourse." He met another girl.

The college boy learned to see himself as an exception. He gambled at cards and didn't always win, yet bragged about his gambling as a source of income. When he lost, he wrote checks that bounced and wore a .357 Magnum in a holster to attend classes. From a car, he hollered racial slurs at a black man in the street, then threatened another person on the road by brandishing a pistol, and said it was funny. He grabbed a classmate in a headlock and squeezed until the guy passed out, and said it was funny. Along with some friends, he killed a deer without a license and dragged its bloody carcass across the dorm carpet and upstairs, butchering the animal in the shower and hanging it there. For meat to send his father, said a friend. For a prank, the priest said the boy told him. He was caught by the game warden and paid a fine, but then he appealed the fine and the judge dismissed the appeal because the letter of the law was clear. What happened to the meat was unclear. Who cleaned up the stains was unclear. The incident was reported in newspapers.

A doctor at home prescribed Librium for the college boy at Christmas break, not long after the deer incident, because he seemed apprehensive.

Around Valentine's Day, the college boy "tied down" the girl who would become his pretty bride, who had been a member of Future Homemakers of America and Queen of the Youth Fair. At first, she was studying science in order to be a pharmacist, later to become a biology teacher. One day he hung from one hand outside the balcony of his dorm room on the seventh floor and called down the street to impress her. The college boy would not have imagined then that he could ever hurt her, though there were suggestions about what certain kinds of women should like in plenty of magazines at the time. For example: *Man's Favorite Pastime, Men Today, For Men Only, Man's Exploits, Man's Action, Cocktail, Cavalier,* and *Adam*.

In his letters to her before the engagement, he asked if his fiancée would help him get car insurance. He posed as expert in the rules of engagement, writing that he didn't like how her father had all but accused him of wanting to have relations because that was the last thing he wanted to do. He talked about Walter, who he said was not a queer, at least he hoped not, and recommended an article from *Modern Bride*, which urged any woman to have a premarital exam.

On the weekend of his twenty-first birthday, he visited the girl and her family in the small Texas town with its sprawling rice fields and tidy streets. Her mother baked him a cake. He took his girl to meet his priestly father, and the announcement came swiftly afterwards, though he asked his girl to order the rings. Meanwhile, he studied for summer school exams and got drunk with friends on Independence Day. In a hungover letter, he told his fiancée that he wanted to share something about his state of mind, but he did not write down what it was. He secured a new apartment, then wrote to her about the chain lock he attached to the bedroom door.

The priest was supposed to get permission for the marriage as required by church law at the time, which was technical and strict. Permission would have been slippery since the bride was a Methodist who did not plan to convert. The priest also needed permission from the pastor of the church in the bride's hometown. All we know for sure is that he showed up to the ceremony, presided there, and signed the license.

After the wedding reception, the car was loaded with clothes hanging across a wire in the backseat. The couple's names were painted on the windows, and streamers were tied to the antenna. The groom drove his new wife to a Houston hotel for one night, then drove the next day to New Orleans, where he treated her to steaks and Hurricanes on Bourbon Street.

He took her to a strip-tease show where ladies on a platform shimmied out of sequined scarves the way it was expected. He took her to the My-O-My Club on the wharf at Lake Ponchetrain, where men in wigs, lipstick, and sparkling gowns belted out sad and bawdy songs. Like other men in the crowd, the groom could put two fingers in his mouth and whistle. Somehow he had learned, and decided, that this was how it all started.

Within six months of marriage, the newlywed lost his military scholarship due to poor college performance. (Or: he sabotaged his performance because he wanted to leave Texas.) He returned to active duty with the Marines in North Carolina. His new wife dropped out of school and lived with him in a cinderblock apartment for about six months. On maneuvers three days a week, he learned judo and proper handling of a machine gun. He talked of getting a job at a nightclub six nights a week, as a bouncer. He tried to convince his wife to have a baby, but she returned to school without him instead.

By the time he was shipped out to Cuba, the newlywed was making his own rules, which got him into trouble because the Marines kept careful track of injuries and violations. He ran a

Jeep off a hill and walked away without any scratches (though his passenger had damages to his spleen, also his liver). Another night, he and a serviceman were jumped by a group of men and had to fight them off. He was also court-martialed for possessing an unauthorized firearm, and making usurious loans (which led to threatening another Marine), and for gambling in card games. He was sentenced to hard labor and demoted from corporal to private.

The Marine started a journal during his time in the brig. He wrote with pencil and then with ink, pressing hard to bruise the pages. He would take the time for A+ penmanship or print in block letters. In his pages were the rhythms of the catechism, and the altar boy handbook, and a dose of L. Ron Hubbard, and *Poor Richard's Almanac*, and the Boy Scout pledge, and the five-paragraph theme, and *Life Is Worth Living* (until it wasn't).

He wrote that his wife did not do enough for him when he asked her to. He wrote that his mother could not come to the phone one night because she was sick. He spoke of how calls from his Daddy lifted his spirits, and how Daddy was so generous because he paid all his phone bills. He described his worry that his wife got pregnant when she visited him for his court martial, because they had been carefree and not used contraception. He wrote that there was something unusual in his mental state, and that he might explode, but he would not say what he was thinking, except that he didn't know if it was his imagination or if his feelings were valid. He wrote that he was going to explode. He wanted the military to stop hindering his life. He wrote that the other Marines and the "Jewish-type" man he worked for at a clothing establishment were like crude animals when it came to describing the sex act. He described one lieutenant as the most stimulating person he had ever conversed with, who was being forced from the corps but had a wife in France that was going to get him a job as a pilot, and how it was a shame that military rules kept them from fraternizing very much, and how the lieutenant took him to his apartment to show him his stereo and offer him Scotch, which he drank casually to conceal his dislike for the taste.

He talked about the bad girls who wanted to go to bed or shack up with him and how he laughed in their faces because he didn't care about sex with whores anymore, since he had "matured." At a nightclub called Jazzland, when a woman touched him on the stomach, he said he felt she had violated his wife's property. In entry after entry, he said he couldn't live without his wife—though he did live without her for the greater part of two years. He told others that he never cheated, and he said they looked at him in awe. He said he didn't want a child yet, but that he wanted to raise his own son differently. (He didn't disclose his fear of being sterile, although others mentioned this later.)

He wrote that he had always felt physically inferior until joining the Marines, and that people, including his wife and her family, only thought of him as big because they'd never known him as a boy. He wrote about wishing his father hadn't forced him to do what he didn't want to do. He did not say what he didn't want to do.

The boy who was a husband was court-martialed yet honorably discharged from the Marines because his father wrote letters and made phone calls: to a lawyer, a Senator, a Congressman. Upon returning to Texas and college, he had trouble keeping jobs that were easy to get. His wife prepared her notes for final exams. She sliced sandwiches for his study groups and made handkerchiefs for the scout troop he helped lead at her Methodist church. He worked as a scoutmaster for only a few months, and then quit. He gained weight and was self-conscious, but he ran his finger behind picture frames, pointing out dust, and he teased her, in front of friends, about exercising her legs.

On paper and index cards, the son's motivational words remained childlike and borrowed. Key words were typed in all caps at the beginning of each motto: STOP, CONTROL, SMILE, DON'T, STOP, APPROACH, PAY, LISTEN, CONTROL, DON'T LET IT, YOU HAVE TO WORK MUCH HARDER THAN THE AVERAGE, NEVER FORGET, ROUGH. He wrote in parenthesis: "Remember the lad and the man." He could have been referring to some lesson from *Boy's Life*, or to some legend a relative might have told on camping trips, warning about tramps that preyed on young boys by enticing them with egg-salad sandwiches. The college boy who was a husband had made up standards of lad-hood versus manhood in his own mind: about sex and marriage, about bouncing checks and paying the bills, about a pinup slut and the virgin mother.

There were ways to appear normal, as he had learned. He bought a new deer rifle for himself and a fur coat for his wife. She posed wearing the coat for a pair of married friends, who later argued about whether the rifle and the fur reflected poorly on their own relationship.

☨

Six months before the murders, the boy's mother called long distance. Eleven hundred miles away, at the house with the woozy palm trees where the boy had grown up, a police car had parked outside because a neighbor reported a disturbance. The boy made the long drive to take his mother away with him to Texas. As he carried bags and boxes to the car, two officers said his father and mother were yelling at each other in the yard. One officer called it "all nonsense."

Something changed and also stayed the same. The wife whose bruises marked her to submit, whose church taught women to obey, had saved up some money, had gotten away, had secured her own job at a cafeteria. She got her own lawyer. The father now used the telephone to yell and lecture and threaten from a distance. Hear that phone ring, interrupting suddenly, as dreaded. Picture the twist of phone cord—likely too short for pacing in multiple rooms—at the boy's house, at the mother's new apartment. Feel the perspiration and oil from your cheek and ear against the plastic receiver, the tight crook of your shoulder aching. Feel the bedroom suddenly smaller, the curtains across the kitchen going yellow to orange, orange to ash. Don't you hang up on me, boy. I'll hang up this phone right now, boy.

The son who no longer prayed or went to confession made one appointment for counseling, which was not a sacrament but was still a secret until after the murders. He told the doctor he assaulted his wife on two occasions, and how he didn't want to hurt her again, but also that she seemed less afraid of him lately. He talked about his parents' separation and how he feared becoming like his father. He added that he sometimes felt like going to the top of the tower with a deer rifle to shoot people.

Weeks passed, and the boy did not make another appointment with the psychiatrist. He did see the priest who was now a military chaplain. On one of the priest's last visits, the boy presented the arsenal of firearms in the garage. The priest would later say that the weapons were obviously a source of pride for the boy but that he did not recall the number of weapons. This last comment was an odd over-emphasis of mathematics, given that the priest had an arsenal himself at one time, and had been trained in small arms by the Air Force.

☦

After the college boy stabbed his mother and his wife and tucked them into their beds, and before he packed his trunk and climbed the tower and killed people he would never know by name, he wrote a letter to the brother who loved boys but tried to hide it, and a letter to the brother who had been drinking and doing lewd things in public, and a letter to his father, and a letter to the parents of his wife, oh highly favored daughter.

He also wrote letters To Whom It May Concern, which were really letters to himself, and he made notes in the journals as he re-read them in the quiet house with the dead body of his wife in the bedroom. He printed a note at the top of his motivational mottoes and said that he could never quite make it, that the thoughts were too much for him. He had been taking illegal amphetamines, but he didn't mention them. He talked about headaches and violent impulses and consuming large bottles of Excedrin. He said he couldn't explain his recent actions, though he did not say which actions, and also he didn't want to cause his wife embarrassment, so he decided to kill her "as painlessly as possible." For the first time, he wrote about witnessing his mother's beatings. He also said that the world was not worth living in, and that he wanted any of his remaining resources donated anonymously to a mental health foundation after his debts were paid.

He printed another letter on yellow legal paper and left it on his mother's body. He said that his hatred for his father was indescribable, and that his father had treated his mother like a slut. She deserved relief from her tribulations, and now was in heaven or at least out of pain. The boy had ruled that it was best.

✙

In the Marines, he had learned techniques for rifle fire, and for concealment and camouflage, and for scouting, defined in his notes as when an individual "detached from his parent organization for reconnaissance." According to his own records, he had studied fire control and discipline, range determination, how to create and cross obstacles in the field, and why to take the high ground.

He prepared carefully in the morning. He purchased the dolly at a small shop, and purchased the new shotgun from Sears and then sawed off its barrel in his garage. He packed his footlocker carefully and loaded up the car and entered the campus through a service driveway. He parked in an administrator's space, as if he belonged there, and then rolled the trunk on the dolly into the service elevator of the tower. At first the elevator didn't work, but a smiling attendant helped him with the switches and controls. And then he rose. And he rose.

The first victims were not following his rules at the reception desk and in the stairwell. He built a makeshift barricade with pieces of furniture, and then he stepped through the door with glass panels and onto the viewing deck that had four sides, one for each side of the tower. Above his head on each side was a giant clock with the golden border and Roman numerals and long hands that told time. The August sun had no mercy.

He staged and loaded his weapons as he had trained to do, though he had never seen combat—at least not officially, and not with an equal opponent. The rainspouts provided cover for shooting, as he had noticed on a previous visit, and the farthest injury would be five hundred yards away. He wrapped a bandana around his head and took a position and pointed his scope and rifle first at a woman with a broad pregnant body. When he pulled the trigger, the child was killed. The woman had to live.

Two years before, a man at a diner had complimented the boy for his cleanliness. He said the boy looked as if he had just taken a shower. That day the boy described the compliment in his journal and said how grateful he was to have been brought up right, and also to have the standards he had set for himself.

There were prayers for gratitude, and also for cleanliness of mind and contrition, but he hadn't prayed in a long time. Still, the altar boy knew the words: *Mea culpa, mea culpa, mea maxima culpa.* The rules were old and matched up now and also violated in a way that wasn't funny. The boy aimed and shot as more bodies fell below him, and then the men came as he knew that they would. And then they shot him, too.

The bodies of the boy's mother and his wife were not discovered until after the shooting stopped. Across the country, eleven hundred miles away, the father holed up in his house with the two other sons, and with a priest from the parish where his wife had been faithful until she moved away.

Somehow father and the local priest decided that the son and the mother would have a Catholic funeral together, as well as a burial together, and that the boy's coffin would be draped with the American flag while the mother's coffin would be topped with sprays of red roses, also a crucifix. (Far away, the boy's wife was mourned by parents and classmates. The boy's father reportedly sent no word, not even a flower.) During the rosary service, meditations were confined to the sorrowful mysteries, beginning with Christ's agony in the garden. In one photo from the funeral, the father's face twists in conspicuous grief, and the blonde son next to him has turned as if to notice, as if to say, you've got to be kidding me.

No serious crime could be imputed to the boy, explained a priest who spoke with approval from the diocese in the name of the church's rules. (Not even the abortion by gunshot, though the womb was sacred. Not even the murder of his mother or his bride.) In effect, according to the rules of the Church, this meant that the boy had committed mass murder but died in a state of grace.

The priest who was the boy's friend and other father had been assigned to an Air Force base in Alaska the previous week, so he could not attend. Once he heard the news, it is possible that he offered a mass or other prayers for the dead. There was no rule that would compel him to do so.

The policies and practices of the FBI and its director were meticulous and incredibly secretive, and so when agents tapped phone calls and tracked movements of the boy's father after the atrocities, he did not know it. A government psychiatrist had assessed the father as a paranoid, "psychopathic personality" with "homicidal tendencies," likely to commit a berserk crime like his son's. This assessment of the patriarch was "furnished to The White House and Secret Service for information purposes."

So what if he wanted to secure the guns left at his son's house and also all of his deceased wife's belongings? So what if he contested his son's wishes for any remaining money to be donated to a mental health study, or if he yelled at his middle son during one police interview (the son had no shoes on, and didn't speak up properly), and if he was allegedly selling his story to *LIFE* or *McCall's*? None of these behaviors exactly indicated that this father would lug weapons into a public place and shoot people. He saw himself as a sober man collecting his due, the way he had taught himself. And tried (fought?) to teach his children.

Approximately three months later, someone typed and sent the father a threatening letter, which launched an additional investigation that extended into the year following the killings. The writer said that he or she had witnessed what happened to the boy that night years ago in the swimming pool. The writer said the father was to blame for everything at the tower, and that the father would be shot on Christmas Day. The writer used a few words in Latin and referred to a .357 Magnum. The FBI investigated the two sons who were still alive, and some former classmates, and an unidentified woman. Finally, based on fingerprints, a man with a Polish name was indicted. He surrendered and received a suspended sentence.

The FBI had been mistaken about the father as a threat. Or: The FBI arrived too late, and left too soon. There was of course no second siege at any funeral, in any town square or government building. Christmas came and went and the father was not harmed. Within a year of the killings, he had already broken off a relationship, then married and divorced. He soon married a third time. It is reasonable to infer that while he was calling his son to bring the fearful mother home, he was already satisfying his romantic needs elsewhere. The second wife divorced him after finding bruises on her son's body. The third wife would stay, and leave, and return again. He broke her arm, knocked out her teeth, split her lip. But she said that he apologized.

The father accepted money to talk about himself for many years, until he became demented and was involuntarily hospitalized. But before that his youngest son got in trouble with drinking and with drugs and was shot in a bar parking lot on a local street corner, then died in the early hours of the Fourth of July. The father sued the bar. He also took custody of his son's daughter, whose name blended the names of her murdered grandmother and murdered aunt, and the father indulged her with treats including a pony. His middle son moved from Florida to California and died of AIDS not long after a partner committed suicide.

People would call the father a survivor. People would say he was punished. He outlived them all.

He always referred to his eldest son's murders as The Accident. He blamed the psychiatrist more than anyone, more than himself. For a time he told anyone in his house not to move ashtrays or other items from the places where his dead wife had kept them, or had been instructed to keep them. The granddaughter insisted that he never hurt her, but she witnessed what he did to the women: He told them when to use the toilet and where they could buy groceries, and if he got angry, he locked them in a bedroom.

The father's rules remained meticulous until it was clear that he could not tell one thing from another thing. Perhaps he never could tell, or perhaps he did not think he ever needed to. The roots piercing clay pipes were oaks tangled in Spanish moss were Liberty ships sliding from their massive lanes and foremen with clipboards were bricks and shovels were ledger lines and the shotgun shells were jerry cans the crown of thorns the venison his wife's face ice cubes in a washcloth and the eyes and hands of his sons, laughing behind glasses.

A few years before he died, according to one writer who visited him, the father kept a loose license plate on a table. The plate read, "Love thy neighbor, but don't get caught." The father also still wore a large metal buckle shaped like a German Luger on his leather belt. Imagine hearing that buckle, any buckle, before you could see it. Metal on metal. Click.

August 1, 1966

Litany of Dead and Wounded

Margaret Hodges Whitman
Kathleen Leissner Whitman
Edna Elizabeth Rose Townsley
Marguerite Gabour Lamport
Mark Jerome Gabour
Mary Frances Lamport Gabour
Mike Gabour
Claire Wilson James
Baby Boy Wilson
Thomas Frederick Eckman
Dr. Robert H. Boyer
Thomas Aquinas Ashton
Karen Joan Griffith
Thomas Ray Karr
Paul Bolton Sonntag
Claudia Rutt
Harry Walchuck
Officer Billy Paul Speed
Roy Dell Schmidt
David H. Gunby
John Scott Allen
Tom Herman
Roland Ehlke
Ellen Evganides
Avelino Esparza

F. L. Foster

Robert Frede

Irma Garcia

Nancy Harvey

Robert Heard

Aleck Hernandez, Jr.

Morris Hohmann

Devereau Huffman

Homer J. Kelley

Abdul Khashab

Janet Paulos

Adrian Littlefield

Brenda Littlefield

Della Martinez

Marina Martinez

David Mattson

Dolores Ortega

Lana Phillips

Oscar Royvela

Billy Snowden

C. A. Stewart

Sandra Wilson

Carla Sue Wheeler

Charles J. Whitman

Notes

I. The Sins of Special Men

page 41 Information about the teaching of "ontological change" can be found here: http://www.vatican.va/roman_curia/ congregations/cclergy/documents/rc_con_cclergy_doc_18061996_ intr_en.html. See also Marie Keenan's *Child Sexual Abuse in the Catholic Church: Gender, Power, and Organizational Culture* (2012) for her discussion of the connection between a belief in "ontological change" and a culture of entitlement among clerics in the church (154-179). A priest source also directed me to *Crimens Solicitationis*, the Vatican's 1962 imposition of secrecy in cases of clergy abuse, which used Canon Law to pressure bishops under penalty of excommunication from reporting offenders to the public or to law enforcement—with ontological difference as the basis for the argument: http://www.vatican.va/resources/ resources_crimen-sollicitationis-1962_en.html

page 42 The vast spectrum of characters inside the clergy: Joseph Gallagher's *The Pain and the Privilege: Diary of a City Priest* (1983) offered this insight: "Human weakness in clergymen no longer scandalizes me. As with other professionals, such as doctors and lawyers, the wounding often results from the very attempt to heal, and from learning too much about human nature. It has been said that to get a person out of hell, you have to go there yourself" (16). At least two interviewees from the *SMSU* ordination class of 1955 mentioned Gallagher to me as a model student, brilliant scholar and translator of the Vatican II documents, and example of "moral courage." One priest sent me his personally autographed copy of Gallagher's book. Accounts of the man's example were compelling, even second hand, and his letter to the National Council of Catholic Bishops in 1968 (found in appendices for *Pain and Privilege*) is a fascinating and intelligent artifact, calling out the American clerical hierarchy on its hypocrisy about warfare and sexual morality. Unfortunately, when I first went searching for contact with Gallagher myself, his name appeared in a list of priests accused of abuse in the Diocese of Baltimore: http://www.baltimoresun.com/bal-te. md.priestlist26sep26-story.html#page=1. Gallagher publicly objected to his inclusion on the list, admitting to "inappropriate conduct" but "no genital contact": http://www.baltimoresun.com/ bal-te.md.abuse26sep26-story.html. Gallagher's case did not go to court. As I searched more, his name and his situation had to be untangled from reports that sometimes confused him with Philadelphia's Rev. Joseph J. Gallagher, who (along with one other) was deemed "unsuitable for ministry" in 2013, following a grand jury investigation after the suicide of a victim: http://www.cnn. com/2013/04/07/us/pennsylvania-priests-barred/. Much later, I was intrigued to find Gallagher's name in the acknowledgements of Richard Sipe's comprehensive study, *A Secret World: Sexuality and The Search for Celibacy* (1991). Sipe told me personally that he believed the accusations against Gallagher were completely false, a distorted version of contact with a nephew he was caring for after his brother died. Sipe also did not think it far-fetched that Gallagher's inclusion on the public list of accused priests amounted to a political punishment for his public challenges to the hierarchy. Gallagher died in 2015.

page 42 Despite hundreds of years of art: Some early examples of literature exploring the flawed, corrupted humanity of Catholic priests can be found in British works of the 1400s: *The Book of Margery Kempe* as well as Chaucer's *The Canterbury Tales.* Much more contemporary accounts—all of which have been made into films—include José Maria de Eça de Queirós's *O Crime do Padre Amaro* (1875), Willa Cather's *Death Comes for the Archbishop* (1927), Georges Bernanos's *Diary of a Country Priest* (1936), Graham Greene's *The Power and the Glory* (1940), Henry de Montherlant's play, *La Ville Dont le Prince Est en Enfant* (1955), and Colleen McCullough's *The Thorn Birds* (1977). Documentary films exploring criminality and conspiracy in the priesthood to date include *Twist of Faith* (2004), *Deliver Us from Evil* (2006), *Sex Crimes of the Vatican* (2006), and *Hand of God* (2007). A key theme is often the secondary trauma victims suffer when finally seeking acknowledgement, apologies, legal recourse, or mediation years and years after abuse.

page 43 One group preserves: The Grand Jury Report included broad statements, calling Whitman "a crazy, deranged individual who had suddenly gone completely berserk with no warning to his family or friends." The jury also asserted that a pecan-sized brain tumor discovered in the autopsy *"undoubtedly caused* him much mental pain and possibly contributed to his insane actions" (emphasis added). While the jury called for a "medical-legal case study," it also suppressed public release of Whitman's file for twenty years, emphasizing the final letters discovered by investigators: "[These notes] contain unverified statements of an insane killer concerning an innocent individual which could be misunderstood." The public display of deference to Charles Whitman's father under the circumstances seems remarkable now. While the "blame" of a tumor for Whitman's actions is popular, it is also highly disputed by experts; see Eva Frederick's article.

page 44 According to Vincik: See Whitman's thoughts on Catholicism, heaven and hell, and the nature of God and forgiveness in "Who Was Charles Whitman?" For the most part, Whitman's reflections struck me as fairly typical middle-class American undergraduate dabbling with Transcendentalism and "non-Western" thought.

page 45 mid-century book of Catholic etiquette: See Kay Toy Fenner's *American Catholic Etiquette*. Frawley-O'Dea explains the deference of laity to priests during this generation: "To question the integrity of a priest was unthinkable to most Catholics... [who had] a deeply felt need to think only the best about Father" and who lived under "the demands for loyalty placed on laity by the clerical caste" (186-87).

page 46 Catholic education: *Know Your Mass* (first published in 1954) was ostensibly a handbook for all children, but it was clearly directed at Catholic boys as potential future priests; it used the style of a comic book to explain the theology of the mass, the priest's vestments and preparations, and every step from the sacristy through each part of the Tridentine rite (also called the "Traditional Latin Mass"): http://www.ccwatershed. org/media/pdfs/14/06/26/12-34-30_0.pdf. American Catholic kids of this generation were also indoctrinated through the church's own comic book, *Treasure Chest of Fun and Fact* (published from 1946 through 1972). *Catholic Boy* Magazine was also popular in the 1950s and '60s.

page 46 By all accounts: The FBI files include a list of multiple Whitman family addresses in the early 1940s. One relative told investigators that Whitman's parents for a time lived in Savannah in order to work on Liberty Ships for the war effort. Statements from various witnesses recount family conflicts involving sticks and guns, as well as the welts on Charlie's back. The 1930 Federal Census lists Charles A. (CA) Whitman as an "inmate" at the Bethesda Orphanage in Chatham County, Georgia, Militia District #5. Some context about conditions at the orphanage from the late 1800s through 1920 can be found in "Fired for Flogging Orphan Boy" and "Fought Their Teachers: Bethesda Boys Take to the Woods," as well as "Historic Orphanage to Raise Large Sum." More recent first-hand accounts of violence from neighbors of the Whitman family as well as statements from CA Whitman's second wife and his granddaughter can be found in Paul L. Lomartire's article "Demons and Doom" published in the *Palm Beach Post* on Sunday, July 30, 2006 (forty years after the shootings). CA Whitman's second wife alleged that his "erratic" behavior "was endangering her physical condition" (she was pregnant at the time) in a separation lawsuit filed in January 1967. See "Whitman's Wife Cites 'Remorse' in Support Suit." Nelson Leissner also told me he witnessed at least one tirade during a family visit in summer 1962 (see Scott-Coe). *LIFE* published an extensive collection of Whitman family photos in its August 12, 1966 issue.

page 47 Boy Scout Jamboree in California: Charles Whitman was the only member of Troop 119 listed as attending the Jamboree July 17-23, 1953, at Irvine Ranch in California. See "23 Scouts, Three Leaders Going to 'Jamboree.'" Three scoutmasters were listed as accompanying the group. This event took place in the summer, but it is unclear whether Leduc attended with the troop during seminary break. The often-mentioned legend that Whitman was the youngest boy ever to achieve Eagle Scout status is actually traceable to a *Palm Beach Post* article in 1953, including a rare public comment from his mother; see "Lake Worth Eagle Scout May Be Youngest."

page 47 After the murders in 1966: CA Whitman qtd. in Gary Lavergne's *Sniper in the Tower*, p.3.

page 47 Before hitting puberty: The *New St. Joseph Baltimore Catechism* includes a series of illustrations ("this is good" vs. "this is better") that emphasize the traditional view that the lay, married state is inferior to the religious life: http://publishing. capuchin.org/Page%20Content%20Images/Sal_Cordaro_Vocations/ catechism%202.jpg.

page 47 By 1950-51, Charlie was old enough to crave: St. Mary's Seminary and University was founded in 1791 in Baltimore by the Society of St. Sulpice: http://www.stmarys. edu/seminary/about-us/history-mission/. The Sulpician order originated in France to direct the formation of diocesan priests. In part, the order's mission can understood in the context of a Counter-Reformation response to Protestant outrage about poorly educated parish priests and widespread corruption in monasteries: http://www.newadvent.org/cathen/13378a.htm.

page 48 Records show: Catalogs at SMSU 1951-52 and Joseph Leduc FBI Statement. For Leduc's fishing trips see "Fishing Catches" (1952) as well as "Offshore Catches" (1956). Leduc's ordination was announced in two publications only available through on-site library microfiche searches: "Priest to Sing First Solemn High Mass," June 5, 1955, *Waterbury Republican*; and

"Graduates of St. Mary's Ordained," May 28, 1955, *The Houston Chronicle*. The trailer of Edward Dmytryk's *The Sniper* can be viewed here: https://www.youtube.com/watch?v=79HdimrnCHc. The film was nominated for an Academy Award for Best Writing, Motion Picture Story.

page 49 During this time: Two sources identified June 12, 1955, as the date of Leduc's first mass in Lake Worth: "John Klein Is Elected Grand Knight of Lodge" and "Coastal Deanery Holy Name Rally Scheduled Sunday"—the week following his trip to say mass in Waterbury. These sources also indicate Leduc's association with local parish groups, the Holy Name Society and the Knights of Columbus.

page 50 But in the mid-fifties: One retired priest I interviewed, Msgr. Peter Riani, shared his view that even the Catholic "renaissance" in 1950s America had been vastly exaggerated, and that what people overstated as turmoil in the following two decades really amounted to "time to get real." Mid-century (post-WWII) films in Europe depicted much darker storylines than Hollywood (including corruption, illness, sexual themes, and spiritual struggle/failure), and they also featured more idiosyncratic, less triumphant-looking, actors in the roles. Two most striking contrasts with American images were *Diary of a Country Priest* (1951) and *Léon Morin: Priest* (1961), both based on novels. The latter film has a distinctly anti-Communist angle. Both visually emphasized the poverty of priests, an element mostly missing from American movies. A more idealized, heroic European portrait of priesthood can be found in *Le Sorcier du Ciel (The Wizard of Heaven)* (1949), a French film about the life and temptations of St. Jean Vianney, patron saint of priests. I remember watching this movie in a church basement when I was about ten years old.

II. Looking for Father Leduc

page 54 Local chancery archives: See Doyle, Sipe, and Wall's analysis of diocesan files in *Sex, Priests, and Secret Codes: The Catholic Church's 2,000 Year Paper Trail on Sexual Abuse* (2006); the authors discuss at length the restrictions set forth in Canon 487, 488, 489, and 490.

page 55 The first time I discovered: Leduc statement to FBI. Information about the Feast of the Assumption can be found at New Advent, http://www.newadvent.org/cathen/02006b.htm, and American Catholic, http://www.americancatholic.org/Features/Saints/Saint.aspx?id=1108. The teaching of Mary's Assumption did not become official church doctrine until 1950, Leduc's first year of seminary. I can't help but notice how this word poetically marks significant moments and places throughout his story: the name of his prep school, his date of interrogation by the FBI, his last known parish assignment in Houston, and his rumored parish residence in Pompano Beach when sought after by a creditor in the 1978. Catholic doctrine and imagery aside, Leduc appears to have been equally good at eliciting as well as disrupting assumptions about his identity.

page 55 At casual glance, Leduc seems a device: In 1927, the Klu Klux Klan used the Catholicism of Andrew Kehoe in its propaganda following the massacre at a school in Bath, Michigan: "The Greatest Premeditated Murder Since the St. Bartholomew Massacre Murdering 30,000 French Protestants." The gruesome and bizarre murder trial of Father Hans Schmidt (a German immigrant) more than a decade earlier, in 1914, was another early 20th century bellwether for American suspicion of Catholics (and by extension, non-natives) (see Gado's *Killer Priest*). It intrigues me that Whitman's religious background has been rendered mostly through signal flares or outright omissions about his Catholicism rather than any textured examination.

page 57 For this reason in part: See James M. O'Toole's *The Faithful: A History of Catholics in America* (2008) for extensive historical context. He discusses at length how early American Catholics had to adapt their practice because of the shortage of priests during their own time, a fact not readily known.

page 58 Whitman and Leduc met during a generation: See SMSU *Catalog and Announcements* June 1951 and June 1952. Rev. Edward Tarte now has more than 2000 videos on YouTube, where he discusses atheism and his memories of priesthood, and also teaches math and performs on the piano: https://www. youtube.com/user/edwardtarte. Because the unnamed priest here quoted did not want to be associated with Leduc, I have chosen to keep his identity confidential.

page 59 This dynamic was not conducive: McGinnis stressed that dioceses have improved their approach to alcoholism and other substance addictions: "I don't think it could happen that way now. I haven't heard of denial and cover-up for alcohol abuse. The dioceses won't tolerate it." When I visited St. Mary's Seminary in Houston, Rector Rev. Trung Nguyen explained how he had moderated drinking on the campus during the Super Bowl (the students asked for three beers each—he approved no more than two); he also explained that teachers now had to address many problems young men might bring with them to seminary, including online gaming, pornography, and substance abuse. He said, "Priests come from society, from the same fabric as everyone else."

page 60 Several priests repeated to me: A list and total of all seminarians by name, year of study, and diocesan sponsor can be located at the end of SMSU catalogs available in the SMSU archives in Baltimore—a remarkable resource. In a speech given on the 110th anniversary of St. Mary's Seminary, Archbishop Joseph Fiorenza quoted the 1951 rector's description of crowded facilities at La Porte and a smaller population: "[T]he classrooms are too small....The library was moved from the second floor to the first to keep it from falling through the floor. In one building 60 men live, there are six bathrooms and six showers and the other building has 40 men with plenty of wash basins but only two showers and two rest rooms." In this speech, he also recalled problems with rain and with rats. The La Porte location was is the first place Leduc lived when he arrived in Texas. The speech is linked here: http://www.archgh.org/http://www.archgh.org/ http://www.archgh.org/default/Documents/Home/Bishop%20State- ments/St.%20Mary%20Seminary%20-%20110th%20Anniversary.doc.

page 60 Individual seminarians were discouraged: Many sources discuss discouragement against "particular friendships" during earlier generations of seminarians. Books that touch on the subject include Richard Sipe's *A Secret World* (1990), Marie Keenan's *Child Sexual Abuse and the Catholic Church: Gender, Power, and Organizational Culture* (2012), and John Cornwell's *The Dark Box: A Secret History of Confession* (2014). The problem is also explored in *The Fire That Burns*, a 1997 film treatment of Henry de Montherlant's play, *La Ville Dont le Prince Est un Infant* (1955). Slippage between the Church's concern about pedophilia and its blame of homosexuality, especially under Pope Benedict, was explored in JoAnn Wypijewski's article, "Roman Inquisition," published by *Mother Jones* in 2005: http://www. motherjones.com/politics/2005/12/roman-inquisition. Frawley- O'Dea also discusses "secreted and scapegoated" homosexuality at length (p. 109-127).

page 64 There were occasions: In Texas, there were at least two priests who could have had the opportunity to meet Whitman and then remember his face or name later in connection with Leduc. Both men are long-deceased. Rev. Gilbert Pekar, pastor of St. Michael's parish in Kathleen's home town of Needville, had to consent that his church could be used for the wedding ceremony performed by Leduc in 1962. Rev. Ernest ("Ernie") Michalka was Leduc's pastor at Philip Neri Parish 1961-62, and could have been the priest who bailed him out after an alleged speeding arrest described by one of Whitman's friends (see later notes regarding conversations with Schuck). Recollections prompted by the shooting and/or images in news coverage would easily resemble the experience reported by Dr. Jan D. Cochrum, the counselor who first met with Whitman at UT: "He remembered treating Charlie only after seeing a picture of him four months later…[Charlie] was every bit as nice a guy as he looked in the picture" (qtd. in Lavergne 70). In Florida, at least two Miami/ St. Augustine priests would have known of the connection: Fr. Thomas Anglim and Fr. Matthew Morgan, both Leduc's classmates at SMSU (though of different cohorts) who spent significant time at Sacred Heart Parish. Morgan was also active in Troop 119, and named in Leduc's statement.

page 65 June 1963: Whitman's UT transcript from February 12, 1963 documents his withdrawal. All classes are listed as "W" for that term. A letter from Kathleen to her mother dated February 14 announced the bad news and explained her plans to withdraw from UT to join her husband as he returned to active duty in Camp Lejeune.

page 67 During a week of combing through: FBI Files, Letter to Assistant to the Director De Loach, August 12, 1966.

page 68 Leduc's name comes up again: See Francis J. Schuck, FBI Statement. I suspected, then later confirmed, that "Gileus" was a Latin-referencing nickname/linguistic pun used by Whitman and his male friends. To my ear, it sounds not exactly disrespectful, but over-familiar and intentionally absurd; "Gileus" certainly was not French. More than three years later, upon gaining access to private letters that had not been included in the public files, I located three more references to "Fr. Gil" in Whitman's handwriting: two prior to the wedding (June and July 1962), and another in 1963 where his name is included in a list of intended Christmas card recipients.

page 69 Nominal slippages and errors: One priest who had known Leduc in Houston repeatedly called him "Giles," an obvious American, Southern pronunciation of "Gilles." In two different articles from the early 1960s—one from a Texas newspaper and another from *The De Andrein* newsletter archived at DePaul University—his first name is mis-identified as "James Gil" (see LeFevre). One of the initial sources that confirmed his death date was a 2010 issue of a monthly diocesan publication from Galveston-Houston called *Clergy News*, but even it mis-identified his middle name as "Gilbert" in a list of deceased priests. The very first time Leduc's name appears anywhere, it appears in a 1930 US Census record taken when he was one year old, and even there it's misspelled as "Gell."

page 70 The FBI Investigation: The "Autobiography" can be found in the Austin PD/FBI Files. According to interviews in the record, Charles Whitman's father displayed a great deal of vigilance about whether the document could be shared.

page 70 Founding of the troop at Sacred Heart: One fellow seminarian at SMSU during Leduc's first year there (1950-51) was Matthew Morgan. He was ordained in 1951, and his first assignment as an assistant priest was at Sacred Heart Parish, where he served as a scoutmaster and later returned to serve as parish administrator in 1958 after several other assignments. Leduc grew up in New England and did not arrive in Florida until 1950-51, so it's perhaps unsurprising that I discovered no evidence of sustained peer friendships in Lake Worth. His cousin knew of no surviving friends, and my efforts to locate acquaintances from the parish community and the neighborhood were unsuccessful. I found no trace of any enduring relationship between Morgan and Leduc after Leduc returned to Florida in the 1970s. Leduc's latest reference to Morgan would be dated 1966, in his statement to the FBI, as a resource for information about Whitman.

III. SHADOWS AND DISCREPANCIES

page 71 In September 1952, at age 23: See "Honor Is Paid to Scout Leaders." The article indicates a fairly large public ceremony ("an impressive court of honor") for a joint event between Troop 4 and Sacred Heart's Troop 119. The text also indicates Leduc's role as "former scoutmaster" and still refers to him as "Gilles" rather than "Joseph," consistent with other public references prior to his ordination. Leduc's former classmate at St. Mary's Baltimore, Fr. Matthew Morgan, is named as one of the awards presenters, suggesting again a clerical friendship or alliance that likely, in part, facilitated Leduc's transition to the Galveston-Houston diocese. While Leduc was nearly ten years older than the average Eagle Scout at the time, adult men were still allowed to receive the recognition until age limits were introduced in 1952.

page 72 In 2004, two years after the Boston Globe: The
John Jay Report can be read at the US Conference of Catholic
Bishops link here: http://www.usccb.org/issues-and-action/
child-and-youth-protection/upload/The-Nature-and-Scope-
of-Sexual-Abuse-of-Minors-by-Catholic-Priests-and-Deacons-
in-the-United-States-1950-2002.pdf. Bishop Accountability
estimates of percentage of abusers can be found here: http://
www.bishop-accountability.org/AtAGlance/data_priests.htm.
Watchdogs such as Terence McKiernen question the objectivity
of the John Jay document as suspect given the official interests
of the NCCB, and also dismiss specific theories in the document
about the influence of sixties culture on priest behaviors (sometimes called "the Woodstock defense"). Mark Silk, a professor of
Religion in Public Life, published a critique in *The Guardian*:
https://www.theguardian.com/commentisfree/belief/2011/
may/25/woodstock-defence-abuse-catholic-church

page 72 But not all priestly troubles are criminal ones:
Sipe is perhaps most famous now for his writings and expert testimony in cases of sexual abuse; his study of priest sexuality and
psychology is extensive. See: *A Secret World* (1990); *Sex, Priests,
and Power: Anatomy of a Crisis* (1995); *Celibacy in Crisis: A Secret
World Revisited* (2003); *The Serpent and the Dove: Celibacy in
Literature and Life* (2007).

**page 73 I learned firsthand how the official church
response:** During early research to understand Leduc's seminary
pathway, I came across another seminarian named Leduc who
had attended St. Mary's Baltimore/Roland Park between 1951-
1955. It took some time for me to determine that no family
relationship existed. Lucien ("Luke") was remembered warmly

by classmates. In his seminary photograph, he resembles a young Eddie Fisher. In the late 1960s, Luke Leduc met and fell in love with a figure skater, teacher, and professional skier named Natalie (neé Bombard), for whom he left the priesthood to marry. He went on to become a doctor of psychology and died at age 58, only six weeks after being diagnosed with cancer.

page 74 Coleman's story: On Monday March 28, 1966, the Associated Press report about Rev. Coleman's intervention with the gunman was syndicated widely in newspapers across the United States. I have included only a sampling of coverage in my list of sources. I do wonder whether Whitman saw or heard the story. According to UT Health Center records, Whitman sought professional mental health treatment for the first time that same week, on March 29. Dr. Jan D. Cochrum prescribed Valium and referred Whitman to Dr. Maurice Dean Heatly, who saw him the same day. Heatly's report recorded Whitman's descriptions of his father as "brutal, domineering and extremely demanding," as well as Whitman's admissions that "his tactics were similar to his father's and that he had on two occasions assaulted his wife physically." Heatly wrote that Whitman "could talk for long periods of time and develop overt hostility while talking, and then during the same narration may show signs of weeping." He also infamously included Whitman's reference to "thinking about going up on the tower with a deer rifle and start [sic] shooting people." Whitman did not return for his recommended follow-up appointment. Leduc's FBI statement indicates two meetings with Whitman after the meeting with Cochrum: one in May, the other in June.

page 75 The worst-case scenario: Bishop Accountability, Database Publicly Accused Priests in the United States: http://

bishop-accountability.org/priestdb/PriestDBbylastName-A. html. Complete database of *The LA Times* investigation can be found here, "Inside the 'Perversion Files': Tracking Decades of Allegations inside the Boy Scouts": http://spreadsheets. latimes.com/boyscouts-caseshttp://spreadsheets.latimes. com/boyscouts-cases/.

page 75 The Galveston-Houston diocese participated: The Archdiocese of Galveston-Houston Letter issued in 2004 by Bishop Joseph Fiorenza can be read here: http://www.bishop-accountability.org/usccb/natureandscope/dioceses/galveston-houstontx.htm. Listing of public settlements can be viewed here: http://www.bishop-accountability.org/settlements/#largest_settlements. A list of known priests who served in Galveston-Houston and were accused of abuse can be located here: http://www.eurekaencyclopedia.com/index.php/Category:Archdiocese_of_Galveston_Houston. There is one important error in the Eureka listing: Rev. Donald Stavinoha was born in 1943, so he was not ordained in 1949, and thus was too young to be a contemporary of Leduc's.

page 76 Rev. Jesse Linam's case and the statute of limitations in TX: Felicia Peavy, a Houston attorney, had pushed against the statute on appeal when representing a client alleging abuse by Rev. Jesse Linam in 1973-74. The complaint alleged that officials in the Galveston-Houston diocese knew of, and covered up, abuses by Linam--and others--as early as 1961. The appeal was denied, but the diocese did settle during mediation and Linam was removed from ministry. See *Doe v. Linam*.

page 77 Former classmates, if not friends, in high places: See *OCD* listings. Following ordination, Rev. Msgr. William Pickard (SM's Class of 1954; d. 2015) went to Catholic University, where he earned his doctorate in Canon Law then returned to Houston to serve as an ecclesiastical judge and secretary of the Diocesan Tribunal from 1959-1966. Rev. Joseph Fiorenza (also SM's class of 1954) was Vice-Chancellor in 1972 and Chancellor from 1973-1979, when he was named Bishop of San Angelo. Fiorenza became Bishop of Galveston-Houston in 1985 and served until 2004. Rev. James J. Madden (SM's Class of 1955, Leduc's class; d. 2009) served as Vice Chancellor from 1961 to at least 1969. Vincent Rizzoto (SM's class of 1956) also a canon lawyer, served on the diocesan tribunal from 1967-1972 and also was Vicar General and chair of Priests Personnel Board before being appointed Auxiliary Bishop from 2001-2006. Rev. Anton Frank (d. 1982), Leduc's senior pastor in 1955 at Annunciation, was Promoter of Justice from as early as 1952 (Leduc's first year in seminary) until 1977, and Frank was also serving as Diocesan Consultor in 1972, Leduc's first year of leave. Rev. John McCarthy (SM's class of 1956) later became Bishop of Austin from 1985-2001. Both Fiorenza and Rizzotto retain "emeritus" status in the GH chancery office. In his will, Leduc requested that Rev. Madden say his funeral mass, assisted by Rev. Anton Frank and another priest, Rev. Ed Missenda (d. 1996). Madden was still alive to honor this last wish when Leduc died in January 1981, but Rev. Frank appears to have been too old/too ill; I could not verify whether Missenda attended. I also found no record indicating whether former Florida associates—Rev. Matthew Morgan, for example—attended or participated in the funeral. Given his proximity to significant leaders in the GH diocese, I was fascinated that Leduc named a layperson as the executor of his will and explicitly stated, "[I]t is my desire that my executor of this will and my estate shall not be hindered in any way by any of the clergy" (see Leduc Last Will and Testament). Fond feelings, it seems, were limited to a few. I believe Frank must have been an early protector or advocate of some kind, at least in Leduc's mind.

page 77 I had already crossed off names of potential contacts: Very early on, I began building a list of priests whose names appeared in the *OCD* with Leduc at each GH parish where he served between 1956-1972. The vast majority were out of reach or had already deceased by the time I began my search.

page 80 Many Catholics had brought grievous complaints: *Betrayal: The Crisis in the Catholic Church* by the Boston Globe, was first printed in 2002. Cited here are documents in the appendices from Cardinal Medeiros and Bernard Law in response to a letter from Margaret Gallant (222-229). Descriptions I've included also refer to two physical meetings documented by the Globe investigation: one, between five mothers of molestation victims and a chancery official; the other, a meeting where two young men were asked to repeat details of their complaints in front of their fathers, church officials, and their alleged abuser (56-58). Other accounts of Cardinal Medeiros and Law can be found in France's *Our Fathers* (2004). For insightful discussion of appeals to a Church doctrine of "mental reservation" employed by clerics "as a defense to justify not telling the truth" and circumstances "when it is permissible to lie," see Keenan, p. 154-55.

page 81 The questions I had prepared: This month of emails regarding possible contact with Bishop Fiorenza took place in January-February 2014.

page 82 The encounter drove me to understand: A sequence from the bishops' correspondence about Rev. David Holley can be located here: http://www.bishop-accountability. org/news/1997_08_31_DMN_PathOf.htm. More on Holley's case can be found in David France's *Our Fathers* (2004). Craig Malisow's story, "Parish Predators," can be found in *Houston Press*: http://www.houstonpress.com/news/parish-predators-6545483. The earliest public report I could find linking Holley's case to Fiorenza's correspondence with other bishops was published in 1997, in the *Washington Post* article "Church Long Knew of Priest Pedophilia"—the key here was that Holley was "moved along" to another diocese where he committed crimes rather than being immediately referred to legal authorities when his "problems" surfaced in San Angelo: https://www.washington-post.com/archive/politics/1997/09/01/church-long-knew-of-priests-pedophilia-files-indicate/9fd36723-1fe4-4837-a011-c1cf1ba10bbd/

page 82 Fiorenza went on to serve as President: see National Conference of Catholic Bishops history webpage, as well as GH Chancery Fiorenza biography page. See *John Does I, II, II v. Roman Catholic Diocese of Galveston-Houston,* et al: http://www.leagle.com/decision/2005680408FSupp2d272_1650/DOE%20v.%20ROMAN%20CATHOLIC%20DIOCESE%20OF%20GALVESTON-HOUSTON. For information about the Patino-Arango case, see Cindy George's "Settlement Reached in Houston Church Sex Abuse Case": http://www.chron.com/life/houston-belief/article/Settlement-reached-in-church-sex-abuse-case-1771874.php

page 83 There was no evidence that someone this long-invested: I do imagine if I had asked about Pickard, the response would have inspired at least some details. Fiorenza's friendship with Pickard is openly and warmly included in Pickard's obituary: http://www.legacy.com/obituaries/houstonchronicle/obituary.aspx?pid=175654924

page 84 Located during an on-campus interview: I visited with Very Rev. Trung Nguyen, Rector of St. Mary's Seminary Houston, in early July 2013. He gave me a comprehensive tour of the seminary grounds, including the classroom building and a peek at the original dorm.

page 86 Nearly a year later: Yearbook photograph obtained courtesy of Assumption Preparatory alumnus Roger Chagnon. Two years later, I was able to secure a copy of the entire yearbook, *Memini 1947,* from an online vendor. In other sections beyond the class photographs, the *Memini* revealed that Leduc was also member of the yearbook editorial staff as a photographer, as well as a highly-invested member of Cercle St. Jean, which lists him as vice-president, secretary, and treasurer his senior year. In the "Class Prophecy" there is a single reference to Leduc that reads either as either friendly ribbing or veiled denigration of sexual (in)experience or identity: "…tells of a discovery by explorer GILLES LEDUC of the true grave of Joe Phknae" (capitals in original, p. 69).

page 87 Together and separately, the images are difficult: I sent two letters to one of Leduc's surviving cousins in early 2013. When she did not respond, I felt obligated to make a personal visit. She and her husband sat and talked with me for approximately half an hour. While she provided me information for subsequent communications, follow up contacts from me were not returned. To protect their privacy, I have chosen not to name them. Any quotes attributed to "cousin," "family," "husband," or "niece" came from the live exchange.

page 87 Waterbury's role in Catholicism: See Douglas

Brinkley and Julie M. Fenster's *Parish Priest: Father Michael McGivney and American Catholicism* (2006). Fantastic Waterbury history resources can be found at Waterbury Time Machine http://www.freewebs.com/waterburyct/. A tour of the landmark Waterbury Clock Tower at Union Station can be viewed here: https://www.youtube.com/watch?v=QpqRxTTijUU . UT Austin's clock tower stands 67 feet taller than Waterbury's: https://tower.utexas.edu/history/

page 87 Originally from a family in French Canada: All addresses, occupations, and census records were located via city directories and other documents on genealogy websites.

page 88 As a child, Leduc could easily walk from home to church: Waterbury historian Robert Bisaillon's *St. Anne Parish and Her People* (1986) includes photographs of Leduc's 8th grade class in 1943 as well as group images of Scout Troops at St. Anne's Parish in the 1930s and 1940s; his name is included in a list of priest vocations from the parish. Bisaillon was deceased by the time I began this project. When I visited Waterbury in 2013, I was able to see how tightly the neighborhood had been built around the church, the school, and neighboring (no longer standing) factory.

page 90 Leduc helped Whitman marry: While Whitman was male, white, alienated, and of typical age, his marriage set him apart from the majority of mass killers, who tend to be single. However, despite his repeated and superficial gushing in letters and diary entries about his wife (and praising himself for his lack of cheating), his actual behavior from early on suggests that he was not successful at married life. Repeated periods of physical separation indicate that he was not comfortable with the realities of married partnership, either.

page 91 Leduc's language on the surface: See Leduc FBI statement as well as A.J. Vincik's comments in *The Texas Observer*, 19 August 1966. One can now find many sources now about the proliferation of mid-century "men only," "lad, and "stag" magazines in the U.S. See Magforum http://www.magforum.com/mens/mensmagazinesatoz.htm as well as Stagmags http://www.stagmags.com/. A discussion of men's adventure magazines in the post-WWII milieu can be found here: http://www.artofmanliness.com/2010/05/26/vintage-mens-adventure-magazines/

page 91 expedited the mixed-marriage ceremony See Kay Toy Fenner's *American Catholic Etiquette* (1961), which includes an entire chapter titled "The Mixed Marriage." The chapter lays out the social norms for interfaith marriages and their basis in Catholic teachings and traditions. Charlie's fixation on his parents' wedding anniversary as the date for his own ceremony was later gruesomely referenced when he crushed the fingers of mother's left hand, mutilating her engagement ring the night he killed her, the same night he murdered his wife.

page 92 Whitman and Catholicism: All letters cited here from June through August 1962, along with photographic records and wedding invitation, courtesy of Nelson Leissner. In his last letter dated a few days prior to the wedding ceremony, Whitman wrote to Kathy that she needed to decide whether she would attend mass with him the morning of their marriage. This communication indicates formal attachment to the ritual, and/or a fulfillment of another request from his mother, despite what he also was reportedly assuring his in-laws. Whether he in fact attended mass, and where, is unknown. Fr. Pekar or an assistant would have said daily mass at St. Michael's, but Whitman could have driven into Houston for morning mass with Fr. Leduc as well.

page 94 Leduc's presence at wedding ceremony: I discussed Leduc's presence with Nelson via email and in multiple occasions by phone over an extended period of time; his story did not change. When I asked Schuck about the unknown woman, he at first said he did not recall seeing her, but subsequently offered that it must have been a mutual friend of Charlie and Kathy's, whom Leduc might have picked up for the wedding. Schuck's description of this guest, however, as a blonde woman nearly 6 feet tall and "homespun" looking, did not match with Nelson's description of her as a "vivacious" blonde of average size. A woman who was extremely tall would have been impossible not to notice next to someone as short as Leduc when they stepped from the car. Nelson repeated to me more than once, "I kept thinking: why was she with the priest?" To date, the identity of Leduc's driving companion has not been confirmed. I have also not been able to locate the person named by Schuck to cross-check the perception once and for all.

V. White, Washed Hands

page 95 Leduc's difficulties likely surfaced: See Leduc's FBI statement. The obituaries/funeral notices, which I discovered early on, presented challenges because they included errors and important omissions. *The Palm Beach Post* obituary stated that Leduc in 1950 had entered "Baltimore Minor Seminary," but multiple documents later confirmed that he was enrolled in the major seminary at Roland Park, not the "minor," which was St. Charles College at the time. The *Post* obit also made no reference to Leduc's prior attendance at University of Ottawa starting in 1947. To the untrained eye, the chronology indicated a straightforward move from "minor" to "major" seminary. The *Texas Catholic Herald* obituary included Ottawa as part of a simple transfer chronology, omitting all dates except ordination. The *Herald* also stated that Leduc had been "on sick leave" for more than 11 years—omitting the first five years of regular "leave" as recorded in the *OCD*. By contrast, the *Post* referred to Leduc's "recent illness," suggesting erroneously that Leduc had served actively in Galveston-Houston until just before his death.

page 96 Seminary expectations: The SMSU Catalogs 1951-52 stated clearly that general results of exams were made public, and that a complete grade report was sent to each seminarian's bishop; the seminary rector and the seminarian's home pastor were instructed to communicate under strict seal about the candidates activities, as well as his "habits of life both present and past," inside and outside of school. Sipe discusses seminary practices, church law, and conventions in *Sex, Priests, and Power* (1995) and (with Thomas Doyle and Patrick Wall) in *Sex, Priests, and Secret Codes* (2006). See also David France's *Our Fathers* (2004).

page 97 Precise explanations for "clipping": In 1961, categories of reasons for removal were formally explicated in *Religiosorum Institutio: Instruction on the Careful Selection and Training of Candidates for the State of Perfection and Sacred Orders*—including sexual categories, mental health categories, and inappropriate family or financial pressures: https://www.ewtn.com/library/CURIA/CCL1961R.HTM

page 98 Records of Leduc's name during seminary pathway: Information from emails with the University of Ottawa archivist and SMSU archivists, Sept. 2013. See also *The Voice of St. Mary's Seminary* (Nov. 1950) and SMSU Catalogue 1950-52.

The date of Leduc's enrollment at SMSU in 1950 suggests a possible problem at Ottawa—it would have taken him until 1951 to complete his bachelor's degree. In the beginning, I glossed over this gap, hoping that Leduc had been an advanced and dedicated student. In fact, according to the Ottawa archivist, Leduc's BA degree did not even post in Ottawa until 1952, where he was listed as "étudiants extramuraux" (suggesting possible correspondence/extension work), and still with a Waterbury CT address. How then had Leduc enrolled at SMSU as a first year Theology student without a full undergraduate degree? One can envision here a scenario where he hit a roadblock as a student in Ottawa and attempted to jump the queue, perhaps with the recommendation of a professor or clerical ally—a priest relative?—only to be stopped again when final documentation did not come through. This scenario would be consistent with the trickster element displayed in the patterns of borrowing and defaulting on significant debts over a period of fifteen years from 1961-1975. A trickster path to priesthood, however, would raise more disturbing questions. It reads more like compulsive desire than a rational or spiritual aspiration.

page 98 too-easily approved for seminary transfers: One notable case is that of Pueblo, CO, Bishop Charles Buswell, who ultimately approved candidate Daniel Maio for ordination, despite Buswell's recorded reservations along with documented concerns of the seminary rector and other relevant parties between 1957-1966. Maio was eventually sued in 2010 by two different plaintiffs for sexual abuse that appeared to occur among an "inner circle" of youths who sang at church and camped together in the late 1960s. See Sipe's expert testimony about the case here: http://www.awrsipe.com/Docs_and_Controversy/DECLARATION.pdf. A report about the confidential settlements for both plaintiffs can be found in Jeff Tucker's article here: http://www.chiefads. com (search for "Maio Settlements"). France documents correspondence about the seminary "bumps" in the case of Rev. John Geoghan ("Jolly Johnny") in *Our Fathers*, including a letter from Geoghan's uncle, "a powerful monsignor" who "noticed difficulties" but "blamed the seminary"(p. 24-25).

page 99 Of the five students: According to July 2015 emails from the archivist at SMSU, Martin J. O'Toole had begun his studies in 1948 (at the School of Philosophy on Paca Street). His name is listed as a 1st Theology student at Roland Park the same year Leduc began, in 1950. O'Toole departed November 15, 1951, two days after Leduc left. I was not able to locate him, but it does not appear he was ever ordained. (For those who do check the *OCD,* there is a different Martin J. O'Toole already listed as a priest by 1950.)

page 99 he no longer used the name he had used in Ottawa and in Baltimore: Diocesan priests typically do not change names in their progression to ordination, unlike men and women who join religious orders (Dominicans, Jesuits, Franciscans, etc.). As late as May 25, 1952—approximately four months before his transfer to St. Mary's Houston—Leduc was still using the initials "G.R." A *Palm Beach Post* report about a fundraising spaghetti dinner at Sacred Heart for Troop 119 lists "G.R. Leduc" as a scoutmaster along with Rev. Matthew Morgan, identified as "spiritual advisor." See "Scouts Planning Dinner to Help Buy Equipment." The announcements in 1955 for each of Leduc's first masses in Waterbury and Palm Beach indicate his name as "Joseph G. Leduc" or "J. Gilles Leduc." The "R," at that point, was gone.

page 100 Leduc's first two masses; a Canadian priest

relative: See "Priest to Sing first Solemn High Mass" 5 June 1955 (*Waterbury Republican*), and a week later, "Coastal Deanery Holy Name Rally Scheduled Sunday" (*Palm Beach Post*), which mentions Leduc's first mass at Sacred Heart in Lake Worth. Photograph and records of Real Beauregard from Chancery of Diocese of St. Hyacinthe, via email dated 26 Sept. 2013. Tom Rastrelli describes the "unwritten tradition" of a mentor honoring his protégé by preaching at his first mass—in his own case, it had been a priest who has assaulted him during confession: http://tinyurl.com/p39y3qu. Sipe explores the shock and trauma experienced by seminarians and/or new priests at the hands of "mentors" or clerical superiors at length in *Sex, Priests, and Power* (1995).

page 100 Leduc seemed "threatened" and "uncomfortable": Interview with Jack McGinnis, 1 November 2013. "Joseph" was Leduc's father's first name, according to obituaries and his death certificate. "Joseph" was also a reference to the foster father of Christ—among Catholics, a model of paternal constancy and chastity. It was also Charles Whitman's middle name.

page 101 Twenty-nine years to the exact day; "dog whistle" reference to Catholic doctrine: Rev. Thomas M. Anglim's death date can be seen at Find A Grave: www.findagrave.com/cgi-bin/fg.cgi?page=gr&GRid=55647791. I was unable to secure a full text of Anglim's statements. Excerpts of his comments were published in articles syndicated by UPI (see "Priest Justifies Whitman Rites," *Modesto Bee and News Herald* 5 Aug. 1966) and in Paul L. Lomartire's 40th anniversary article ("Demons and Doom," *Palm Beach Post* 30 July 2006). The most important segment of Anglim's statement makes a direct reference to the three conditions for mortal sin: "Catholic moral theology teaches that no *serious crime* may be imputed to an individual unless he has committed it *with sufficient knowledge* and *full consent of the will*" (emph. added). The press release referenced in the *Palm Beach Post* the day before the funeral stated that Anglim's words had been approved by diocesan officials—presumably, the bishop—and essentially proclaimed that Whitman had been in "a state of grace" when he died. Catholics who had been shamed about eating meat on Friday, missing mass, divorce, pre-marital sex, out-of-wedlock pregnancies (never mind artificial contraception, abortion, and certainly masturbation) would have been understandably confused and appalled. As France puts it succinctly in *Our Fathers*: "Catholic theologians considered self-pleasure to be a mortal sin, pretty near the gravest on the depravity scale—like murderers and blasphemers, the unrepentant masturbator would be denied a place in heaven" (22). Perhaps most vividly, even a priest expressed how fearful "self-abuse" was in comparison to any other sin he could reasonably commit: "I began to wonder if I was *guilty of murder*" (emphasis added, qtd. in Keenan, p. 136). During the hours when he reportedly "holed up" with local priests following his son's murders, Whitman's irreligious but politically savvy and narcissistic father likely negotiated, or demanded, this kind of public pronouncement. Why church officials agreed is another matter. A thoughtful priest could have buried and prayed for Whitman and comforted his family without grandiose commentary about the nature of his acts. One of the most ubiquitous pictures after the shootings shows C.A. Whitman holding a press conference on his front lawn. What's often not seen is the full image, including Rev. Eugene Quinlan (Anglim's assistant at the time), eyes cast down, standing awkwardly behind Whitman as if brought to heel, while his Catholic son Patrick and wife cling to each other, far off to the opposite side—a strange and painful image.

page 101 Msgr. Anglim would be posthumously accused: See *Jimmy Wilkins v. Archdiocese of Miami*, 27 April 2010, as well as Gillespie's article "Diocese Responds to Sexual Abuse Lawsuit." Rev. Anthony Mercieca's 2006 admissions about abuse of Congressman Mark Foley can be found in an article at *Herald-Tribune*: http://www.heraldtribune.com/article/20061019/NEWS/610190725 . Mercieca's assignment record, including his assignment listing from 1965 to 1967 at Sacred Heart in Lake Worth, can be viewed here: http://www.bishop-accountability.org/assign/Mercieca_Anthony.htm. An independent newspaper report confirming Mercieca under supervision of Anglim as early as 1965 can be found at "Altar and Rosary Society" in Works Cited and Consulted. Jon Ombres, one of Foley's childhood friends and fellow altar boys from Sacred Heart, alleged that another cleric fraternized with the boys during this period: "He and Foley would hang out in the apartment of an older Irish priest who let them smoke and drink—until the priest grabbed for his fly." Ombres ran off after this incident, but Foley continued to visit that priest, who remains to date unnamed. See "Priest Admits He Fondled Foley." Southern Florida was inundated with Irish priests during this generation, but the two "Irish" priests at Sacred Heart at the time were Thomas Anglim (until late 1966) and Eugene Quinlan. Both presided at Whitman's funeral and burial.

page 102 Another in Leduc's cohort at Baltimore: Although the allegations against Rev. Bryan O. Walsh were dismissed, one appeal judge expressed vehement dissent in the Third District Court, arguing that the plaintiff should have the opportunity to present his evidence. Original links have been lost, but articles are preserved here: http://www.bishop-accountability.org/news2009/09_10/2009_09_15_Weaver_Dismissal0f.htm. Walsh's photo appeared in the centerfold of *The Saturday Evening Post* in May 1954 (the year Leduc should have been ordained), see Landers' article: http://www.bishop-accountability.org/news5/1994_05_24_Landers_PriestHonored.htm. In *The Voice of St. Mary's* (November 1950), both Anglim (front row, center) and Walsh (very back row, center) stand on the steps in the group photo of SMSU for the Class of 1954. Leduc stands on the step in front of Walsh, three shoulders away.

page 102 The steeple of an old church: Dedicated in 2005, the steeple includes a plaque to honor the service of Rev. Anglim at St. Francis Xavier Church and School in Ft. Myers, Florida, from 1966 to 2004: "This steeple is dedicated in honor of the very Reverend Thomas M. Anglim, beloved and devoted pastor... Fr. Anglim will be forever remembered as a 'good and faithful servant' of our Lord, our Parish, and our people." Photographs are available here: http://www.waymarking.com/waymarks/WM9GWO_St_Francis_Xavier_Church_Steeple_Ft_Myers_FL_USA

page 103 Leduc must have seen Morgan as an ally: Matthew Morgan's name is listed as 4th year Theology Student in the SMSU catalog for 1950-51, and as an Alumni Ordained Priest by the end of that same year. Aside from academic, sexual, spiritual, or temperamental reasons for Leduc's departure, I considered the possibility that he might have disclosed or alleged abuse by another student or religious superior. Accounts in criminal cases as well as Andrew Madden's memoir, *Altar Boy* (2004), provide examples of young men being summarily dismissed from seminary because they confided in senior priests about their sexual abuse at the hands of someone else. Whether Leduc was identified at SMSU as a "problem" for his own behaviors or for implicating someone else, the available evidence suggests that Morgan was some kind of ally at least during that time. For Morgan's role in local scouts and K of C, see "Scouts Planning Dinner" and "50 Initiated by KC Council" in Works Cited and Consulted. For Leduc's mention of Morgan, see his FBI statement.

page 103 Supply and demand: See SMSU Catalogs 1951-52. Also see *OCD*, Dioceses of St. Augustine and Galveston-Houston 1950-1952—diocesan stats appear in a summary at the end of each listing every year.

page 104 necessary for active members of the faith: See James O'Toole's *The Faithful: A History of Catholics in America* (2008) for a comprehensive discussion of the evolving roles of Catholics within their own congregations, American society, and the larger church—from colonial to contemporary times.

page 104 Interviews: with Showfety 18 Sept. 2013 and Riani 9 Sept. 2013.

page 106 I finally located and communicated via email: Briganti was certain that Leduc referred to Florida in this comment, yet it is documented that Leduc had belonged to a club of young students interested in the priesthood between 1945-47 at Assumption Prep, and had been enrolled in seminary before his parents moved to Lake Worth. Was Leduc's story a gratuitous fabrication, fusing memories of a priest from CT or Canada with the later FL location in order to avoid questions about where he had really come from, or had Leduc's desire for ordination simply not taken its fullest shape until his time in FL? Whether he was cynical or honest here, the response is consistent with Leduc's apparent ability to "misdirect" attention, whether by intention or erratic temperament. As I looked for names of priests who served at Sacred Heart in the early 1950s, one name came into focus as a possible model of the "soft" life. In 2006, Fr. John Skehan was accused, along with another priest, of skimming hundreds of thousands of dollars from collection plates over decades: to pay "girlfriends," purchase real estate (even in his native Ireland), gamble, and take vacations. Skehan pled guilty to grand theft and was sentenced to 14 months in prison. Leduc would have encountered Skehan at Sacred Heart when Skehan served there between 1952-54. At thirteen years old, Charles Whitman represented Sacred Heart School and Boy Scout Troop 119 at a sendoff for Skehan at the parish in December 1954 (see "Farewell Fete Given Pastor"). More than thirty years later, in 1982, Rev. Matthew Morgan sold a 16th floor high-rise apartment on Singer Island to Skehan (see Morgan Warranty Deed), and Palm Beach County court records also document that Skehan served as executor for Morgan's estate when he died in 2003.

VI. CATHOLIC CULTURE

page 107 Two basic categories of priesthood: The distinction between "religious" and "secular" priests can be explored easily online—you can start with Catholic Answers: http://www.catholic.com/quickquestions/what-is-the-difference-between-secular-priests-and-religious-priests . During Leduc's generation, there was one exception to the usual division of pastoral labor prior to racial desegregation: religious orders were specifically tasked with ministry at "colored" or "Mexican," parishes within dioceses. Well into the 1960s, Catholic parishes were segregated in the *OCD* listings across the United States; a quick browse can give anyone a good idea.

page 108 Seminary instruction at the time: Interview with Jack McGinnis 1 Nov. 2013.

page 109 The timing of the shootings: Many sources provide a window into Catholic culture and politics during this period: *LIFE Magazine's* cover story, "Pope Paul VI in America," appeared on 15 Oct. 1965. Gallagher's *The Pain and the Privilege* includes an up-close account of priest protests and social action during the mid to late 1960s. By 1968. Priests in locations such as San Antonio and Baltimore were banding together against hard-line bishops about the church's official stance on artificial birth control; their efforts gained media attention and in some cases led to dramatic rifts with church leadership; see "Bishops Reject Request" and "Panel to Probe San Antonio Priest Controversy." One very public case that came later was Rev. Charles Curran, famously fired from Catholic University in 1986. Curran wrote and published *Loyal Dissent: Memoir of a Catholic Theologian* (2006). O'Toole's *The Faithful* provides a good historical overview of American Catholic lay activity before, during, and after Vatican II.

page 110 Even establishment figure Bishop Fulton J. Sheen: Bishop Sheen's radio and television presence is well-preserved: see Thomas C. Reeves's article at Catholic Education Resource Center, http://www.catholiceducation.org/en/culture/media/archbishop-fulton-j-sheen-catholic-media-s-greatest-star.html. Sheen's archived programs are viewable on YouTube, as here, https://www.youtube.com/watch?v=FmMBLTz6Pp8 and programs are also indexed at FultonSheen.com. In 1952, Sheen was awarded an Emmy for "Most Outstanding Television Personality," defeating Edward R. Murrow and Lucille Ball. Sheen's popularity later came under fire by the right when, in July 1967, he called for withdrawal of troops in Vietnam. Cardinal Spellman's rivalry with and "revenge" upon Sheen is explored in Reeves's biography, *America's Bishop: The Life and Times of Fulton J. Sheen*

(2001). The first time I read Whitman's letters from the night of the murders, I recognized an inverted reference to Sheen's "life is worth living" motto: "I truly do not consider this world worth living in." There is a similar moment in one of Whitman's diary entries in 1964. Sheen's upbeat slogan was a phrase (and a program title) Whitman would have heard over and over again as an American Catholic of the period.

page 111 Starting in the Middle Ages: See John Cornwell's *The Dark Box* (2014) as well as Doyle, Sipe, and Wall's *Sex, Priests and Secret Codes* (2006). A thoughtful discussion of the problematic role sacramental confession plays in "externalizing" behaviors and also depersonalizing offenses against other people can be found in Keenan (p. 166-171).

page 112 The Church teaches that it is a grave canonical crime: The text of *Crimen Solicitationis* can be found here at Vatican resources: http://www.vatican.va/resources/resources_crimen-sollicitationis-1962_en.html See also Thomas Doyle's discussion of the subject: "The 1922 and 1962 Instructions: 'Crimen Solicitationis' Promulgated by the Vatican" http://www.awrsipe.com/docs_and_controversy/2010-03-04-solicitation.html

page 114 Even in third person monotone: Austin PD, Texas DPS, and FBI Files, witness interviews.

page 116 The second of two priests Leduc mentioned: Leduc FBI statement; Neyrey's description of Samuel Hill Ray can be found here: http://ourladyoftheoaks.com/wp-content/uploads/2013/10/OurLadyoftheOaksRetreatHouseBiographies.pdf; information about Ray in Anderson's book can be located here: http://tinyurl.com/h8w74mr . It is clear from newspaper coverage in West Palm Beach that, once assigned to St. Ann's,

Ray circulated to deliver many speeches to secular and religious groups. See Works Cited and Consulted for examples.

page 117 He was not keeping a low profile: Most articles I located announced merely the audience and topic of Ray's speeches; one rare article including large excerpts is Garland White's report in the *Palm Beach Post* from May 1958: "Communist Danger Sounded as Kiwanians Mark Birthday." By 1964, after a transfer to Texas, Ray was addressing Republican groups—certainly not keeping a low profile in public.

page 117 the Latin rite at the time: See Campion Children's Missal: *Know Your Mass* (1954): images include instructional drawings depicting each stage of the mass as part of an ascending staircase, where only "the faithful" are permitted to reach the tabernacle at the top—the complete text can be seen here: http://www.ccwatershed.org/media/pdfs/14/06/26/12-34-30_0.pdf. Another powerful artifact of the period is the Knights of the Altar handbook intended for altar boys and steeped in medieval language and imagery, including chalices as well as swords: http://www.sanctamissa.org/en/serving/knights-of-the-altar.pdf At St. Ann's High School, where Whitman attended, the mascots were the Crusaders.

page 118 the primary spiritual duties of the priest: Catholic teaching emphasizes the duty of all the faithful to be Christlike, as suffering servants; see the Catechism: http://www.vatican.va/archive/ccc_css/archive/catechism/p122a4p2.htm. Shaw's insightful discussion about the conflict between clericalism (emphasizing the stature/status and privileges of priests) contrasted with a pastoral role (emphasizing "selfless service") can be found in a 2009 article published in *Our Sunday Visitor*: https://www.osv.com/TheChurch/ChurchStructure/USCCB/Article/

page 118 some of the most powerful images of hands are both violent and sensual: Catholic perspective on the "Song of Songs" can be explored here: http://www.newadvent.org/cathen/03302a.htm. The US Conference of Catholic Bishops has information about reception of Holy Communion here: http://www.usccb.org/prayer-and-worship/the-mass/order-of-mass/liturgy-of-the-eucharist/the-reception-of-holy-communion-at-mass.cfm. Among some traditional Catholics, the practice of communion-in-the-hand remains controversial; the practice was not truly widespread until the late 1970s and early 1980s. The teaching that the sacrament of holy orders can only be received by "a baptized man" is explored in Vatican resources from the current catechism: http://www.vatican.va/archive/ccc_css/archive/catechism/p2s2c3a6.htm

page 119 Witnesses after the shootings: See Austin PD, Texas DPS, and FBI Files for accounts from friends, neighbors, acquaintances, and other figures in Whitman's life

page 120 McGinnis drew parallels: McGinnis also referred me to the Adverse Childhood Experience Study, a collaboration of research between the Center for Disease Control and Kaiser Permanente; you can read about their research here: http://www.cdc.gov/violenceprevention/acestudy/

VII. DRINKING, DRIVING, AND OTHER DEEDS

page 121 Interviews with Felix Scardino 19 May 2015, Jack McGinnis 1 Nov. 2013, and Houston Priest 31 Aug. 2013.

page 124 but then someone who knew both men: Schuck had contacted me on a genealogy website using a different first name and different spelling of a last name I recognized. I was cautious in verifying this party, unsure at first whether this was another writer, perhaps, or a person who'd appropriated Schuck's identity out of some fixation on Whitman's story. In the very first message, without prompting, Schuck independently described visiting Leduc's cabin property with Whitman and friends (information I had not shared with anyone). I informed Schuck that I had tried to locate him and had sent multiple emails nearly a year earlier, with all but one returning to me. Once we began email and phone exchange using our names in late 2014, I was more certain that Schuck was in fact who he said he was. I still thought it was necessary to meet him face-to-face during Jan. 2015.

page 125 Leduc at St. Philip Neri parish: A narrative history of St. Philip Neri can be found here, including correspondence between Apostolic Administrator Louis Morkovsky (later bishop of Galveston-Houston) and the Very Rev. Maurice J. Hymel, Vice-Provincial of the Vincentian order set to take over administration of the parish as it became a "predominantly Negro" church in the diocese: http://www.stphilipnerichurch.org/index.php?option=com_content&view=article&id=50&Itemid=27 Morkovsky refers to Leduc by name as an assistant to one of the Vincentians until an additional priest could be sent: "It will be satisfactory for Father Joseph G. Leduc to remain at SPN as assistant until it is possible for the Vincentian Fathers to send one of their priests. ...I would not like this situation to continue for any longer than one year, and I would much prefer that it be for a shorter period." Leduc had been moved to Philip Neri after only a few months in 1960-61 at St. Pius V in Pasadena where, according to the OCD, Rev. John McCarthy, future Archbishop of Austin, was also assigned; the webpage refers to Rev. Ernest Michalka as "a Vincentian" (abbreviated C.M.), though neither the *OCD* nor the 1972 diocesan yearbook identify him with that religious order.

page 125 During Fall 1961 and Spring 1962: In the research, legal cases, and public media reports about sexual abuse or other dysfunctional priest behavior, activities at a priest's "private home" or "cabin" away from the rectory frequently served as enticements to make targeted victims feel special and other guests feel complicit. Secular culture was exploring the boundaries of sexuality and power in corporate structures, as well: *The Apartment* was released in 1960, a popular film about a salesman who loaned out the keys to his NY apartment to his boss and co-workers for extramarital liaisons.

page 127 Another incident: Schuck sent his memories of the arrest to me as a narrative attached to an email. Leduc's assignment trajectories in and around Houston between 1956 and 1962 would have required a great deal of driving, and trouble on the road seemed like a realistic and probably recurring problem, especially for a heavy drinker. Frank Briganti had shared a story he had heard that Leduc "was a chaplain to Houston Fire and had been seen scooting around Houston with a light flashing atop his car." I never found evidence that Leduc was chaplain to any fire departments, but of "scooting around," there certainly had been plenty. It's reasonable to assume that during this time, before breathalyzers and before drinking and driving was treated as a serious crime, Leduc would have likely received a pass more than once. Until 2001, Texas drivers could still legally drink at the wheel as long as they were not drunk.

page 128 Leduc in "serious" mode? These descriptions track with accounts of how priests were beginning to fraternize more casually with the young in the early 1960s, often outside the parish premises: "The black suit and Roman collar were coming off, and priests were often undistinguishable from the laity in all but their special status...A new spirit of permissiveness had arisen among priests" (Cornwell, *The Black Box* 177). See also Keenan for discussion of troubles arising when priests seemed to treat young people as "friends" and "equals" (235-239).

page 129 Whitman, alcohol, and other self-medication: In an entry from January 1964 in his Memoranda notebook, Whitman meditated on his trouble concentrating and his dislike for the Marines, along with his mixed feelings about drinking: "Lately (in the past 10 days) I have been either tight or drunk 3 or 4 times. I don't like to be like that." The following month, he wrote about drinking Scotch "as casually as [he] could, without giving away [his] distaste for it," because he had been invited to the personal apartment of a Marine officer he admired ("the most stimulating person I have ever conversed with") despite rules discouraging fraternization. The statement of Francis J. Schuck to the FBI in 1966 includes a reference to Whitman using a "bracer" of bourbon during an exam sometime in 1961-62 after drinking due to nerves the night before. In a brief letter to his fiancée on July 5 1962, an admittedly hung-over Whitman expressed concern about his "state of mind" (enough to alarm his fiancée in her subsequent letter) following heavy drinking the day before, on the July Fourth holiday—only a week and a half after his twenty-first birthday, when he had visited with his future in-laws and taken Kathy to meet Father Leduc. Statements made by Richard Owen Clark and Robert Don McCrary, both classmates of Whitman, include information about Whitman's "heavy" use of tranquilizers as well as amphetamines and aspirin to self-medicate during 1965. Clark also explicitly stated that he had asked Whitman about whether he was concerned about possible legal consequences: "[He] was never concerned, he always had a very causal attitude about the drugs."

page 130 Considered altogether: Schuck repeatedly requested that I send him the deed with Leduc's signature, but I did not comply (he had already identified himself as a realtor); early on, he indicated his perception that, by 1964, Leduc had sold the property, suggesting that he didn't know about, or didn't want to talk about, Leduc's financial situation.

page 131 Nearly one year before my contact: "Police Report," *Brazosport Facts* 21 January 1962.

page 132 notorious "pranks": See accounts in *Texas Observer*, "Who Was Charles Whitman?"

page 133 Guns in clerical culture at the time: The only Houston story I located about a priest and a gun ended with murder and arson in 1973—see Muril Hart's "Proving Murder of Priest" in Works Cited and Consulted. Rev. Laumer Schoppe (ord. 1956) of Channelview, TX was murdered by an intruder who also burned down the entire parsonage—reports state that guns and two typewriters (!) were found ditched in a nearby reservoir. The shooter went to prison. Rev. Jesse Linam (ord. 1961) replaced Laumer Schoppe and continued to serve for more than two decades in Channelview before being suspended for sexual abuse. The murdered priest's brother, Charles (ord. 1949), was later suspended for sexual abuse himself. In 1974, to honor Rev. L. Schoppe's memory, a statue of "Jesus and the Little Children" was dedicated at St. Andrews Parish. One haunting photograph shows Bishop Morkovsky standing between Revs. Linam and C. Schoppe—two now-known abusers. See Hart's "Memory of

Pastor's Death Honored in CV." Regarding violence against clergy within this same period: Two months after Laumer's murder, in March, Bishop Morkovsky was assaulted at his home by two robbers. One of the intruders beat Morkovsky severely, causing blindness in one of his eyes. The intruder received an extreme sentence of 45 years in prison—see "Man Sentenced for Robbery." The assault accounted for the reason behind a sober expression one priest had shared with me about diocesan leadership in the early 1970s: "Two bishops, one eye." Wendolin Nold had already lost his sight; and, after the attack, Morkovsky was partially blind. It seems that physical blindness was also an unfortunate metaphor.

page 133 While diocesan priests do not take a vow of poverty: As addressed previously, differences between diocesan ("secular") and religious priests are explained here at Catholic Answers: http://www.catholic.com/quickquestions/what-is-the-difference-between-secular-priests-and-religious-priests

page 135 Liverpool, TX: Information about Liverpool can be found here: https://en.wikipedia.org/wiki/Liverpool,_Texas. A source I consulted at the Alvin Public Library was useful for context about religious groups and the local cemetery: J. W. Moore's *The History of Liverpool, Texas, and Its People* (1996), published by the Liverpool History Book Committee. Since Leduc's deeds do not include street addresses, I consulted with Christian Harder, a friend and expert at ESRI. After repeated examination of the surveys and maps, he figured out the physical location, later confirmed by my own visits as well as a drive to the property with Schuck, who had gone himself on previous occasions.

page 136 Why would "discretion" be necessary? In an email dated 11 Dec. 2014, Schuck wrote, "I believe that GL remained a 'Silent Partner' in all of this. Had he not, there were too many violations of priestly behavior, along with the drinking, plus violations of vows sorta, that would have otherwise made him very vulnerable." I followed up about these "violations of vows sorta" in one in-person interview, asking what he meant: was there blue humor once in a while, a guy who brought *Playboys*, some gambling, maybe some overnight visits with girls? Schuck would not answer the question. The thing is: Whitman and his friends couldn't violate any priestly vows; they hadn't taken any. What Leduc (or any other ordained person) was doing or might have facilitated in this location, however, would have been his responsibility.

page 136 Leduc went a step further: J.G. Leduc Promissory note; A. Guy Crouch II was a prominent and well-connected figure in the Brazoria County area, as documented by newspaper articles between 1955 and 1965: he was a leader in Brazoria as well as Alvin Boy Scouts; he represented Alvin/Brazoria County in the Democratic Party as a delegate in the state convention; he served as chairman for the Brazoria County Tuberculosis Association and was a director for the Brazos River Authority Board; he owned (and eventually sold off) shares in *The Alvin Sun*; he served on the board of the First National Bank of Alvin and was later a director for the First Savings and Loan of Alvin; in 1959, he was the court appointed defender for an Alvin man in a sensational rape/fondling case (1959). His son, A. Guy Crouch III, decades later landed in trouble with the federal government for questionable financial dealings—A. Guy Crouch II was named as a possible witness in the case: see *US v. A. Guy Crouch III and Michael J. Frye* (1995): https://scholar.google.com/scholar_case?case=11567218548707866372&hl=en&as_sdt=6&as_vis=1&oi=scholarr

page 136 Seminary tuition at the time: The SMSU Catalog in 1952 lists student expenses ("for Board, Tuition, and Doctors' Fees") as $750 per year—approximately $6,739 in today's dollars. I found no record of the cost for study at SMH, but would estimate it to be slightly less expensive because it was at the time a much smaller institution.

VIII. LEAVE NO TRACE

page 139 Sam Houston Area Council scout history: Emails with historian Nelson Block, Jan. 2014. Interview with historian Marvin Smith, 20 Jan. 2014. Information about Order of the Arrow in Sam Houston Area Council can be found here: http://oa.samhoustonbsa.org/about-us

page 141 the height of his activity as regional chaplain: An article in the *Baytown Sun*, "Comaux [sic] Boys Will Receive Awards at Sunday Service," placed Leduc at St. Pius Catholic Church for a Catholic scouting event as "Catholic area chaplain" in Pasadena in February 1960. The National Boy Scout Jamboree in Colorado Springs took place that summer. Other articles name Leduc as a leader at Catholic scout events as late as February 1963 in Baytown, even while he was assigned by this time to St. Philip Neri in south Houston.

page 140 Leduc's Vigil Honor is significant: The Vigil Database for the Colonneh Lodge/Order of the Arrow of the Sam Houston Area Council can be found here: http://oa.samhoustonbsa.org/vigil-honor-database. Marvin Smith, a recognized figure in Catholic scouting in the area, was awarded the St. George Emblem in 1968, one year before Leduc received it. Like Msgr. Brady, Smith also eventually received the ultimate scouting recognition, the Silver St. George Emblem, in 1997-98.

page 143 But the only clue: The following year, in 1970, the recipient of the St. George Emblem was the Most Rev. J. Morkovsky, then coadjutor and apostolic administrator of the diocese of Galveston-Houston, and the named successor to Bishop Wendolin Nold. From 1959 to 2014, out of nearly two hundred awards, only fourteen priests are named recipients. For a gap of nineteen years, from 1974-1993, no priests at all are listed. Recipients from 1994 onward include significant figures in local diocesan leadership: Joseph Fiorenza (1994), Frank Rossi (1999), Vincent Rizzotto (2004), and Cardinal Daniel DiNardo (2009). You can see the complete list here: http://www.dccs-dgh. org/st-george-emblem.html The St. George was not an award handed out to just anyone.

page 144 The summer of that year: FBI letter and attachments regarding Whitman's employment and addresses, dated 3 August 1966. See Texas DPS Files, John Morgan statement regarding his friends' marriage during summer 1965. Details of Leduc's official military assignments are included in USAF Chronological Listing of Service record for Joseph G. Leduc. The August 3 FBI letter also documents that Whitman's dates as an engineering aide at NASA began July 6 and ended September 16, 1965. However, in a June 13 letter to his in-laws and already using a League City, TX return address, Whitman advised that he would be taking classes four days a week at Alvin Community College (ACC) from June 13 through July 16, starting nearly a month before his internship began. My records inquiry with ACC via email confirmed that Whitman indeed registered that summer.

page 145 In an extensive interview dated July that year:

See transcript of John E. Groh's 1976 interview with Deputy Chief of Chaplains, Brigadier General Thomas M. Groome, Jr.

page 147 Whitman's father lobbied heavily: FBI files recorded that Whitman's father, as a member of the Palm Beach County Democratic Executive Committee, solicited assistance from attorney and then-chairman of the committee, Alvin B. Zalla, who wrote to then-Senator Spessard Holland to plead Charlie's case. There are also letters recorded from Representative Paul G. Rogers to the Under Secretary of the Navy. Likely taking direction from his well-placed advocates, Charlie reportedly made a personal appeal in his letter to the Under Secretary of the Navy on July 13, 1964 (a document not available). Even after his "honorable discharge" and early release, Whitman typed a letter to his father in 1964 (copied for his wife) complaining that the date didn't seem soon enough. The pattern shows how Whitman expressed entitlement not only when it came to absolution but also to reward: after brushing with trouble and getting a reprieve, Whitman simply made more demands—something he likely observed in other male role models.

page 147 The record also indicates lax supervision: See "Rev. J.C. LeDuc Will Be Serra Speaker Monday." See Leduc USAF assignment record. According to the *OCD,* Rev. Drouilhet served as Director of Catholic Scouting from 1956-1966.

page 147 Leduc's commission was much different: Early on, I wondered whether Leduc might have been inspired by one maternal cousin (deceased in 2012) who served in the Army's 101st Airborne Division (a.k.a. the Screaming Eagles), though I could not confirm whether that cousin had enlisted or been drafted by 1964. No facts to date suggest that Leduc would be inclined to such a grand gesture of solidarity. Leduc's family members mentioned no such thing; when I asked whether he had seen combat, both his cousin and her husband said unequivocally "no."

page 148 What did Whitman think of Vietnam? See the 1992 account of Fuess's discussion with Whitman about Vietnam and other topics (including fingernail biting and purchasing land on the shores of Canyon Lake) on p. 51 of Time/Life *Mass Murderers*; Fuess later maintained that he didn't recall deep discussions about Vietnam on this or any occasions (see Lavergne, *Sniper in the Tower*, p. 94).

page 148 One of the most notorious cases Alaska: Sipe's observations in the Dallas case of Rev. Robert Peebles can be accessed here: http://www.awrsipe.com/reports/sipe_report. htm#FR.%20ROBERT%20R.%20PEEBLES,%20JR. An AP report by Matt Kelley about the church's problems with scandal in the military can be found here: http://www.deseretnews.com/article/515038186/ Catholic-scandal-expanding-in-military.html?pg=all

page 149 Priests in Alaska: The first official listings of any kind for the new Diocese of Anchorage appear in the *OCD* 1966 and 1967. The 2006 settlement in the case of Frank Murphy, alleging abuse back in the 1960s, totaled $1.4 million: see O'Malley's article, http://www.bishop-accountability. org/news2006/07_08/2006_08_04_OMalley_14Million.htm. The Anchorage diocese helped cover settlements by selling off property in 2006: http://juneauempire.com/stories/092806/ sta_20060928012.shtml#.VqASn_EupiU

page 150 Leduc's statement and content of military experience: Leduc FBI Statement and Joseph Leduc USAF records. The historic SDN number code directory and related lawsuit information can be found in this document, a plaintiff's exhibit from

AF Manual 300-4: http://www.apfn.org/pdf/AF-Manual-300-4. pdf. Leduc's code can be found under Section IV titled "Release from Extended Active Duty—Voluntary."

page 151 Contacts with Ordinariate and NY Archdiocese: Emails in March 2014

page 152 Contacts with Elmendorf historian: Emails with Joe Orr exchanged from November 2013 to February 2014

page 153 Former Elmendorf chaplains: Interview with William Rhett, 15 Jan. 2014. I eventually sent a large copy of a photograph via snail mail and Rhett reported that he did not recognize Leduc's face. Interview with Rabbi Azriel Fellner, 16 Dec. 2013

IX. A PRIEST IN THE GAPS

page 156 Professor's recollections of Whitman: See Bill Kimmey's article, "UA Professor Recalls Whitman as Student with Many Problems," published in *Tucson Daily Citizen* 5 Aug. 1966.

page 157 One of the darkest gaps: Charles Whitman Letter July 31, 1966, begun at 6:45 PM

page 159 The lapsed Catholic was making a transparent effort: The problems with this "strategy" are multiple when considered within framework of Catholic teaching on mortal sin and sacramental reconciliation in grave circumstances: http:// www.vatican.va/archive/ccc_css/archive/catechism/p3s1c1a8. htm. Sins cannot be confessed and absolved "in advance" of commission ("I've decided to rob a bank.... I'm going to kill my father"), and they must be articulated in person to a priest. In addition, Whitman's letters along with the sequence of crimes themselves reflect a high degree of consciousness and attention to planning, suggesting knowledge of stakes, seriousness, and "consent of the will." Furthermore, Whitman commits one murder, then another, and then a mass of murders across a twelve-hour period—not counting the number of days (at least two) during which he had indulged the intention of murder—indicating zero "purpose of amendment." See Keenan, however, for the discussion of "legalistic-orthodox" tendencies in Catholic moral instruction at the time, an approach that on many levels fostered rationalization, undermined empathy, and "defined morality that was devoid of internal and critical reflection and engagement [and was also] marked by the absence of a relational ethic" (p. 169).

page 160 a version of the lavabo he witnessed at mass: Fr. Demetrius Manousos's text for *Know Your Mass* (1954) includes the English translation for the priest's prayers during the washing of hands in the Tridentine ritual: "I will wash my hands among the innocent, and I will walk around thy altar, O God, to hear the voice of thy praise and to tell all thy wondrous deeds. O Lord, I love the beauty of thy house, and the place where thy glory dwells. Destroy not my soul with the impious, O God, nor my life with men of blood…But as for me, I will walk in my innocence" (42). This ritual occurs immediately after the offering of bread and wine, and as a prelude to the "high point" or center of the liturgical ritual, the consecration on the altar that re-enacts Christ's sacrifice.

page 160 Call from his mother Margaret: Descriptions from the Lake Worth Police Department included in the FBI files indicate a dismissive and laissez-faire attitude on the part of law enforcement towards the March 1966 incident(s)—certainly not surprising for the time, especially within the context of a marriage where this was not the first occasion of trouble. On the evening of March 2, anonymous caller #68342 "stated that the people at [the Whitmans' address] were going to kill each other," but the report also states that two officers "report all quiet on their arrival and all quiet when they left," not indicating investigation or questions about parties' safety. Charles Whitman himself made a long distance phone call a few hours later to police, referring to the earlier caller and saying that he was en route to pick up his mother. The record also includes a notation that Margaret called for police to come to her home on March 4 "while she removed her personal effects." According to the report, the officers "stood by for one hour and fifteen minutes [while] complainant and husband were arguing, *giving each other all kinds of trouble* for the entire time, *all nonsense*" (emphasis added).

page 160 Whitman was still a struggling college student: According to a written statement from UT during the investigation, Whitman had an "uneven" record prior to 1966, but had maintained a "B" average and a course load of 19 units in Spring 1966. Transcripts also substantiate this record. By summer, Whitman would take on a "heavy load" of 14 hours.

page 161 Whitman made a single visit: See report of M. D. Heatly, MD, 29 March 1966

page 161 An odd incident around this time: see Lavergne p. 68. There is a minor disagreement about whether this was Debussy's or Beethoven's version.

page 161 Also that spring: For an account of Whitman's seemingly frantic and abrupt resolve in spring 1966 to quit school (again?), leave his wife, and "become a bum" see Time/Life *Mass*

Murderers p. 49. See also Lavergne p. 69. One statement from a classmate in the FBI files noted that Whitman volunteered an odd comment that spring, apropos of nothing in particular: "Something like 'I wonder what would happen if I left Kathy and school and went to Japan and got my black belt in Karati [sic].' "

page 162 Catholic teaching about divorce: A classmate of Leduc's, Rev. William Pickard, wrote a dissertation titled *Judicial Experts: A Source of Evidence in Ecclesiastical Trials*—his sponsoring bishop at the time, Wendolin Nold, offered the imprimatur and received formal acknowledgement by Pickard in his foreword. The text explores all manner of ritual and law about how to verify lack of consummation and/or impotence when alleged for annulment purposes. Casual conversations often equate "annulment" with "divorce" when they are not interchangeable terms. Many Catholics who seek divorce reject annulment because it puts them in a position to deny the validity of marital histories that may include children. Some reforms of the Church's position on divorce and annulment have been discussed under Pope Francis: http://www.catholic.com/blog/jimmy-akin/pope-francis-reforms-annulment-process-9-things-to-know-and-share; Francis's *Amoris Laetitia*, released in April 2016, calls for more understanding of divorced Catholics but does not yet reverse church teaching on the sacrament of marriage or communion for divorced Catholics who have remarried; see Yadley and Goodstein in the *New York Times* http://www.nytimes.com/2016/04/09/world/europe/pope-francis-amoris-laetitia.html as well as Damian Thompson's realistic analysis in *The Spectator* http://www.spectator.co.uk/2016/04/the-battle-of-pope-franciss-footnote/

page 163 Whitman's father faced no such dilemma: FBI files suggest a broken engagement and indicate a new marriage for CA Whitman by November 1966. An account of his second wife's desire for divorce in 1967 can be perused in "Whitman's Wife Cites 'Remorse' in Support Suit." CA Whitman married again the following year. First-hand descriptions of violence in both marriages—as well as his abuse of Margaret—can be found in Lomartire's article, "Demons and Doom."

page 163 Margaret sought her own lawyer: Returning home to secure her own attorney was a big deal. Margaret had lived a long time within a circle of her husband's male alliances—including doctors and lawyers. Alvin B. Zalla, her husband's long-time friend and lawyer, had played a central role in lobbying for Charlie's "honorable" discharge and early release from the USMC after his court martial. Even the "family physician" reported calling both Charlie and Margaret in May 1966 to urge her to return to Florida, all at the request of Charlie's father.

page 164 Leduc's relationship to his own bride: Traditional teachings about the church as "bride of Christ" can be found at these Vatican resources: http://www.vatican.va/archive/ccc_css/archive/catechism/p123a9p2.htm; a priest's reflections on his role as "groom" are offered by Msgr. Andrew R. Baker: http://www.cuf.org/2003/05/here-comes-the-groom-the-priest-as-the-bridegroom-of-the-church/ See also *Living the Celibate Life* for Sipe's discussion of how theologians have equated priestly celibacy with the "marriage bond," to frightening effect (43-45).

page 164 Whitman's counseling visit: Psychiatrist form filled out by Charles Whitman, 29 March 1966

page 165 Johnnie had gotten into trouble: FBI files, statement from a source dated August 3, 1966, about Johnnie Mike's refusal of a judge's offer to return home to his father in exchange for suspension of a fine for possession of alcohol; the same source stated that Johnnie Mike had "come to the attention of the [police] department as a window peeper and also came to his personal attention when a local doctor had ordered John off his premises and to stay away from his daughter"; other sources, including Kathy's brother Nelson, recall Patrick and his wife taking up temporary residence in Austin during spring 1966.

page 165 Whitman's acute distress: See Maurice Heatly's report 29 March 1966. In July 1966, Whitman himself re-printed a poem he had originally composed when on duty in 1964, suggesting a reprise of distress he was keeping below the surface. While not profound in literary terms, as an artifact, it speaks to the blatant circumstances of anxiety: "To maintain sensibility is the greatest effort required./To slip would be so easy.../To burden others with your problems—are they problems?—is not right./However, to carry them is akin to *carrying a fused bomb./I wonder if the fuse can be doused*" (Austin PD files, emph. added). One element rarely mentioned about Whitman is that, while he was bent on destruction of others, his own death was clearly an ultimate goal.

page 166 the purchase of a book: *Love Without Fear*, Eustace Chesser, p. 110 and 79. All letters cited here courtesy of Nelson Leissner. See also *Diary of CJ Whitman*, Feb. through March 1964. Keenan's discussion of how priests' training about sexuality impacted the laity by passing on a "rule book" mentality: "[Priests] understood sexual sin as direct offense against God but not as a direct offense against a person...." Two of the worst results could be an inability to "engage with moral behavior in specific terms, in specific situations, regardless of what the apparent rules seemed to suggest or omit," as well as "thinking of bodies more than people" (p. 166-169).

page 167 his psychological and sexual questions: For reflection on how lay Catholics have been often confused and damaged by an over-emphasis on sexual purity, see Eugene Kennedy's *The Unhealed Wound* (2001). In the context of clergy abuse, Marie Keenan has extensively studied the troubling difference between a "purity ethic" and a "relational ethic" in Catholic moral teaching and practice (see *Child Sexual Abuse & the Catholic Church: Gender, Power, and Organizational Culture*, 2012). To glimpse how a blend of high-minded theology, medieval tropes, and venereal preoccupations were handed down by priests and teachers to mid-century Catholic young people, see Tihamer Toth's *Youth and Chastity* (1934): "Should anyone use this physical organ in any other way, either himself alone or with others, for gaining pleasure and delight, he would commit a grievous sin against himself and against society as a whole, against human nature, and against the Holy Will of his Creator...'Why did God so ordain?' someone may further ask. 'Why,' might be the answer, 'God is the Supreme Lord...'" (20).

page 167 Whitman's correspondence: The primary documents discussed here are contained in the private archive of Nelson Leissner. In multiple conversations between 2015-2016, Nelson shared with me his vivid impression that Whitman downplayed his Catholic identity to appease Kathy's Methodist family. The difference between Whitman's language and voice when compared with Kathy's in the pre-marriage letters is a vivid contrast in maturity and social intelligence, a subject I have explored at length in the anthology, *Wives: Roles, Representations, Identities, Work* (Demeter Press).

page 168 Marriage did not make Whitman a good partner: For a more comprehensive and first-time analysis of Whitman's attitudes about women and sexuality as expressed in his diaries and letters, see my essay in *American Studies Journal,* "Invisible Women, Fairy Tale Death: How Stories of Public Murder Minimize Terror at Home" `http://www.asjournal.org/62-2017/` `invisible-women-fairy-tale-death-stories-public-murder-` `minimize-terror-home/`. In 2016, fifty years after Kathy's murder, I was granted permission to study primary sources that provided powerful new insight into Kathy's experience and her perceptions of Whitman's attitudes and abuse. See *Listening to Kathy* as well as "But What Would *She* Say? Reframing 'Domestic Terror' in the 1966 UT Austin Shooting."

page 169 After the murders: See "Who Was Charles Whitman?" in *Texas Observer,* 19 August 1966.

page 169 Some have dismissed the account: See Gary Lavergne, *Sniper in the Tower,* p. 251. Pornography to be shown or sold to minors would be shocking and seedy enough, but that didn't mean that the images necessarily depicted kids. The original *Texas Observer* article did not report that the photos included children. See "Who Was Charles Whitman?" The article does emphasize, however, how Whitman spoke of the pictures: "He was very technical about it…as a pure business venture—no sentiment whatsoever." Whitman displayed a similar "flat affect" in his writings the night he committed the first two murders. Whitman's final violent acts and his matter-of-fact descriptions of these acts in letters ultimately reflect an unsurprising compartmentalization and lack of empathy fostered by the "rule book morality" of Catholic training in the era (see Keenan 169), coupled with the contradictory messages growing up in his family system. As far as the timing and/or temporary nature of Whitman's possible interest in pornography as a Catholic college adolescent, Richard Sipe's observations can be helpful: "For the average priest or the average religious layperson, pornography is not the subject of prolonged or undue interest. The most apt similarity to the interested priest is the adolescent—curious and afraid of sex, relatively inexperienced, yet eager to learn about it and not quite certain of *an avenue that is both safe and acceptable to his conscience*" (*A Secret World*, p. 200, emphasis added). In this context, quick marriage after one year of college would have appeared to provide a legitimate "avenue" for sexual expression. Andrew Greeley reflects on the connection between "impersonalism" and "false spirituality" in his analysis of the way chastity was taught to seminarians (qtd. in Sipe SW, p. 54)—an approach that certainly would have trickled down in formal "lessons" and informal messages about sexual morality in Whitman's Catholic upbringing and contact with clergy. Explicit sexual fixations already discussed, along with flares of moral indignation and repetitive "god bless you"'s in Whitman's letters and diaries, all express the ethos to which Greeley refers. I would argue that this ethos—not a simple "yes" or "no" about pornography—was a significant root of Whitman's warped thinking about himself and other people. This distortion clearly had sexual and emotional consequences. In a letter to Whitman from August 1963, his wife expressed that she had at times felt "used" by him sexually. For more exploration about the impact of Catholic sexual teaching on personal development, see Eugene Kennedy's *The Unhealed Wound* (2001). In the context of sexual abuse survivors, Frawley-O'Dea examines how dissociation is frequently experienced and expressed (p. 23-36).

page 168 When Whitman wrote about Kathy: The entry cited here is from 23 Feb. 1964 in Whitman's *Daily Record*. It is also the diary entry he returned to and wrote notes upon ("I still mean it 8-1-66") his last hours alive, after he abandoned her stabbed body in their bedroom, early in the morning before the massacre. I examine this text at length in "Invisible Women: Fairy Tale Death" in *American Studies Journal.*

page 170 In his journals: See Whitman's journal entries about Kathy's role, temperament, and physical attributes in Feb. 1964. Most often cited is the entry from 23 Feb., which he later scrawled notes upon the night after he had killed her—including the contextually bizarre imprimatur he added at the end: "My wife was a true person." An earlier entry from a previous notebook dated Jan. 22, described his frustration that Kathy was not meeting his expectations during their separation: "I put myself out of the way to do things for her…but it doesn't seem to be a 2-way process." The irony of his own circumstances at the time, and the consequences of his court martial (a brig sentence plus hard labor and a demotion from Corporal to Private), seemed to escape him entirely.

page 170 The post-WWII milieu: Russ Meyer's filmography can be found at IMDB http://www.imdb.com/name/nm0000540/. The stripper and adult model from Texas, Candy Barr, was well-known in the mid-twentieth century, appearing in one of the first "underground" pornographic films, *Smart Alec* (1951), at the age of sixteen. Bettie Page's popularity and influence extended far beyond her relatively short pinup career in the 1950s http://www.imdb.com/name/nm0656114/bio. Cheesecake in calendars and ads thrived during the fifties and sixties: http://www.express.co.uk/life-style/style/473044/Pin-up-queens-The-real-women-behind-Gil-Elvgren-cheesecake-paintings. David Allyn's *Make Love, Not War: The Sexual Revolution: An Unfettered History*, underscores the false "innocence" of the 1950s, documenting many examples of printed material and films at the time, along with the relatively easy access to highly explicit material for kids—often following the examples of male mentors. Allyn notes one extreme example: a stag party in Washington, DC where "197 boys, ages eleven to seventeen, gathered to watch erotic films (the party was organized by a father of one of the boys)." These and lesser activities were a more explicit extension of "satiric" but misogynistic messages in the 1930s, such as Jack Hanley's *Let's Make Mary: A Gentleman's Guide to Seduction in 8 Easy Lessons,* which leads with a preface from Ogden Nash: "Seduction is for sissies; a he-man wants his rape." For current analysis of how male social activities have shaped and reinforced degrading and violent attitudes towards women through rituals of drinking and pornography, see Walter S. Dekeseredy's essay in sources.

page 171 he can easily indulge and be appalled by sexual material: In an entry of *The Diary* on March 6, 1964, Whitman writes how his employer ("a Jewish-type hustler") called him a "hustler" and said he couldn't understand why Whitman didn't "fuck all the whores in town." Whitman goes on at length about how he thinks his love for Kathy would "set some kind of record," and that other men's surprise at his faithfulness to her "makes [him] feel good and superior," reflecting on "how little sex with some whore means to me since I have matured." One of the final—and longest—entries dated March 13 includes his account of "a little blonde girl with a Polaroid camera" who approached him at the Jazzland nightclub. Whitman indulges her flirtation in an extended and detailed description, including how she asked him to be "her secret lover." He states that his wife would have been "proud" that he rebuffed her: "Now I only notice other women to compare them with [Kathy]...When the girl in J-Land touched my stomach I removed her hand and felt as though she definitely had done something she shouldn't have done. *It disgusts me* to be touched by anyone but Kathy. *I never realized before now* how much I could be repulsed by something similar to that" (emphasis added). Importantly, this entry came more than a week following a letter from his wife dated Feb. 23, where she expressed some understandable jealousy in response to his apparent accounts of "propositions" from women who had flirted with him. She also enclosed an article titled "Sexual Communication." During their pre-marital letters in June 1962, Whitman referred to his own Polaroid camera. One letter during between July 1963 and December 1964 mentions a mutual female friend getting stopped at the Mexican border "after a weekend with a boy" because she was carrying "dexidrene" [sic] and "obscene pictures." For context on Polaroids, see "Before Sexting, There was Polaroid" in *Atlantic*—1 Oct. 2012: http://www.theatlantic.com/technology/archive/2012/10/before-sexting-there-was-polaroid/263082/

page 172 In a police interview after the shootings: See Austin PD files, interview with John Morgan, who was a next-door neighbor and college classmate. The FBI files contain the family doctor's statement about Whitman's father joking about his son's sex life after Kathy's operation for an ovarian cyst. Regarding Whitman's ugly connection of sex and economics in the marriage of his parents in the letter he left on his mother's body, it's worth noting that Whitman's "business" of capitalizing on others' debt while in the military has interesting religious associations: "debt" is associated with sin and "payment" with forgiveness/redemption. The power/ability of "forgiveness" was an important theme in his conversations with A.J. Vincik (see "Who Was Charles Whitman?") as well as a central problem described in a letter from Whitman's mother-in-law in January 1963, where problems of his younger brother, Patrick, were at issue. The idea of morality measured on a scale also evokes Catholic categories of sin (which ones have more "gravity"?), as well as the "exchange" of confession for penance and absolution. Whitman had learned that threats of physical violence could render any exchange moot, enabling the debtor to walk way free and clear without making anyone whole: At one point during a high-stakes poker game at his dorm in 1961-62, Whitman turned a gun on a "local gangster" who confronted him about his bad checks; see Nick Kralj's interview at *Out of the Blue: A Texas Standard Documentary*: http://towerhistory.org/profiles/nick-kralj/ Clearly, when it came to dispensing forgiveness, Whitman claimed the arbitrary power to withhold it from others—but again and again, he expressed entitlement to claim it for himself. This mirrors the clerical culture of the time, which claimed absolute privileges without accountability (see Frawley-O'Dea's discussion of clerical narcissism p. 151-169). Even Kathy's mother, Frances Leissner, referred to Whitman's harsh attitudes about forgiveness in a letter from Jan. 1963

page 173 Whitman had such acute anxiety: FBI files: medical record from Lake Worth, Florida, lists all treatments from family physician from July 27, 1957 through September 1, 1964, and the 1961 Librium prescription is included here. There are abundant indications of "high risk" and erratic behaviors during the 1961-1963 window, and any experimentation with pornography would have not contradicted the pattern. Leduc mentioned in his FBI statement the regional publicity of Whitman's deer poaching incident (which he represented as "a prank") in November 1961, and the Austin History Center archive includes two article clippings from 1961 in the papers of Grover Simpson, a Texas game warden. A County Clerk record in the police files shows a record of Whitman's fine for "unlawful possession of a deer" on 20 November 1961, followed by Whitman's brash motion for a new trial filed 28 November (a motion simply dismissed). One vivid account describes Whitman in the driver's seat of his car with Kathy and another friend, making "pejorative remarks" at a black pedestrian and pointing a pistol at him (see Lavergne, p. 23). Kathy's brother Nelson recounted to me an occasion when he witnessed Whitman display road rage in the car and raise his hand as if to strike Kathy when she urged him to calm down, later saying he was sorry and didn't mean it. Newly-available letters underscore that Whitman was accident-prone in the car when carrying passengers, including his wife: Whitman's mother reported to his in-laws about a car accident en route back to Texas post-honeymoon; a letter from Kathy to her parents indicated an accident en route to Camp Lejeune; she also makes reference to his Jeep accident in Cuba—where Whitman walked away with no injury while the passenger suffered severe internal injuries. Other accounts of Whitman's reckless and aggressive behaviors related to money, gambling, and local gangsters are well synthesized in Lavergne (pp. 16-35) as well as in "Who Was Charles Whitman?" in the *Texas Observer*. Nick Kralj, in a brief interview for a documentary project at *The Texas Standard*, said that he distanced himself from Whitman in 1961-62 once he realized "Whitman was a guy out looking for trouble, and he ran into some guys that trouble was their business."

page 173 Johnnie Mike's troubles in Florida: In the FBI files, one interviewee in Lake Worth stated that Charlie's youngest brother, Johnnie Mike, seemed to have the most obvious and public problems: he had thrown a rock through a large plate glass window "to get back at his father for something." He moved out of the house in early 1966 and was subsequently fined for "possession of an alcoholic beverage," but when the judge offered to suspend the fine if John returned home, John refused. One witness statement reported that he had landed on local police's radar "as a window peeper," and was ordered by a local doctor to get off his premises and "stay away from his daughter."

page 173 Mothers, virgins, temptresses, or martyrs: For analysis and context about the problematic "role" or "placement" of women in Catholic theology and tradition, see Frawley-O'Dea, p.67-72. Particularly applicable to Whitman's written expressions about his first two victims, women he repeatedly claimed to love, are the following insights: "Idealization is a form of objectification and oppression. The idealized person becomes an object, not a subject, and is not free to move out of the positions that render her able to be idealized" (70). In this way, "women (and by extension, children) ...are rendered unable to say *no* to abuse and oppression" (71).

page 174 In a newly-discovered letter: I was first informed that this letter existed during a phone interview with Nelson Leissner; he subsequently allowed me to read the document when I met him in person. Several months later, he granted me permission to write about its contents. A much more complete discussion of this artifact was published by *American Studies Journal* in 2017; see my essay titled, "Invisible Women, Fairy Tale Death: How Stories of Public Murder Minimize Terror at Home."

X. IF YOU LEAVE—OR DON'T

page 175 Different types of mobility: Doyle, Sipe, and Wall discuss layers of church law regarding canonical penalties for sexual misconduct *in Sex, Priests and Secret Codes* (2006). How "leaves" versus "suspensions" are determined or recorded presents difficulties for parishioners, who do not consistently get explanations about the reasons for a priest's sudden or long-term absence.

page 176 I told you I was sick: I found the gravestone online and then visited the grave in person. He was borrowing the phrase, sure, but it's definitely there on Gagne's stone.

page 176 One priest on leave starting in 1971: When I asked Schuck if he knew of any priests Leduc actually liked, Schuck described someone whom Leduc "grew up with, who was here in Houston." When I subsequently mentioned Gagne, Schuck said he recognized the name, but he also said that he had never seen this friend in person. I was never able to get an independent confirmation of the association between Gagne and Leduc. My hypothesis is that they did know each other, and that Gagne in the early 1970s decided to, or needed to, break off the connection. See also OCD listings of leave for Diocese of Galveston-Houston, 1970-1982.

page 176 Gagne had come to St. Mary's around 1953: Email exchanges with Jeffrey Meadows, Jan-July 2015.

page 177 Leduc returned from Alaska: Leduc's Florida obituary lists his membership in the Veterans of Foreign War—a designation that could only have been earned through assignments that could give him "overseas" credit. An Air Force historian with whom I communicated doubted that assignment in Alaska at that date would have counted; according to him, only remote islands in AK would have earned this designation. Leduc's official service record does show a change in his assignment code to "information officer" on the same date the FBI decided via correspondence to locate him for interview, but there is no adjustment in base assignment location on the record. There are three possibilities: Leduc's AK assignment did qualify him for credit "off mainland;" the obituary contained yet another inaccuracy; or Leduc had been able to "pass" as a member of the VFW in social circles after returning to Florida, without much scrutiny. The latter two seem the most plausible given the rest of Leduc's story.

page 177 one significant step to get his affairs in order: Joseph G. Leduc, Last Will and Testament from Leduc Probate File; the Will also included a desire to be buried in Arlington Cemetery if he was still in active or reserve service at the time of death; city directories and the US Dept. of Veterans Affairs BIRLS files show that Charles F. Ashy lived from 1921 to 1993. An Army veteran of WWII, Ashy's last known address was in Pearland, TX; during the 1950s, he worked as a linotype operator in Houston; his widow did not respond to contact. Leduc also refers to Rev. Ralph Diefenbach in his will, a priest who bequeathed Leduc his mass field kit. Diefenbach was well-known in Galveston-Houston as a WWII veteran who had served under General Patton; he was also legendary locally in 1952 for racing into a church fire to rescue the blessed sacrament and for chasing after car thieves: see "Priests Recover Stolen Car, Capture Two Suspected Youths" and "Priest Risks Life to Rescue Holy Sacrament." Diefenbach died suddenly in 1959 along with three other people (laypeople) when he crashed his Cessna 170 shortly after takeoff in a field south of Houston.

page 178 Leduc as parish administrator: See *Texas Catholic Herald* 24 Jan. 1969. According to *The National Catholic Reporter* in 2011, an increasing number of "parish administrators" are now laypeople: http://ncronline.org/news/catholics-america/how-parish-life-has-changed. Differences between duties of "pastor," "administrator," and "parochial vicar" are discussed at Catholic Education Resource Center http://www.

page 178 Assumption parishioners: Phone interviews during a visit to Houston, July 2013

page 178 The longtime pastor at Assumption: The *OCD* in 1961 shows that when Perusina was pastor at St. Pius X in Beaumont, he had supervised Rev. Charles K. Schoppe, who was later forced to retire (in 1992) after the diocese confirmed his sexual abuse of one child in the early 1960s. Three other adults came forward in 2002, the year Archbishop Fiorenza informed Schoppe that he could no longer present himself as a priest See Ackerman and Dooley's article from 2002: http://www.bishop-accountability.org/news3/2002_06_23_Ackerman_RetiredPriest_Charles_Schoppe_1.htm

page 179 The Houston Knights of Columbus sued: See *Daily Court Review* 26 May 1970 and Original Petition from Houston KC. A memorial essay about the prosecutor, George F. Luquette, known mostly for his work as a defense attorney, can be found in a cover profile in *Voice of the Defense* (Spring 1990). Highlights include his commitment to "preventing abuse of children" (noted by the author as unique for a defense attorney) and his Catholic upbringing, repeating a story about a priest who rewarded Luquette with a hamburger every time he broke in a horse. Luquette was a veterinarian at the Houston Zoo before he became an attorney and leader in the Texas Criminal Defense Lawyers Association. He died in a car accident.

page 180 The old jail in Houston: Information about the 1991 case in the Fifth Circuit Court of Appeal regarding poor and overcrowded conditions at the 301 San Jacinto jail facility can be viewed here: http://openjurist.org/937/f2d/984/

alberti-v-sheriff-of-harris-county-texas-richards. A description of the 301 San Jacinto jail prior to 1982 can be located here: http://web.archive.org/web/20030222131554/www.co.harris.tx.us/so/ih_301.htm

page 180 Barring an outright error on the form: Arrest/booking records require an offense date and location in order to perform a search, so I was unable to confirm details of any arrest. Leduc's name (in all iterations) turns up zero hits in the Harris County District Court records, both criminal and civil—even though *Daily Court Review* shows that he was indeed sued in civil court.

page 180 By 1972: See *OCD* 1972, Galveston Houston Archdiocese.

page 181 his bishop would have remained financially responsible: One case of a Brooklyn priest who pled guilty to grand larceny and still received his monthly stipend can be found here: http://www.bishop-accountability.org/news2005_07_12/2005_12_07_Eisenberg_PriestWho.htm

page 181 County Clerk Records: *Serabia v. Leduc*, 29 Oct. 1974. There appears to be an important typo in the original petition and citation, which both identify Leduc's address as *402* Cottage Street; the attached billing/invoice exhibit, however, lists Leduc's house number as *702* W. Cottage. The process server may simply have walked three blocks in the wrong direction. Harris County Appraisal District records accessible online go back to 1984, so I was unable to discern the owner of the properties at the time. The 4-bedroom house stands three blocks from Christ the King parish, where Leduc had served as an assistant from August 1956 through June 1961.

page 182 In that day and age: Correspondence with Serabia

June-July 2014.

page 183 correspondence in his file: Emails from GH archivist 2013-14 and emails from archivists at Dioceses of Miami and St. Augustine Sept. 2013.

page 183 Priests' relationship to "home" diocese: Webpage of the United States Conference of Catholic Bishops states, "Deacons and priests are ministers of the community and as such are representatives of the bishop." Some discussion of protocols for excardination and incardination can be viewed here: http://www.usccb.org/beliefs-and-teachings/vocations/diaconate/protocol-for-the-incardination-excardination-of-deacons.cfm. Questions related to movement of priests from one diocese to another can be located in O'Reilly and Chalmers's *The Clergy Sex Abuse Crisis and the Legal Responses* (2014).

page 184 Johnnie Mike's shooting death: See Lavergne, pp. 289-291, as well as "Whitman Claims Body of Second Son" in *Corsicana Daily Sun* 5 July 1973. CA Whitman eventually sued the owner of the bar where his son had been shot. Patrick Whitman's 1984 lawsuit contesting the will and estate of a partner who committed suicide can be found here: http://law.justia.com/cases/california/court-of-appeal/3d/152/813.html

page 184 Florida newspaper report in 1976: See Brenda Bell's articles in Works Cited and Consulted

page 185 Msgr. Rowan "Rasty" Rastatter: his obituary can be found at the *Sun-Sentinel*: http://articles.sun-sentinel.com/1996-01-11/news/9601100539_1_florida-catholics-catholic-charities-five-bishops. An article that connects Rasty to Whitman appeared in *Express and News* 6 Aug. 1966, page 4. See also Rastatter listings in *OCD*.

page 186 Despite the length of his absence: See again

Leduc's obituary in *Palm Beach Post* 22 Jan. 1981 and *Texas Catholic Herald* 30 Jan. 1981.

page 188 the effects of radiation upon the body: Susan Griffin, *A Chorus of Stones,* p. 38.

page 188 data suggests it was too early for that: Timeline of HIV/AIDS: https://www.aids.gov/hiv-aids-basics/hiv-aids-101/aids-timeline/. Despite improvements in health treatments and public policies, the CDC reported recently that HIV/AIDS was Florida's "most distinctive cause of death" http://www.cdc.gov/pcd/issues/2015/14_0395a.htm

page 189 Leduc died as an inpatient: St. Mary's Hospital (founded in 1939) and Doctors Hospital (founded in 1973, now closed) can be seen in a Palm Beach County timeline here: http://www.pbchistoryonline.org/page/hospitals-timeline. See Probate File, Estate of Joseph G. Leduc

page 189 one final strangeness: *Leduc v. Gregory,* Docket Case No. 80-1953 CA(L) 01 G; Voluntary Dismissal with Prejudice filed 14 April 1982.

page 191 a slab transformed into a platform: During a summer visit in 2014, my husband and I secured permission from the inhabitant of the house to explore and take close-up photos of the slab. There was an old cement patch adjacent to it, with sides and corners overgrown, and it seemed to match measurements on the mechanic's lien for a patio. But we had also found the remainder of a severed plastic drainage pipe in the foundation—and that looked much too new. Schuck's thought was that, after Leduc went away, the original structure could have been damaged or washed out by one of the area's many floods, leaving someone else to rebuild on the slab until the most recent owners tore it down. I had asked the woman in the surviving house: What about the slab? She said that it had been a "drug house" when they arrived in the late 1970s, and that they had indeed demolished it. (That didn't necessarily mean it was Leduc's original structure.) Further research yielded interesting images prior to the demolition of structures: Google map photos dated from 2008 revealed four structures on Leduc's lots that year, including a house on the slab that appeared to have 1970s features. The oldest-looking dwelling, a weary clapboard house on stilts tucked behind the trees, seemed familiar in appearance to Schuck when I sent him screenshots, but he said the placement didn't feel right to him. He said that the garden slab was more likely the original spot.

page 192 located in a partially dry county: The history of restrictions on alcohol in Texas is complex: laws varied from county to county, and even from town to town. A history of Brazoria County's votes on the subject can be found at a county clerk document here: https://brazoriacountyclerk.net/recorder/assets/History_Alcoholic_Beverages_and_Liquor_Elections.pdf

XI. CONCLUDING RITE

page 194 the competing gospel: See USMC training film, *The Rifle* c. 1960: https://archive.org/details/TheRifle-Usmc-TrainingFilm1960s. The entire creed, accredited to Major General William H. Rupertus, can be located at the USMC History Division available online: http://www.mcu.usmc.mil/historydivision/pages/frequently_requested/Rifle_Creed.aspx. The creed is famously savaged in a scene from Stanley Kubrick's *Full Metal Jacket* (1987): "This is my rifle, this is my gun": https://www.

youtube.com/watch?v=4kUOXCVey_U. Kubrick's film also refers to Charles Whitman as an example (along with Lee Harvey Oswald) of the ideal sniper who "shows what one motivated Marine and his rifle can do": https://www.youtube.com/watch?v=a5IWK9sRYTs

page 194 American Sniper exceeding all box office records: "Box Office: American Sniper Stuns with $105.3 Million MLK Weekend" in *Variety* 19. Jan. 2015: http://variety.com/2015/film/news/box-office-american-sniper-stuns-with-105-3-million-mlk-weekend-1201408725/

Works Cited and Consulted

Literature, Theory, and Films

Bernanos, Georges. *The Diary of a Country Priest.* Cambridge: Da Capo Press, 1965. Print.

Chesser, Eustace M.D. *Love without Fear: How to Achieve Sex Happiness in Marriage.* New York: Signet, 1947. Print.

Dekeseredy, Walter S. "The Role of Male Peer Support in Intimate Partner Sexual Violence Perpetrators' Offending." *Perpetrators of Intimate Partner Sexual Violence: A Multidisciplinary Approach to Prevention, Recognition, and Intervention.* Eds. Louise McOrmond-Plummer, Jennifer Y. Levy-Peck, and Patricia Easteal. New York: Routledge, 2017. Print.

Full Metal Jacket. Dir. Stanley Kubrick. Warner Brothers, 1987. DVD.

Gartner, Richard B. *Betrayed as Boys: Psychodynamic Treatment of Sexually Abused Men.* New York: The Guildford Press, 1999. Print.

Girard, Rene. *Violence and the Sacred*. Baltimore: John Hopkins University Press, 1972. Print.

Greene, Graham. *The Power and the Glory*. New York: Penguin, 1940. Print.

Griffin, Susan. *A Chorus of Stones: The Private Life of War*. New York: Doubleday, 1992. Print.

Hanley, Jack. *Let's Make Mary: A Gentleman's Guide to Seduction in 8 Easy Lessons*. Hillman-Curl, 1937. Print.

Kyle, Chris, Scott McEwen and Jim DeFelice. *American Sniper: The Autobiography of the Most Lethal Sniper in U.S. Military History*. New York: Harper Collins, 2012. Print.

McOrmond-Plummer, Jennifer Y. Levy-Peck, and Patricia Easteal, eds. *Perpetrators of Intimate Partner Sexual Violence: A Multidisciplinary Approach to Prevention, Recognition, and Intervention*. New York: Routledge, 2017. Print.

The Sniper. Dir. Edward Dmytryk. 1952. DVD.

HISTORIES

Allyn, David. *Make Love, Not War: The Sexual Revolution: An Unfettered History*. New York: Routledge, 2016. Print.

Anderson, R. Bentley. *Black, White, and Catholic: New Orleans Interracialism*. Nashville: Vanderbilt University Press, 2008. 89-91. Print.

Bisaillon, Robert R. *Franco-American Biographies of the Greater-Waterbury Area.* Waterbury, CT: Waterbury Printing, 1993. Print.

——. *Mariages de la Paroisse de St. Anne of Waterbury, Connecticut 1886-1982.* Montréal: Bergeron, 1985. Print.

——. *Sainte Ann Parish and Its People: Waterbury, Connecticut 1886-1986.* n.p., c. 1988. Print.

Botham, Fay. *Almighty God Created the Races: Christianity, Interracial Marriage, and American Law.* Chapel Hill: University of North Carolina Press, 2013. 167-169. Print.

Brinkley, Douglas and Julie M. Fenster. *Parish Priest: Father Michael McGivney and American Catholicism.* New York: Harper Perennial, 2006. Print.

Carroll, James. *Constantine's Sword: the Church and the Jews. A History.* Boston: Houghton Mifflin Company, 2001.

Courtwright, David T. *Violent Land: Single Men and Social Disorder from the Frontier to the Inner City.* Cambridge: Harvard University Press, 1996. Print.

Giles, Robert C. *Changing Times: The Story of the Diocese of Galveston Houston in Commemoration of its Founding: 125th Anniversary, 1847-1972.* Houston: The Most Reverend John L. Morkovsky, STD. Print.

"History & Mission: America's First Seminary." St. Mary's Seminary and University. StMarys.edu. 2014. Web. 10 Oct. 2014.

"History of Alcoholic Beverages: Brazoria County, TX, 1919-2006." Brazoria County Clerk.net. 20 March 2007. Web. 5 March 2015.

"History of the UT Tower." UTexas.edu. 2016. Web. 16 Aug. 2016.

"Hospitals Timeline." Palm Beach County History Online. Historical Society of Palm Beach County, 2009. Web. 27 May 2014.

Lavergne, Gary M. *A Sniper in the Tower: The Charles Whitman Murders.* Denton, TX: University of North Texas Press, 1997. Print.

McKay, Brett and Kate McKay. "Weasels Ripped My Flesh! Vintage Men's Adventure Magazines." ArtofManliness. com 26 May 2010. 7 July 2015.

Men's Magazines: An A-Z. Magforum.com. 21 Nov. 2012. Web. 7 July 2015.

"Nick Kralj, Recent Graduate, Galveston, TX." *Out of the Blue: A Texas Standard Documentary.* 2016. Web. 31 Aug. 2016.

"Our Patron Saint, Philip Neri." St. Philip Neri Catholic Church. stphilipnerichurch.org. n.d. Web. 4 Oct. 2013.

Reef, Catherine. *Alone in the World: Orphans and Orphanages in America.* New York: Clarion Books, 2005. Print.

Reeves, Thomas C. *America's Bishop: The Life and Times of Fulton J. Sheen.* New York: Encounter Books, 2001. Print.

"Society of Saint-Suplice." *Catholic Encyclopedia.* 2012. Web. 10 Sept. 2013.

"The Tower." *Mass Murderers.* Alexandria Virginia: Time-Life Books, 1992. 44-51. Print.

"The Waterbury Clock Tower." WTNH News 8. YouTube 28 June 2012. Web. 6 Dec. 2013.

"Waterbury Time Machine: Vintage Views and Memories of the Brass City." Brad Brassity. 15 March 2010. Web. 6 Dec. 2013.

CATHOLIC THEOLOGY, CULTURE, AND RITUAL

"Ban Criticized." *The Capital* 5 August 1968: 2. Newspapers. com. Web. 19 April 2015.

Bohn, Carole R. "Dominion to Rule: The Roots and Consequences of a Theology of Ownership." *Christianity, Patriarchy, and Abuse: A Feminist Critique.* Eds. Joanne Carlson Brown and Carole R. Bohn. New York: The Pilgrim Press, 1989: 105-116. Print.

"Canticle of Canticles." *Catholic Encyclopedia.* 2012. Web. 4 May 2015.

Carey, Patrick W. *Catholics in America: A History.* Westport, Greenwood Publishing, 2004. Print.

Carlson Brown, Joanne and Carole R. Bohn, eds. *Christianity, Patriarchy, and Abuse: A Feminist Critique.* New York: The Pilgrim Press, 1989. Print.

"Church Has No Funds for Nuns Who Retire." *The Amarillo-Globe-Times.* 17 Nov. 1972. Newspapers.com. Web. 9 Feb. 2016.

Cornwell, John. *The Dark Box: A Secret History of Confession.* New York: Basic Books, 2014. Print.

D'Antonio, Michael. *Mortal Sins: Sex, Crime, and the Era of Catholic Scandal.* New York: St. Martin's Press, 2013. Print.

"Feast of the Assumption." *Catholic Encyclopedia.* 2012. Web. 6 April 2014.

Fenner, Kay Toy. *American Catholic Etiquette.* Westminster, MD: Newman Press, 1961. Print.

France, David. *Our Fathers: The Secret Life of the Catholic Church in an Age of Scandal.* New York: Broadway Books, 2004.

Gautier, Mary. "How Parish Life Has Changed." *National Catholic Reporter.* 24 Oct. 2011. Web. 2 Dec. 2014.

Greeley, Andrew. *The Catholic Myth.* New York: Charles Scribener's Sons, 1990. Print.

Goodstein, Laurie. "Trail of Pain in Church Crisis Leads to Almost Every Diocese." *New York Times* 12 Jan. 2003. Web. 29 Aug. 2016.

The Investigative Staff of the Boston Globe. *Betrayal: The Crisis in the Catholic Church.* Boston: Little, Brown, and Company, 2002. Print.

Kelly, Gerald, S.J. *Modern Youth and Chastity.* St. Louis: The Queen's Work, 1941. Print.

Kennedy, Eugene. *The Unhealed Wound: The Church and Human Sexuality.* New York: St. Martin's Griffin, 2001. Print.

Knights of the Altar Handbook. Sanctamissa.org. n.d. Web. 6 June 2015.

Loh, Jules. "American Catholics Opposed Infallibility." *Brazosport Facts.* 31 August 1962: 4. Newspapers.com. Web. 21 May 2015.

Manousos, Fr. Demetrius, OFM Cap, and Addison Burbank. *Know Your Mass.* Catechetical Guild Society, 1954. Web. 5 Sept. 2013.

The New St. Joseph Baltimore Catechism Vols. 1 and 2, 2nd edition. Totowa, NJ: Catholic Publishing Corporation, 1991. Print.

Ochs, Stephen J. *Desegregating the Altar: The Josephites and the Struggle for Black Priests, 1971-1960.* Baton Rouge: Louisiana State University Press, 1993. Print. 446-453.

O'Toole, James W. *The Faithful: A History of Catholics in America.* Cambridge, MA: The Belknap Press of Harvard University Press, 2008. Print.

"Part One: The Profession of Faith." *The Catechism of the Catholic Church.* Vatican.va. n.d. Web. 10 Oct. 2015.

"Part Two: The Celebration of the Christian Mystery." *The Catechism of the Catholic Church.* Vatican.va. n.d. Web. 10 Oct. 2015.

"Part Three: Life in Christ." *The Catechism of the Catholic Church.* Vatican.va. n.d. Web. 10 Oct. 2015.

Pope Francis. *Amoris Laetitia: On Love in the Family.* Vatican Press, 2016. vatican.va. 17 May 2016.

Pope Paul VI. Encyclical Letter: *Humanae Vitae.* 25 July 1968. vatican.va. Web. 10 March 2015.

Radford Ruether, Rosemary. "The Western Religious Tradition and Violence against Women in the Home." *Christianity, Patriarchy, and Abuse: A Feminist Critique.* Eds. Joanne Carlson Brown and Carole R. Bohn. New York: The Pilgrim Press, 1989: 31-41. Print.

"The Reception of Holy Communion at Mass." United States Conference of Catholic Bishops. 2016. Web. 3 Feb. 2016.

Redmond, Sheila A. "Christian 'Virtues' and Recovery from Child Sexual Abuse." *Christianity, Patriarchy, and Abuse: A Feminist Critique.* Eds. Joanne Carlson Brown and Carole R. Bohn. New York: The Pilgrim Press. Print. 70-88.

Reeves, Thomas C. "Archbishop Fulton J. Sheen: Catholic Media's Greatest Star." Catholic Education Resource Center. 2000. Web. 7 Feb. 2015.

Saunders, Fr. William. "Pastors, Administrators, and Parochial Vicars." Catholic Education Resource Center (CERC) 2005. Web. 7 Jan. 2015.

Shaw, Russell. "Symposium Sheds Light on Pastoral Difficulties: Clericalism and Being Spread Too Thin Add Stress to Priest-Laity Relations, Participants Say." *Our Catholic Visitor.* 24 Nov. 2009. Web. 20 Jan. 2016.

Sipe, A.W. Richard. *Living the Celibate Life: A Search for Meaning and Models.* Missouri: Liguori, 2004.

"Solemnity of the Assumption of Mary." *American Catholic.org.* 1996-2016. Web. 4 July 2013.

Thompson, Damian. "The Beginning of the End for Pope Francis." *The Spectator* 16 April 2016. Web. 16 April 2016.

Toth, Tihamer. *The Young Man of Character.* Angelus Press (reprint), 2012. Print.

——. *Youth and Chastity.* Toronto: Garden City Press, 1934. Print.

Yardley, Jim and Laurie Goodstein. "Francis' Message Calls on Church to Be Inclusive." *The New York Times* 8 April 2016. Web. 16 April 2016.

Young-Eisendrath, Polly and Demaris Wehr. "The Fallacy of Individualism and Reasonable Violence against Women." *Christianity, Patriarchy, and Abuse: A Feminist Critique.* Eds. Joanne Carlson Brown and Carole R. Bohn. New York: The Pilgrim Press, 1989: 117-138.

CLERICAL TEACHING, SEMINARY FORMATION, AND INSTITUTIONAL PRACTICE

Baker, Andrew R, Msgr. "Here Comes the Groom—The Priest as the Bridegroom of the Church." *Lay Witness Magazine* May/June 2003. *Catholics United for the Faith. cuf.org.* May/June 2003. Web. 10 May 2015.

Berrigan, Daniel. *To Dwell in Peace: An Autobiography with New Afterword by the Author.* Eugene, OR: Wipf & Stock, 2007. Print.

"Bishops Reject Request." AP. *San Antonio Express* 13 Nov. 1968: 91. Newspapers.com. Web. 21 May 2015.

"Cardinal Penalizes 11 Priests for Defending Freedom of Conscience." AP Report. *Lubbock-Avalanche Journal* 19 September 1968: 102. Newspapers.com. Web. 21 May 2015.

"Church Long Knew of Priest's Pedophila, Files Indicate." *The Washington Post* 1 Sept. 1997. Web. 10 Oct. 2014.

"Church Suspends a Priest Who Claims He Is Gay." *Florida Today* 18 Nov. 1981: 4B. Newspapers.com. Web. 14 June 2016.

Crimen Solicitationis: Instruction on the Manner of Proceeding in Causes involving the Crime of Solicitation. Vatican Polygot Press, 1962. Vatican.va. Web. 14 June 2014.

Debien, Noel and Tiger Web. "Sex Abuse and International Secrecy Imposed by Vatican." *Religion and Ethics Report* 6 June 2014. Web. 7 July 2014.

Doyle, Thomas P., OP, JCD. "The 1922 and 1962 Instructions: 'Crimen Solicitationis' Promulgated by the Vatican." 4 March 2010. Awrsipe.com. Web. 21 March 2014.

Doyle, Thomas P., A.W.R. Sipe, and Patrick J. Wall. *Sex, Priests, and Secret Codes: The Catholic Church's 2,000-Year Paper Trail of Sexual Abuse.* Los Angeles: Volt Press, 2006. Print.

Eisenberg, Carol. "Priest Who Admitted Grand Larceny Still Receives Pay from Brooklyn Diocese." *NY Newsday* 7 Dec. 2005. BishopAccountability.org. Web. 19 Nov. 2015.

Frawley-O'Dea, Mary Gail. *Perversion of Power: Sexual Abuse in the Catholic Church*. Nashville: Vanderbilt University Press, 2007. Print.

Gado, Mark. *Killer Priest*. Westport, CT: Praeger, 2006. Print.

Gallagher, Joseph. *The Pain and the Privilege: Diary of a City Priest*. Garden City, NY: Image Books, 1983. Print.

Greeley, Andrew M. *The Catholic Priest in the United States: Sociological Investigations*. Washington, DC: United States Catholic Conference, 1972.

The John Jay College of Criminal Justice. *The Causes and Context of Sexual Abuse of Minors by Catholic Priests and Deacons in the United States, 1950-2002*. New York: City University of New York, 2004.

Keenan, Marie. *Child Abuse and the Catholic Church: Gender, Power, and Organizational Culture*. Oxford: Oxford University Press, 2012. Print.

Kelley, Matt. "Catholic Scandal Expanding in Military." *Deseret News* 12 Oct. 2003. Web. 16 April 2016.

"Largest Settlements by Total Dollar Amount." Bishopaccountability.com 2004. Web. 10 September 2015.

Lavoie, Denise. "Files Show Priests Working in Other States, Despite Allegations." AP Report. 5 Feb. 2003. Web. 16 Aug. 2013.

Mattingly, Terry. "Abusive Priests Hiding as Chaplains?" *Get Religion*. 28 March 2011. Web. 15 July 2013.

McCarthy, Bishop John, Jill Grimes and Tom Borders. *Off the Cuff and Over the Collar: Common Sense Catholicism.* Austin: Greenhills Publishing, 2013.

O'Connor, John Cardinal. "The Necessity of Continuing Formation for the Priest." Vatican.va. 18 June 1996. Web. 15 May 2014.

The Official Catholic Directory. 1950-1982 editions. New Providence, NJ: PJ Kennedy and Sons, 1950-1982. Print.

Old, Francis E., Jr. "Tessier and Duluol." *The Baltimore Sun* 26 Feb. 1950: 122. Newspapers.com. 15 Sept. 2017.

O'Reilly, James T. and Margaret S.P. Chalmers. *The Clergy Sex Abuse Crisis and the Legal Responses.* Oxford University Press: 2014.

"Panel to Probe San Antonio Priest Controversy." UPI. *The Brownsville Herald* 12 Nov. 1968: 5. Newspapers.com. Web. 21 May 2015.

Pickard, Rev. William M., JCL. *Judicial Experts: A Source of Evidence in Ecclesiastical Trials.* Dissertation. Catholic University of America. Washington, D.C. 1958. Print.

"Protocol for the Incardination or Excardination of Deacons." United States Conference of Catholic Bishops. 1995 and 2002. usccb.org. Web. 3 March 2014.

Rastrelli, Tom. "Confessions of an Ex-Priest: How Seminary Forms Victims and Forces False Forgiveness." *Huffington Post Blog* 19 Oct. 2012. Web. 5 May 2013.

Sacred Congregation for Religious. *Religiousorum Institutio: Careful Selection and Training of Candidates for the States of Perfection and Sacred Orders.* 2 Feb. 1961. EWTN.com. n.d. Web. 10 June 2014.

"Seminarians Complain to Pope over Priest Firings." UPI. *The Brownsville Herald* 31 Oct. 1968: 7. Newspapers.com. Web. 21 May 2015.

Sipe, A. W. Richard. *Celibacy in Crisis: A Secret World Revisited.* London: Routledge, 2003.

———. *A Secret World: Sexuality and the Search for Celibacy.* New York: Brunner/Mazel, 1990. Print.

———. *The Serpent and the Dove: Celibacy in Literature and Life.* Westport, CT: Praeger, 2007. Print.

———. *Sex, Priests, and Power: Anatomy of a Crisis.* New York: Brunner/Mazel, 1995. Print.

"What Is the Difference Between Secular Priests and Religious Priests?" Catholic Answers. 1996. Web. 9 May 2013.

"What Percent of Priests Were Accused?" bishopaccountability. org. 2004. Web. 30 July 2015.

Williams, R. Seth, District Attorney of Philadelphia. Report of the Grand Jury in RE: County Investigating Grand Jury XXIII. 21 Jan. 2011. Web. 30 July 2015.

Wypijewski, JoAnn. "Roman Inquisition." *Mother Jones.* Dec. 2005. Web. 26 Sept. 2015.

Zagier, Alan Scher. "Lawyer Concludes Church Leaders Used SW Florida as 'Dumping Ground.'" *Naples Daily News* 28 April 2003. BishopAccountability.org. Web. 15 July 2013.

Newspaper and Magazine Sources

"23 Scouts, Three Leaders Go to Big 'Jamboree.'" *The Palm Beach Post* 8 July 1953: 2. Newspapers.com. Web. 10 Feb. 2016.

"25 Get Diplomas at Sacred Heart." *The Palm Beach Post* 31 May 1955: 6. Newsapers.com. Web. 10 Feb. 2016.

"50 Initiated by KC Council." *The Palm Beach Post* 31 March 1958: 2. Newspapers.com. Web. 10 Feb. 2016.

Ackerman, Todd and Tara Dooley. "Retired Priest Penalized for Alleged Abuse." *Houston Chronicle* 23 June 2002. Web. 15 May 2015.

"Alaska Digest: Diocese Sells Property to Cover Settlements." JuneauEmpire.com. 28 Sept. 2006. Web. 8 Nov. 2014.

"All-American Boy." *Newsweek* 15 August 1966: 24-29. Print.

"Altar and Rosary Society." *The Palm Beach Post* 8 Dec. 1965. Newspapers.com. Web. 31 Aug. 2016.

"Alvin Savings in New Building, Opens Branch." *Brazosport Facts* 19 Sept. 1965: 60. Newspapers.com. Web. 22 July 2014.

"Archdiocese of Galveston-Houston: Diocesan Cases." Eureka. com. n.d. 15 Oct. 2015.

"Archdiocese's List of Clergy Accused of Child Abuse." *The Baltimore Sun.* 26 Sept. 2002. Web. 30 July 2015.

"Attorney Andrew Lannie Will Open New Office in Baytown." *The Baytown Sun* 10 June 1966: 10. Newspapers.com. Web. 6 July 2015.

"Aurora G. Leduc: Obituary." *The Palm Beach Post* 1 April 1996: 85. Newspapers.com. Web. 9 Feb. 2016.

"Auto-Motorcycle Crash Suit Basis." *The Palm Beach Post* 1 Oct. 1958: 4. Newspapers.com. Web. 10. Feb. 2016.

Bartlett, Kay. "Priest Asks Americans Not to Judge 'Harshly." *The Lawton Constitution* 5 Aug. 1966: 1-4. Newspapers.com. Web. 16 Nov. 2016.

"Baytown Man Gets 30 Years in Priest Death." *The Baytown Sun* 11 July 1973: 2. Newspapers.com. Web. 20 Aug. 2015.

Bell, Brenda. "Anatomy of a Massacre: Decade Hasn't Dimmed Texas Tower Memory." *The Palm Beach Post* 1 Aug. 1976: 1, 17. Newspapers.com. Web. 12 Feb. 2016.

———. "Charles Whitman's Sniping Still Vivid in Victims' Minds." *The Port Arthur News* 1 August 1976: 3. Newspapers. com. Web. 14 April 2014.

"Best Evidence of Mother's Day." *The Palm Beach Post* 13 May 1951: 12. Newspapers.com. Web. 10 Feb. 2016.

"Bishop Points out Attacker." *The Odessa American* 15 March 1974: 26. Newspapers.com. Web. 19 August 2015.

"Body of Slain Priest Found." *Vernon Daily Record* 2 Jan. 1973: 2. Newspapers.com. Web. 20 August 2015.

Bonanos, Christopher. "Before Sexting, There Was Polaroid." *The Atlantic* 1 Oct. 2012. Web. 2 Feb. 2016.

"Books Discussed at St. Ann's Library." *The Palm Beach Post* 15 March 1958: 2. Newspapers.com. Web. 10 Feb. 2016.

"Boylan Holy Name Society President for Second Year." *The Palm Beach Post* 13 July 1954: 7. Newspapers.com. Web. 14 June 2016.

"Brain Washing Will Be the Subject of a Talk." *The Palm Beach Post*: 14 March 1957: 12. Newspapers.com. Web. 10 Feb. 2016.

"Brantley Invokes 9 pm Curfew Law." *Palm Beach Post* 6 Aug. 1942: 7. Newspapers.com. 15 May 2017.

"Brave Priest Convinces Cuban to Surrender Gun." AP. *Nashua Telegraph* 28 March 1966: 1. Newspapers.com. Web. 6 April 2015.

Burhman, Margaret. "In the Service." *The Palm Beach Post* 18 Oct. 1959: 46. Newspapers.com. Web. 10 Feb. 2016.

"Catholic Daughters Hear Talk by Pastor." *The Palm Beach Post* 13 Oct. 1955: 33. Newspapers.com. Web. 10 Feb. 2016.

"Children Given Christmas Party." *The Palm Beach Post* 21 Dec. 1956: 16. Newspapers.com. Web. 10 Feb. 2016.

"Christ the King Event." *The Montgomery Advertiser* 23 Oct. 1965: 2. Newspapers.com. Web. 28 May 2017.

"Coastal Deanery Holy Name Rally Scheduled Sunday." *The Palm Beach Post* 11 June 1955: 2. Newspapers.com. 10 Feb. 2016.

"Comaux [sic] Boys Will Receive Awards at Sunday Service." *The Baytown Sun* 7 Feb. 1960: 7. Newspapers.com. Web. 26 May 2015.

"Communism Theme for Pastor's Talk." *The Palm Beach Post* 9 Jan. 1958: 11. Newspapers.com. Web. 10 Feb. 2016.

Davis, James D. "Rowan Rastatter: Catholic Priest for Five Decades." *Sun-Sentinel* 11 Jan. 1996. Web. 20 June 2014.

"Disgraced Delray Beach Priest John Skehan Released from Prison." *The Palm Beach Post.com* 26 April 2010. Web. 10 Feb. 2016.

"Dr. Grady Brantley, Longtime Doctor at Lake Worth, Succumbs." *The Palm Beach Post* 10 Feb. 1961: 7. Newspapers.com. 5 May 2017.

Doig, Matthew and Maurice Tamman. "Priest Tells of Foley Relationship." *Herald-Tribune* 19 Oct. 2006. Web. 10 May 2014.

"Editorial Rapped for Boy Scout Opinion: Claims a Boy Scout is 20 Per Cent Girl and Hybrid." UP. *The Baytown Sun* 9 March 1955: 8. Newspapers.com. Web. 23 Jan. 2014.

"E. L. Boston Re-elected by Alvin Bank." *Galveston Daily News* 20 Jan. 1961: 6. Newspapers.com. Web. 22 July 2014.

"Elmendorf Links Airlift Routes." *Fairbanks Daily News-Miner* 9 Nov. 1967: 11. Newspapers.com. Web. 18 April 2016.

"Farewell Fete Given Pastor." *The Palm Beach Post* 17 Dec. 1954: 22. Newspapers.com. Web. 10 Feb. 2016.

"Father Joseph Leduc Dies in Florida, Jan. 19." *Texas Catholic Herald* 30 Jan. 1981: 7. Print.

"Feast of Immaculate Conception to Be Celebrated at St. Joseph's." *The Baytown Sun* 8 Dec. 1968: 8. Newspapers.com. 18 Jan. 2013.

"Fight Is Being Waged to Defeat Amendment for Segregation in Schools." *Monroe Morning World* 17 Oct. 1954: 6. Newspapers.com. Web. 21 May 2015.

"Fired for Flogging Young Orphanage Boy." *The Atlanta Constitution* 25 June 1916: 6. Newspapers.com. Web. 13 Feb. 2016.

"Fishing Catches." *The Palm Beach Post* 23 June 1952: 9. Newspapers.com. Web. 10 Feb. 2016.

"Florida Priests Get Jail for Stealing from Church." Reuters 25 March 2009. Web. 14 June 2016.

"Fought Their Teachers: Bethesda Boys Take to the Woods. Some of Them Return." *The Atlanta Constitution* 9 Jan. 1895: 3. Newspapers.com. Web. 13 Feb. 2016.

Frederick, Eva. "Experts Still Disagree on Role of Tower Shooter's Brain Tumor." *The Daily Texan* 31 July 2016. Web. 20 Aug. 2016.

George, Cindy. "Settlement Reached in Church Sex Abuse Case." *The Houston Chronicle* 4 Feb. 2008. Web. 12 Dec. 2014.

Gillespie, Pat. "Diocese Responds to Sexual Abuse Lawsuit Involving St. Francis Xavier Priest." *News-Press* 29 April 2010. BishopAccountability.org. 2004. Web. 6 July 2014.

"Graduates of St. Mary's Ordained." *The Houston Chronicle* 28 May 1955: A3. Library Microfiche.

"GOP Women to Hear Priest Review Book." *El Paso Herald-Post* 26 June 1964: 19. Newspapers.com. Web. 10 Feb. 2016.

Guthrie, Amy. "Priestin' Ain't Easy." *Broward Palm Beach New Times* 20 March 2008. Web. 10 Feb. 2016.

Hart, Muril. "Proving Murder of Priest: Area Deputy Has Key Role in Suspect Arrest." *Baytown Sun* 4 Jan. 1973: 1. Newspapers.com. Web. 20 Aug. 2015.

———-. "Memory of Pastor's Death Honored in CV." *Baytown Sun* 6 Jan. 1974: 6. Newspapers.com. Web. 20 Aug. 2015.

"Historic Orphanage to Raise Large Sum." *The Atlanta Constitution* 22 Nov. 1920: 6. Newspapers.com. Web. 13 Feb. 2016.

"Homosexual Diseases Linked to Immunities." *The Palm Beach Post* 10 Dec. 1981: 11. Newspapers.com. Web. 14 June 2016.

"Honor Is Paid to Scout Leaders." *Miami News* 17 Sept. 1952: 15. Newspapers.com. Web. 18 Sept. 2017.

Hoye, Sarah. "Philadelphia Archdiocese Finds Two Priests Unsuitable for Ministry." CNN.com 8 April 2013. Web. 6 March 2015.

Hudson, Nan. "She's a $100 Winner." *The Palm Beach Post* 6 June 1965: 26. Newspapers.com. 10 Feb. 2016.

"'Insight' Films to Be Shown at St. Joseph's." *Baytown Sun* 8 Sept. 1968: 4. Newspapers.com. Web. 18 Jan. 2013.

"Introducing: St. Mary's Class of 1954." *The Voice of St. Mary's.* November 1950: 25. Print.

"John Klein Is Elected Grand Knight of Lodge." *The Palm Beach Post* 29 May 1955: 33. Newspapers.com. Web. 10 Feb. 2016.

"John Michael Whitman: Obituary." *The Palm Beach Post* 5 July 1973: 34. Newspapers.com. Web. 12 Feb. 2016.

"Josefa A. York: Obituary." *The Galveston Daily News* 4 Feb. 1998: 4. Newspapers.com. Web. 30 Aug. 2014.

"Joseph Leo Leduc: Obituary." *The Palm Beach Post* 1 Feb. 1986: 44. Newspapers.com. Web. 9 Feb. 2016.

Kimmey, Bill. "UA Professor Recalls Whitman as Student with Many Problems." *Tucson Daily Citizen* 5 Aug. 1966: 2. Newspapers.com. Web. 6 April 2014.

"Kiwanians Hear WPB Priest." *The News Tribune* 4 March 1958: 1. Newspapers.com. Web. 10 Feb. 2016.

"Lake Worth Eagle Scout May Be Youngest." *The Palm Beach Post* 15 Dec. 1953: 12. Newspapers.com. 25 April 2016. Web.

"Lake Worth Notes: Mothers Teachers Club." *The Palm Beach Post* 21 Sept. 1954: 9. Newspapers.com. Web. 10 Feb. 2016.

"Lake Worth Scouts Seek New Sponsors." *The Miami News* 1 Dec. 1946: 5. Google Newspapers. Web. 17 April 2014.

"Lake Worth's Newly Elected and Appointed City Officials." *The Palm Beach Post* 12 April 1939: 5. Newspapers.com. Web. 15 May 2017.

Landers, Peggy. "Priest Honored for 40 Years of Church, Civic Service." *Miami Herald* 24 May 1994. BishopAccountability.org. 2004. Web. 10 Sept. 2014.

Lang, Brent. "Box Office: *American Sniper* Stuns with $105.3 Million MLK Weekend." *Variety* 19 Jan. 2015. Web. 20 Jan. 2016.

LeFevre, J., CM. "New Parishes Added in the South." *The De Andrein.* Vol. 35: 1 (October 1964). DePaul.edu. Web. 4 June 2013.

"Life Has Become Nightmare for 'Texas Sniper's' Father." *Galesburg Register-Mail* 7 July 1973: 10. Newspapers.com. Web. 6 April 2014.

Lomartire, Paul L. "Demons and Doom." *The Palm Beach Post* 30 July 2006. Newsbank: America's News. Web. 19 July 2012.

"Lost Wallet [of Mrs. Margaret Whitman]." *The Palm Beach Post* 15 June 1952: 34. Newspapers.com. Web. 15 Sept. 2017.

"The Madman in the Tower." *Time* 12 August 1966: 14-19. Print.

Malisow, Craig. "Parish Predators." *Houston Press* 17 Aug. 2006. Web. 15 July 2014.

"Man Sentenced for Robbery." *Corpus-Christi Caller Times* 20 Nov. 1974: 18. Newspapers.com. Web. 19 August 2015.

"Mass Murderer's Letter Revealed." *UPI Archives* 8 July 1986. Web. 15 Feb. 2016.

McDonald, Charles M. "George Francis Luquette Memorial." *Voice for the Defense* Spring 1990: 10-11. Web. 1 June 2015.

"Mrs. R.D. Stowell Presenting Pupils." *The Palm Beach Post* 9 June 1956: 11. Newspapers.com. Web. 10 Feb. 2016.

"Navigation, Sailing Talk Heard by Scouts." *The Palm Beach Post* 24 May 1953: 24. Newspapers.com. Web. 10 Feb. 2016.

Neyrey, Fr. Jerome Henry, SJ. "Directors and Associates of Our Lady of the Oaks Retreat House, Grand Coteau, Louisiana, on the 75th Anniversary Celebration of the Dedication." 6 Oct. 2013. Web. 5 May 2015.

"North Brazoria Names Boy Scout District Officers." *Galveston Daily News* 16 Dec. 1955: 23. Newspapers.com. Web. 22 July 2014.

"Offshore Catches." *The Palm Beach Post* 30 Oct. 1956: 13. Newspapers.com. Web. 10 Feb. 2016.

O'Malley, Julia. "$1.4 Million Settles Suit with Ex-Priest--Anchorage: Five Men All Said They Were Abused by Father Murphy." *Anchorage Daily News* 4 Aug. 2006. BishopAccountability.org. n.d. Web. 11 Oct. 2014.

"One Charged in Bishop Morkovsky Case in Houston." *Shiner Gazette* 21 March 1974: 1. Newspapers.com. Web. 19 August 2015.

"Palm Beach County Growing Fast." *The Palm Beach Post* 31 July 1955: 1. Newspapers.com. Web. 5 Dec. 2016.

"Part of St. Mary's Urged for Colored School." *The Baltimore Sun* 17 March 1950: 11. Newspapers.com. 15 Sept. 2017.

"Path of a Pedophile Priest." *Dallas Morning News* 31 Aug. 1997. Bishopaccountability.org. 2004. Web. 11 August 2014.

"Patrick Whitman, Patricia Smith: Wedding Announcement." *The Palm Beach Post* 15 Aug. 1965: 28. Newspapers.com. Web. 12 Feb. 2016.

Pickard, William M., Rev. Msgr. Obituary. Legacy.com. *Houston Chronicle* 27 Aug. 2015. Web. 8 Sept. 2015.

"Pleading with a Gunman." UPI report. *The Los Angeles Times* 28 March 1966: 1. Newspapers.com. Web. 29 June 2017.

"Police Chaplain Talks Gunman into Surrendering." AP. *Portsmouth Herald* 28 March 1968: 89. Newspapers.com. Web. 6 April 2015.

"Police Report." *Brazosport Facts* 21 Jan. 1962: 3. Newspapers.com. Web. 8 April 2014.

"Priest Abuse Case Settled for $1.4 Million." AP Report. *Albuquerque Journal* 4 March 2006. Web. 16 April 2016.

"Priest Admits He Fondled Foley but Denies They Had Sex in Late 1960s." *The Free-Lance Star* 20 Oct. 2006. Web. 31 Aug. 2016.

"Priest Justifies Whitman Rites." UPI. *Modesto Bee and News-Herald.* 5 Aug. 1966: 3. Newspapers.com. Web. 6 April 2015.

"Priest Risks Life to Rescue Holy Sacrament." *Waco Tribune-Herald* 14 Sept. 1952: 30. Newspapers.com. Web. 21 May 2016.

"Priest Talks Refugee Out of Gun, Hostages." AP. *The Mexia Daily News* 29 March 1966: 4. Newspapers.com. Web. 12 April 2015.

"Priest to Sing First Solemn High Mass." *Waterbury Republican* 5 June 1955. Library microfiche, Waterbury Public Library, CT.

"Priest Urges Mercy in Judging Whitman." *Ocala Star-Banner* 5 Aug. 1966: 1. Google Newspapers. Web. 4 Aug. 2015.

"Priests Recover Stolen Car, Capture Two Suspected Youths." *Lubbock Evening Journal* 22 Dec. 1952: 7. Newspapers. com. Web. 21 May 2016.

Pure Oil: Local Establishments (advertisement). *The Palm Beach Post* 27 Aug. 1956: 6. Newspapers.com. Web. 10 Feb. 2016.

"Refugee Talked into Surrendering." AP. *Abiline Reporter-News* 28 March 1966: 10B. Newspapers.com. Web. 12 Sept. 2015.

"Researchers Puzzled by Disease." AP. *The Palm Beach Post* 29 June 1982: 61. Newspapers.com. Web. 14 June 2016.

"Rev. Fr. Joseph (Gille) [sic] Leduc: Funeral Notice." *The Palm Beach Post* 22 Jan. 1981: 59. Google Newspapers. Web. 10 June 2012.

"Rev. Jack McGinnis of Assumption Catholic Church of Houston Will Speak." *The Baytown Sun* 21 Jan. 1969: 2. Newspapers.com. Web. 10 Feb. 2016.

"Rev. J. C. [sic] LeDuc Will Be Serra Speaker Monday." *Port Arthur News* 21 March 1965: 4C. Library microfiche.

"Rev. Linam Is New Priest at St. Andrew's Church." *The Baytown Sun* 18 Feb. 1973: 10. Newspapers.com. Web. 20 August 2015.

"Rites Scheduled Today for Whitman and Mother." *The Palm Beach Post* 5 Aug. 1966: 1, 2. Newspapers.com. Web. 12 Feb. 2016.

Rivera, John. "Priests Upset by Release of Abuse List." *The Baltimore Sun* 26. Sept. 2002. Web. 15 May 2015.

Scott-Coe, Jo. "But What Would *She* Say? Reframing 'Domestic Terror' in the 1966 UT Austin Shooting." *Pacific Coast Philology* Vol. 52.2 (2017): 294-313.

———."Invisible Women, Fairy Tale Death: How Stories of Public Murder Minimize Terror at Home." *American Studies Journal* No. 62 (2017). Web. 18 July 2017.

———."Listening to Kathy." *Catapult* 30 March 2016. Web. 30 March 2016.

"Scout Investiture Rites To Be Held Here Sunday." *The Baytown Sun* 6 Feb. 1963: 1. Newspapers.com. Web. 5 April 2015.

"'Scout Sunday' Is Scheduled." *The Baytown Sun* 10 Feb. 1963: 9. Newspapers.com. Web. 5 April 2015.

"Scouts Planning Dinner to Help Buy Equipment." *The Palm Beach Post* 25 May 1952: 30. Newspapers.com. Web. 10 Feb. 2016.

"Scouts Study First Aid." *The Palm Beach Post* 10 May 1953: 26. Newspapers.com. Web. 10 Feb. 2016.

"St. Joseph's Altar Society Tells Annual Dinner Plans." *Baytown Sun* 3 Nov. 1968: 3. Newspapers.com. Web. 18 Jan. 2013.

"St. Joseph's Church Sets Epistle, Gospel." *Baytown Sun* 13 Oct. 1968: 6. Newspapers.com. Web. 18 Jan. 2013.

"St. Joseph's Church to Hold Area Meeting." *Baytown Sun* 11 Aug. 1968: 8. Newspapers.com. Web. 18 Jan. 2013.

Silk, Mark. "'Woodstock defence' of Abuse Doesn't Hold Water." *The Guardian* 25 May 2011. Web. 11 May 2015.

"Slayer Given 30 Years as Part of Deal." UPI. *Progress Bulletin* 15 July 1973: 8. Newspapers.com. Web. 20 Aug. 2015.

Smith, Bob. "250 Attend Whitmans' Rosary Rite." *The Palm Beach Post* 5 Aug. 1966: 1. Newspapers.com. Web. 12 Feb. 2016.

"Sniper's Brother Shot Dead." UPI. *The Post-Standard* 5 July 1973: 3. Newspapers.com. Web. 6 April 2014.

"Sniper's Dad Tells of Quarrel." *The Pittsburgh Press* 2 Aug. 1966: 1, 6. Google Newspapers. Web. 5 June 2013.

"Sniper Described as Wife-Beater, Gambler, Poacher." *The Miami News* 8 Aug. 1966: 2A. Web. 15 June 2015.

"Sniper's Father, Brothers Talk to Priest at Home." *The Spokesman-Review* 2 Aug. 1966: 2. Google Newspapers. Web. 30 June 2013.

"Sniper's Father Secludes Self, 2 Sons, Priest." *The Bridgeport Telegram* 2 August 1966: 8. Newspapers.com. Web. 14 April 2014.

Springer, Sylvia. "Leven Fails to Stop Pro-Priests Rally." *Express and News* 2 Nov. 1968: 36. Newspapers.com. Web. 21 May 2015.

"Start Marked Today of New K of C Hall." *The Palm Beach Post* 2 June 1957: 35. Newspapers.com. Web. 10 Feb. 2016.

"Suits Filed in District Courts and Courts of Domestic Relations." *Daily Court Review* 26 May 1970: 2. Microfiche.

"Task Force Seeks Reason: 2 Diseases Kill 100 Homosexuals." AP. *The Palm Beach Post* 29 Aug. 1981: 6. Newspapers.com. Web. 14 June 2016.

"Ten Priests of Diocese Get New Appointments." *The Texas Catholic Herald* 24 January 1969: 3. Print.

"The Texas Sniper." *Life* 12 August 1966: 24-31. Print.

"They Will Wed in Summer." *The Palm Beach Post* 15 July 1962: 27. Newspapers.com. 10 Feb. 2016.

Tissot, Capterton. "Natalie Leduc: The Stuff Local Legends Are Made of." *Adirondack Daily Enterprise* 22 Oct. 2008. Web. 30 Sept. 2013.

Tontini, Linda. "Gay Men Asking, 'Why Me?' Diseases Have Homosexuals Reassessing Their Lifestyles." *The Palm Beach Post* 25 Oct. 1982: 18. Newspapers.com. Web. 14 June 2016.

Tucker, Jeff. "2 Priest Sexual Abuse Suits Settled." *The Pueblo Chieftain*. 18 May 2011. Web. 17 Aug. 2016.

"Two Hospitalized after Accidents." *The Palm Beach Post* 25 May 1958: 14. Newspapers.com. Web. 10 Feb. 2016.

"Two New Chaplains Assigned to Maxwell." *The Montgomery Advertiser* 3 Sept. 1965: 11. Newspapers.com. 28 May 2017.

Weaver, Jay. "Dismissal of Suit Protested." *Miami Herald* 15 Sept. 2009. BishopAccountability.org. n.d. Web. 9 Sept. 2014.

White, Garland. "Communist Danger Sounded as Kiwanians Mark Birthday." *The Palm Beach Post* 31 May 1958: 4. Newspapers.com. Web. 10 Feb. 2016.

"White House Wedding." *Newsweek* 15 August 1966: 17-21. Print.

"Whitman Claims Body of Second Son." AP. *Corsicana Daily Sun* 5 July 1973: 17. Newspapers.com. Web. 6 April 2014.

"Whitman, His First Victim Buried after Joint Service." *Express and News* 6 August 1966: 4. Newspapers.com. 16 June 2015.

"Whitman's Priest Prays No Vengeance Follows; Sniper, Mother Buried in Florida." *The Lincoln Star* 6 August 1966: 2. Newspapers.com. Web. 24 Jan. 2015.

"Whitmans' Rites Held in Florida." AP. *Tucson Daily Citizen* 5 Aug. 1966: 2. Newspapers.com. Web. 6 April 2014.

"Whitman Was 'A Thinker' Say Old Friends." AP. *The Bridgeport Telegram* 2 Aug. 1966: 8. 14 April 2014.

"Whitman's Wife Cites 'Remorse' in Support Suit." *The Palm Beach Post* 12 Jan. 1967: 14. Newspapers.com. Web. 21 May 2016.

"Who Was Charles Whitman?" *Texas Observer* 19 Aug. 1966. Print.

"Would-be Jack Tars Greet Head of Navy." *The Atlanta Constitution* 13 May 1913: 3. Newspapers.com. Web. 13 Feb. 2016.

"Young People Presenting Musicale." *The Palm Beach Post* 18 May 1958: 31. Newspapers.com. Web. 10 Feb. 2016.

"Yule Program Given by Lodge." *The Palm Beach Post* 15 Oct. 1956: 14. Newspapers.com. Web. 10 Feb. 2016.

Interviews and Correspondence

Arceneaux, Louis, CM. Personal interview. 15 Jan. 2014.

Brady, John, Msgr. Personal interview. Jan. 6. 2014.

Briganti, Frank. Emails. 15-18 Aug. 2014.

Chagnon, Roger. Personal interview. 2 July 2014.

Coleman, Joseph. Personal interview. 25 Sept. 2013.

Comeaux, Bob. Personal interview. 21 Jan. 2014.

Evans, Lamar. Personal interview. 13 Jan. 2014.

Fellner, Azriel. Personal interview. 16 Dec. 2013.

Garcia, John. Personal interview. 24 Jan. 2014.

Houston Priest. Personal interview. 31 Aug. 2013.

LeBoef, Donny. Personal interview. 1 March 2013.

Leduc, Maurice. Personal interview. 10 Feb. 2014.

Leduc, Natalie. Personal interview. 3 Oct. 2013.

Leissner, Nelson. Interviews and emails: 8 August 2014, 18 Dec. 2014, 18 May 2015.

McGinnis, Jack. Personal interview. 1 November 2013.

Meadows, Jeffrey. Emails. 26 Jan. 2015 – 4 May 2015.

Nguyen, Rev. Trung, Rector of St. Mary's Houston. Personal interview. 3 July 2013.

Olsovsky, Rev. George. Personal interview. 8 July 2013.

Riani, Peter, Msgr. Personal interview. 9 Sept. 2013.

Scardino, Felix. Personal interview. 29 May 2015.

Schuck, Francis J., II, also "Joe" Schuck and Joseph K. Shook. Personal interviews, emails, and phone calls. 29 Oct. 2014 through 21 Jan. 2015.

Showfety, Joseph, Msgr. Personal interview. 18 Sept. 2013.

Sipe, A. W. Richard. Personal interview. 12 Aug. 2013.

Smith, Marvin. Personal interview. 20 Jan. 2013.

Tarte, Edward. Personal interview. 10 Jan. 2015.

Wetzel, George. Personal interview. 15 Feb. 2014.

PRIMARY DOCUMENTS AND OTHER RECORDS (ARCHIVES, COURT RECORDS, AND REPORTS)

"301 San Jacinto." Harris County Sheriff's Department Archive. 22 Feb. 2003. Web. 30 June 2015.

"About Colonneh Lodge." Colonneh Lodge: Order of the Arrow. samhoustonbsa.org. n.d. 10 Jan. 2014.

Alberti v. Sheriff of Harris County Texas, et al. United States Court of Appeals, Fifth Circuit. 25 July 1991. Web. 21 Aug. 2015.

Anglim, Rev. Thomas M. *Find a Grave.* 30 July 2010. Web. 16 June 2014.

"Anthony Mercieca: Assignment Record." BishopAccountabilty. org. 25 Oct. 2006. Web. 18 June 2014.

Austin Police Department (APD) Files. Charles Whitman's Notebooks, The Daily Record of C.J. Whitman, "The Autobiography" of "Charles Whitman." Austin History Center.

Beauregard, Rev. Real. "La Courte Biographie de l'abbé Réal Beauregard." Chancellerie, Eveche de Saint-Hyacinthe Quebec. PDF record via email. 26 Sept. 2013.

Centers for Disease Control and Prevention. "Adverse Childhood Experiences (ACEs)." cdc.gov. 2016. Web. 5 Jan. 2016.

Crouch, A. Guy. Trustee's Deed (including notice of promissory default, auction, and sale). 14 June 1966.

Data Elements and Codes: Volume II—Personnel. Air Force Manual 300-4 Volume II. 1 May 1971. apfn.org. n.d. Web. 5 Sept. 2013.

Database of Publicly Accused Priests. BishopAccountability.org.

Declaration of Richard Sipe in Case Number 2010CV561. *John Doe No. 24 v. Bishop of Pueblo.* Awrsipe.com. n.d. Web. 4 April 2016.

"Diocese of Galveston-Houston, TX" with Letter by Most Reverend Joseph Fiorenza dated Jan. 16, 2004. Bishopaccountability.com. 10 May 2015.

Doe v. Linam, et al. US District Court for the Southern District of Texas. 225 F. Supp. 2d 731 (SD Tex. 2002). 21 Aug. 2002. Web. 1 July 2015.

Doe v. Linam, et al. Civil Action No. 02-41359. Appeal from the US District Court for the Southern District of Texas Galveston Division. Record excerpts. 11. Dec. 2002. Print.

Doe v. Linam, et al. Civil Action No. 02-41359. Brief of Appellant. Appeal from the US District Court for the Southern District of Texas Galveston Division. 11 Dec. 2002. Print.

Doe v. Linam, et al. Civil Action No. 02-41359. Brief of Appellees. Appeal from the US District Court for the Southern District of Texas Galveston Division. 13 Jan 2003. Print.

Doe v. Roman Catholic Diocese of Galveston-Houston, et al. 408 F. Supp. 2d 272 (SD Tex. 2005). 22 Dec. 2005. Web. 1 July 2015.

E. A. Serabia v. Joseph G. Leduc. Plaintiff's Original Petition and related documents. Harris County Civil Court. 29 Oct. 1974.

Estate of Phifer v. Patrick Grady Whitman. No. B001177. Court of Appeals of California, Second Appellate District, Division Two. 6 March 1984. Justia US Law. Web. 10 Nov. 2015.

Ex Libris: Memini (yearbook). Assumption Preparatory High School. Worcester: Les Versificateurs de l'Ecole Superieure de L'Assomption, 1947.

FBI Files. Cole Letters and Reports. 5 and 16 August 1966. APD Files. Austin History Center.

FBI Files. Statement of Joseph G. Leduc. 15 August 1966. APD Files. Austin History Center.

Fiorenza, Joseph A. Archbishop. "St. Mary's Seminary 1901-2011." Text of speech. Archdiocese of Galveston-Houston, 2011.

Groh, John E., Chaplain Major. Interview with Deputy Chief of Chaplains Brigadier General Thomas M. Groome, Jr. USAFR. Washington, DC. 19-20 July 1976. Transcript.

Heatly, Maurice, MD. Charles Whitman Appointment Report. 29 March 1966. APD Files. Austin History Center.

Houston KC Credit Union v. Joseph G. Leduc. Plaintiff's Original Petition, Citation, and Defendant's Original Answer. Case No. 834086. Harris County, Texas. K-152 Judicial District. 19 May 1970.

John Jay College of Criminal Justice. *The Nature and Scope of Sexual Abuse of Minors by Catholic Priests and Deacons, 1950-2002.* New York: CUNY, February 2004.

The Knights of the Klu Klux Klan. "Roman Catholic Dynamites Bath Public Schools." Pamphlet, 1927. Web. 15 Jan. 2016.

Leduc, Joseph G. Certificate of Death. Palm Beach County, Florida. 23 Jan. 1981.

——. Deed from Elmer E. Cary. Brazoria County. 1 Nov. 1960.

——. Deed from L. G. Gaines. Brazoria County. 28 Oct. 1960.

——. Last Will and Testament. Witnesses: Fr. Thaddeus Palmieri and Josefa A. York. Harris County, Texas. 22 Nov. 1968.

——. Promissory Note. Trustee A. Guy Crouch II. Brazoria County. 12 July 1961.

———, Estate of. Petition for Establishment and Probate of Lost or Destroyed Will. Circuit Court for Palm Beach County, FL, Probate Division. 20 August 1981.

Leduc, Joseph G., Rev. Mechanic's Lien. Gene Elkins DBA Air-Vent Awning Co. Harris County, TX. 5 May 1964.

Leduc, Joseph Leo Avila. Declaration of Intention Form 2202-L-A. U.S. Department of Labor: Immigration and Naturalization Service. Waterbury, New Haven County CT. 13 July 1935.

Los Angeles Times Staff. "Inside the 'Perversion Files': Tracking Decades of Allegations in the Boy Scouts." *The Los Angeles Times* 18 Oct. 2012. Web. 15 Oct. 2014.

Morgan, Matthew A. *Warranty Deed*. To John Skehan. 12 March 1982. Palm Beach County Florida.

The Rifle. USMC Training Film. c. 1960. YouTube. 10 Oct. 2014.

Rupertus, William H. Major General. "My Rifle: The Creed of a United States Marine." USMC History Division. Web. 12 Sept. 2015.

Saint Francis Xavier Church Steeple, Fort Myers, FL, USA. Waymarking.com. 2012. Web. 16 June 2014.

"St. George Emblem Recipients 1959-2009." DCCS-Galveston-Houston. dccs-dgh.org. 12 March 2014. Web. 7 April 2014.

St. Mary's Seminary School of Theology Catalog and Announcements. Baltimore: E.J. Horan and Company, 1951. Print.

St. Mary's Seminary School of Theology Catalog and Announcements. Baltimore: E.J. Horan and Company, 1952. Print.

Schuck, Francis J., Jr. Statement to FBI. 13 Sept. 1966. APD Files. Austin History Center.

Special Report of the Grand Jury, 147th Judicial District Court of Travis County, Texas. 5 Aug. 1966. Print.

Tarte, Edward. YouTube Channel. n.d. Web. 10 Jan. 2015.

Vigil Honor Database. Colonneh Lodge Order of the Arrow. samhoustonbsa.org. n.d. Web. 28 Dec. 2013.

Whitman, Charles Joseph. Selected letters to Kathy Leissner (Whitman) and her family. Private archive of Nelson Leissner. Manuscript.

Whitman, Kathy Leissner. Selected letters to Charles Whitman and her family. Private archive of Nelson Leissner. Manuscript.

ACKNOWLEDGMENTS

I wish first to acknowledge and thank the ordained men who helped me gather an up-close view of seminary training, parish life, and church politics in the 1950s, 1960s, and beyond. Some of these men still officially identify as priests; others have different statuses now. But all provided stories and reflections with a candor and generosity that I would most often describe as "pastoral." Many not only made time for lengthy interviews in person or by phone, but also patiently indulged follow-up emails and phone calls: Rev. Jack McGinnis; Joseph Coleman; Msgr. Peter Riani; Msgr. John Brady; Msgr. Joseph Showfety; Felix Scardino; Frank Briganti; and Louis Arceneaux, CM. Two former Air Force chaplains who served in Alaska were of vital assistance in understanding religious-military dynamics in the mid-to-late 1960s: Rabbi Aze Fellner and Rev. William Rhett.

In addition, through a long process that often required traveling and repeated remote communications, I benefited from indispensible direction and clarity from on-site archivists, historians, and experts, both laypeople and religious: Susan Rittereiser, Archives and Manuscripts Curator, Austin History Center; Fr. Trung Nguyen, Rector, St. Mary's Seminary Houston; Alison Foley, Archivist, St. Mary's Seminary and University; Elizabeth Visconage, St. Mary's Seminary and University; Joe Orr, Historian, Elmendorf Air Force Base; Samuel C. Shearin, Air Force Historical Archives; Christian Harder, Esri; Nelson Block, Marvin Smith, and Jim Olive, of Sam Houston Area Council of Boy Scouts (SHAC); Theo-Charles Martin, Archivist, the University of Ottawa; Lisa May, Director of Archives & Records, Archdiocese of Galveston-Houston; Michele Morel, Chancery Secretary for Diocese of St. Hyacinthe; Maria Paxi, Archivist, Diocese of Hartford; Sr. Catherine Bitzer, Archivist, Diocese of St. Augustine; Sr. Elizabeth Worley, SSJ, Archivist, Archdiocese of Miami; Lisa Mobley, Archivist, Diocese of St. Petersburg; Renae Bennet, Archivist, Diocese of Orlando; Anne Barrett Doyle, Bishop Accountability; Rev. Louis L. Renner, SJ (RIP), author and Catholic historian of Alaska; Stephanie Carter, Reference Librarian, Angleton Branch, Brazoria County Library; Rev. George Olsovsky, former pastor of St. Dominic Parish, Houston; George Christian, OP, and Roger Chagnon, alumni of Assumption Prep in Worcester, MA; Edward Tarte, alumnus of St. Mary's Seminary Houston.

A special appreciation to Nelson Leissner, for sharing his recollections and for allowing me first-time access to primary documents and photographs in his private archive, some of which are included here and in references.

Additional thanks go to George Wetzel, for information about his minor seminary experience and the Dignity movement for gay Catholics in Houston; to Lamar Evans, for his memories of the Colonneh Lodge Vigil Ordeal in November, 1955; to Joanna Clapps Herman and Donny LeBoeuf, for their recollections about Waterbury and St. Anne's parish; to Thatcher Carter, for her amazing Waterbury photographs, and her mother, Laurie Chamberlain (RIP), for her memories of living in Waterbury; to Felicia Y. Peavy, for her assistance in understanding the Jesse Linam case; Glenn E. Coe, Esq., for legal counsel and fatherly advice; Amanda Marie Dorado and Clay Hodson for fielding my inquiries about police and court records, as well as legal forms; to Francis "Joe" Schuck, for sharing his impressions about CW and GL; to Nancy Rommelmann, David Rensin, Ana Maria

Spagna, and Michael Steinberg, for their professional commiserations and insights; to Natalie Leduc, for her personal story; to Bob Comeaux and John Garcia, for sharing their memories Catholic scouting in Houston in the early 1960s; to Rev. Tom Doyle, OP, for helping me understand the structure and logistics of the Military Ordinariate; to Jeffrey Meadows (RIP), for his memories of Arthur Gagne; to Leduc's cousin and her husband for sharing what they could remember.

I can't end without sending out my love to a band of fearless, curious, and intelligent friends who asked questions, encouraged me, let me bounce ideas off them, and endured my necessary (and sometimes annoying, I realize) embargoes: Stephanie Barbé Hammer and Larry Behrendt, Donna Hilbert, Julie Ann Higgins, Thatcher and Ross Carter, Victor Sandoval, Lindsey and Grey Frandsen, Christine Sandoval, Bonnie Parmenter and Fred Baines, Jeff and Suzanne Rice, Kaylean and Rob May, Nick Prelesnik, and Molly Scott (sis!). A special appreciation goes to Ann and John Brantingham, for their unwavering support of this project, and of me personally, during a particularly difficult period.

All writers know—or learn—that a book comes to be only through collaboration with a good editor and publisher. I am forever grateful to Mark Givens, of Pelekinesis, for his tireless attention to detail, his sharp eye, his patience and creativity in making *MASS* a reality. Mark's advocacy for writers and books of all kinds is a true inspiration, and I am glad to have him as a colleague and friend.

Finally, I owe a deep gratitude to Richard Sipe, who reminded me that seeking answers can be an act of faith as well as respect, no matter how uncomfortable or sobering the questions may be.

And for Justin, always.

About the Author

Jo Scott-Coe is the author of *Teacher at Point Blank* (Aunt Lute). Her first-ever portrait of Kathy Leissner Whitman, "Listening to Kathy" (Catapult) received a Notable listing in *Best American Essays* and is now available in print. Scott-Coe's nonfiction has appeared in *Talking Writing, Tahoma Literary Review, Cultural Weekly, American Studies Journal, Pacific Coast Philology, Superstition Review, Fourth Genre, Ninth Letter, Salon,* and many other publications. She is an associate professor of English composition at Riverside City College, where she was named 57th Distinguished Faculty Lecturer for her research on the epistolary history of Kathy Leissner. Scott-Coe also facilitates community writing workshops for the Inlandia Institute.

More information at http://www.joscottcoe.com
Twitter: @joscottcoe
FB: @teacheratpointblank

CPSIA information can be obtained
at www.ICGtesting.com
Printed in the USA
FSHW02n1608140718
50418FS

9 781938 349737